THE
GLOBAL
GOD

A
BridgePoint
Book

BridgePoint,
an imprint of
Baker Books,
is your connection
for the best in
serious reading
that integrates
the passion of
the heart with
the scholarship
of the mind.

THE
GLOBAL
GOD

Multicultural Evangelical Views of God

Aída Besançon Spencer
and William David Spencer, editors

A BridgePoint Book

A Division of Baker Book House Co
Grand Rapids, Michigan 49516

Published 1998 by BridgePoint Books
an imprint of Baker Books
a division of Baker Book House Company
P.O. Box 6287, Grand Rapids, MI 49516-6287

Printed in the United States of America

Library of Congress Cataloging-in-Publication Data

The global God : multicultural Evangelical views of God / Aída Besançon Spencer and
   William David Spencer, editors.
      p.   cm.
   "A BridgePoint book."
   Includes bibliographical references and indexes.
   ISBN 0-8010-2163-4 (pbk.)
    1. God. 2. Evangelicalism. 3. Multiculturalism—Religious aspects—Christianity.
I. Spencer, Aída Besançon. II. Spencer, William David, 1947– .
BT102.G574   1998
231—dc21   97-44098

For information about academic books, resources for Christian leaders, and all new releases available from Baker Book House, visit our web site:

http://www.bakerbooks.com

Contents

Litaneia to the Great God

Giving gifts in unexpected places,
sharing rain from cornucopic clouds,
beckoning from unfamiliar faces,
making family members out of crowds,

sentinel against the day of sickness,
wearing mercy like an humble gown,
worthy from the wounds of hate's resistance,
breaking seals that bring the judgment down,

stretching hands that open an escape route,
potently that hold all foes at bay,
comforting the lonely and the destitute,
lifter of the fallen on the way,

neverending source of information,
unfathomed profundity of thought,
opening to honest inclination,
working meaning in all wisdom taught,

striding in high holiness transcendent,
stumbling in the abject in the street,
immanent to all of life's abundance,
sealing walls where love and chaos meet,

God, who is the font of all creation,
source of beauty and all that is true,
work your purpose through our hesitation;
take our hands and form your world anew.

William David Spencer, Aída Besançon Spencer
February 1997

Preface

At first Mary and Joseph must have been puzzled. Was not this child Jesus supposed to be Israel's messiah—sent by God to deliver the Jews? And, yet, here were astronomers from the East, drawn by God's annunciation star in the heavens, waiting in deference to honor this incarnate gift of God as their camels snorted and stamped away the journey and weary, dusty servants unpacked regal treasures. As the years passed, Jesus' family and followers grew accustomed to the steady queue of pilgrims and emissaries dropping in on him from points across the known world—the Greeks in John 12:20–36, the Syrophoenician woman in Mark 7:24–30, the woman cured of a chronic hemorrhage in Mark 5:21–34, identified by Bishop Eusebius as a Gentile because she built in gratitude a bronze statue of herself being healed by Jesus at her gates, and the ruler Abgar, whose reputed exchange of letters with Jesus, requesting a healing and offering sanctuary, were examined by Eusebius in the Record Office of Edessa (Eusebius *History,* 7.18; 1.13).

"I have other sheep that do not belong to this fold," Jesus warned his disciples in John 10:16. "I must bring them also, and they will listen to my voice. So there will be one flock, one shepherd."

This present book is the sound of the other sheep. Through general revelation God has always spoken to all nations and finally through specific revelation God drew people of all nations to be reconciled through Jesus the Christ (God's uniquely commissioned agent).

Speaking of his mission to die to forgive the sins that separated humanity from its Creator, Jesus explained to the seeking Gentiles and to his Jewish disciples in his last public discourse, recorded in John 12:32, "And I, when I am lifted up from the earth, will draw all people to myself." All people, as we see revealed by the context, included the Gentiles, the "barbarians," those who appear to be "other," "different." For each culture "barbarians" differ. For Anglo-Americans, British, and Europeans, the "Gentiles" may be Hispanics, Africans, Chinese, Koreans, and their descendants. For each successive group, everyone else becomes "other," like a rotating compass dial, pointing away from us, when we have fixed ourselves as "north."

Each of us who are not messianic, Christian Jews are among the "other sheep" Jesus promised to draw by the cross to be reconciled to God and to join a new supracultural "Israel." We still remain other sheep, members of our own cultures, contextual within our own contexts, but now united as a rich, diverse panorama of southdown, rambouillet, cheviot, dorset, karakul, suffolk, hampshire, merino, shropshire and many more varieties of sheep in Jesus' great transcultural flock. Drawn from that global flock, this book is produced by Jesus' community of "others." Some of the authors are dear friends; many we have never met, yet we are united through Christ. Each writes from her or his own varied culture with one central message, though the language, context, and history may give us a different perspective. That message has to do with the God who has drawn us together to be one people. This book concerns that global God who calls all people into relationship with God and each other through Christ. This book, in essence, is a Christian communal effort.

We are deeply grateful to each of the contributors as well as to God's body on earth, the supracultural Christian context that made this writing possible. Specifically, we would like to honor four faculty secretaries who helped patch together the multipieced fabric that is the book's final tapestry: Heidi Hudson, Beth Newhall, Diane Newhall, and Laura Gross. Laura especially labored arduously to finalize these chapters in a unified format. Julie Martin, as well, worked on the discs. Elizabeth Geesaman Lynn efficiently completed the Scripture Index.

We could never have had the financial resources or the time to pursue this project without the full support of Gordon-Conwell Theological Seminary. The excellent library staff was particularly helpful, especially our friend and colleague, the most able Dr. Freeman Barton.

We also thank the United Bible Societies for permission to use the New Revised Standard Version. If no version is indicated, the translation is either the NRSV or an author's own translation from the original Hebrew or Greek texts. Special citation must be made of Bob Hosack, who first enlisted the project and championed it through two publishers, and Jim Weaver, who shared Bob's enthusiasm and encouragement, Maria den Boer, our editorial liaison, and Baker Book House, the current cutting-edge publisher of evangelical Christianity with whom we are honored to serve.

Finally, we thank Almighty God, who reached out to each of us in our corners of the globe and made us joint heirs in Jesus' nation.

Other Books by the Authors

(authors listed by order of chapter)

Aída Besançon Spencer and/or William David Spencer

God through the Looking Glass (editors)
The Goddess Revival (editor)
Chanting Down Babylon: A Rastafarian Reader (editor)
Beyond the Curse: Women Called to Ministry
Dread Jesus
The Prayer Life of Jesus
Mysterium and Mystery: The Clerical Crime Novel
Joy through the Night: Biblical Resources for Suffering People
2 Corinthians: A Commentary
Paul's Literary Style

Gretchen Gaebelein Hull

Equal to Serve: Women and Men in the Church and Home
The ABCs of Gender Equality

Dieumème Noëlliste

Caribbean Missions in the Perspective of the Kingdom
Contextual but Not Parochial
Faith Transforming Context: In Search of a Theology for a Viable
    Caribbean
The Importance of Sound Doctrine
Toward a Theology of Theological Education
Options in the Delivery of Education

Tokunboh Adeyemo

Church in Africa Today and Tomorrow
The Church as an Agent of Change in Africa
A Christian Mind in a Changing Africa (editor)
Following Jesus in Africa Today (editor)
The Making of a Servant of God
Reflections on State and Christianity in Africa
Salvation in African Tradition
Selfhood of the Church in Africa

Tsu-Kung Chuang

Ripening Harvest
Interaction and Transformation

Bong Rin Ro

Korean Church Growth Explosion (editor)
Beyond Canberra (editor)
Urban Ministry in Asia (editor)
Christian Suffering in Asia (editor)
God in Asian Contexts (editor)

Christian Alternatives to Ancestor Practices (editor)
The Bible and Theology in Asian Contexts (editor)
Voice of the Church in Asia (comp.)
1995 World Directory of Theological Institutions
1983 Directory of Theological Schools in Asia
1980 Directory of Christian Education in Asia
1979 Directory of Theologians in Asia

Tae-Ju Moon

What Is Happiness, Who Is Happy, and Why?
Love: The Greatest Thing in the World
God of Love and Human Sufferings

Introduction

If one message emerges from the book that follows, it is that God has infused knowledge of Godself into all traditions and, yet, God stands above every tradition calling all people into a new transtraditional relationship with the Supreme God of the universe through Jesus Christ: what the New Testament calls the rule of Christ. Contextual to each of our cultures, we Christians are yet supracontextual in Christ in that we enter a new context: the transcultural reign of God. God has entered human borders, but those artificial boundaries cannot contain the new nation God creates. Into that new nation all people are being called, all cultures are being examined and challenged, all contexts widened to a Christian inclusivity.

This is, therefore, not a "many faces but one God" book. This book is a global Christian manifesto—a chorus of Christ's voices around the world, unique yet harmonious. In a choir, sopranos, tenors, altos, basses, all provide a different tone. Each of our writers looks from a unique historico-cultural perspective at this two-part question: Through what attribute is God most understood in your culture and what attribute of God needs to be more fully apprehended? The point of the book is to build a global theosology—a summary of how God is revealing Godself—in this transmillennial period.

The book is not a potpourri of other voices. Each writer was given the same task: select the attribute of God most evidently operant and apprehended in your culture and supplement for the rest of us what each of our cultures has perhaps missed about that aspect. Then, tell us what attribute of God may have been deemphasized and needs to be appropriated from the revelation emphasized in the Bible and perhaps in other cultures. Essentially, this is a cross-pollination of insights into the general revelation of God, tested against the specific, unifying revelation in the Bible. How each writer went about the task is what makes the book so valuable, and to the editors so marvelous. Each chapter is unique.

Each writer, as both a loyal member of his or her nation, but as well a loyal citizen in the reign of God, assumes the full truth of one religion: Christianity. The dialogue, or more specifically the decalogue, is between Christians in differing cultures. When, as is frequent, culturally indigenous religions contain truths, writers may choose to cite those, but not every writer has restricted herself or himself to drawing from religion as the sole means to understand the positive emphases about God revealed in the writer's culture. Culture, after all, is like a cultivating soil, a nourishing setting in which things grow and then in turn contribute to the whole environment to encourage more growth. Each writer has looked for an opening into each culture to view God at work, using concepts, habits, and institutions, highlighting different disciplines such as history, theology, anthropology, and sociology. Some authors focused on the larger culture; others focused on the church. For coeditor William David Spencer the entrance was through concepts and habits in the past that influence the present; for influential Christian stateswoman Gretchen Gaebelein Hull, it was attitudes to the law. Coeditor Aída Besançon Spencer drew upon personal experience as representative of many others' personal experiences, while the distinguished president of the Caribbean Graduate School of Theology, Dieumème Noëlliste, stood the mirror of biblical truth up against the multifaced Afro-Caribbean theology. The world-renowned Nigerian theologian and noted Ghanaian pastor, Tokunboh Adeyemo and Edward Osei-Bonsu, found the portal in by examining religious institutions and practices in Africa. For the multicultural Grace May, who currently enriches her Chinese American heritage by serving in an African American church, the window in was through the habits of Chinese Americans. For the esteemed pastor Tsu-Kung Chuang and respected church historian Bong Rin Ro, the ingress was the religious concepts of the Chinese and Koreans, respectively. Finally, the astute Canada-based Korean pastor Tae-Ju Moon examined sociological studies of habits and religious institutions to open up the presence of God among Koreans in North American culture.

Working with one's culture has always been problematic for Christians. Emphasizing their new celestial culture of God's rule, some Christians have attempted to be acultural, against all culture. But that is like being a seed that dislikes its soil. It can be placed in another nurturing environment, but it cannot grow without any. To be totally acultural is like proclaiming oneself against the air. The air may be polluted, but without air we cannot live. You either clean the pollutants out of your environment or move to another location with, what you perceive to be, cleaner air, but no human lives without breathing in the air. No human lives without a culture. The person who claims to be against culture often ends up uncritically accepting some alternative (often romanticized) culture as definitive. But all cultures have pollutants or ideas that are not pleasing to God, as so many reformers and utopians have come to realize. However, very few cultures have no concepts pleasing to God, a fact that becomes continually clearer when anti-Christian dictatorships collapse and a strong Christian subculture, often drawing on suppressed cultural values, becomes evident. When a culture is thoroughly bankrupt—Sodom and Gomorrah arrived at that point—the remnant of faithful believers have to leave. But right to the end, Lot was trying to preserve visitors and Abraham was pleading to preserve the cities. The Lots and the Abrahams struggle in every culture. As we read these chapters, we discover many more of them at work than we supposed, and through their inquiry a number of truths about the global God emerge.

Still, this is not a book on religious pluralism. Its premise is that the God revealed in the two written covenants of the Bible is the only Supreme God. Christianity's inclusiveness has to do with all the sheep called into Christ's fold from all nations, not a plurality of divine shepherds to divide them up into parallel herds in God's global flock. In that sense, Christianity is exclusive. Inclusive to all people, it is exclusive to one Supreme God. Each writer has met this one Supreme God, of which his or her culture spoke, in Christ, paralleling in the experience of each of us the testimony of the Bible's eyewitnesses. Over centuries they, as we, have communicated with God. The truths learned through these sacred communications can be verified historically and experientially. As in history, today as well, when one obeys the Bible's teachings in their appropriate applications, one's life will become more wholesome and well integrated. Small wonder, then, that eyewitnesses of God at work throughout the ages into today have championed God's revelations through persecution, even to death. God has always worked in history, and, as this book shows, that work has been global. While the present writers look for God at work in their cultures, they do not gloss over or ignore historical events that are at variance with God's ideals, nor do they mute the negative with the positive. Each chapter resonates with the desire to be truthful and to serve the good.

The book begins in the reign of God, where all its authors begin (chapter 1), examining the attributes of God as revealed in the Bible. Then it had to choose some point on the globe to begin its journey. As the book has been gathered and introduced in North America, that became our port of embarkation. Looking outward, the book begins its journey here with the perspectives of two Anglo-Americans, a man and a woman, examining the United States of America (chapters 2 and 3). Then we move to a Hispanic perspective on the United States (chapter 4), flowing along one of its tributaries to the Caribbean (chapter 5). From there, we follow its Afro-Caribbean ebb back to Africa, specifically visiting Nigeria (chapter 6) and Ghana (chapter 7). That completes our Anglo-Hispanic-Caribbean-African part of our journey. Then we return for part two, our Asian perspective. We begin again at our port of embarkation in the United States, studying the Chinese American perspective (chapter 8) and following it outward to the Chinese viewpoint that it hybridizes (chapter 9). So much of Chinese religious thought has permeated Korean religion that we move across to Korea (chapter 10) and conclude back in far north North America in the Korean American perspective (chapter 11). Part two is organized like a chiasm: American, Chinese, Korean, American. Part one is organized in more parallel fashion: male Anglo-American, female Anglo-American, Hispanic Caribbean-American, Afro-Caribbean, Nigerian African, Ghanaian African. Further, the first North American chapter begins with the United States heritage in Spain and Africa. Emphasizing historical background has guided the organization of the book. At the conclusion, we seek to summarize some of the major points and give our reflections as editors on some of the insights gained from each chapter.

One final caution: in no way do we claim that every global perspective is here included nor that any writer has even begun to exhaust the insights of her or his culture. What we have here are representative, prophetic, God-centered insights from a sample of scholars who glimpse God at work in our world.

May God use this book to bless and grow the church.

The God of the Bible

Aída Besançon Spencer

Aída Besançon Spencer, born and reared in Santo Domingo, Dominican Republic, is professor of New Testament at Gordon-Conwell Theological Seminary and pastor of organization with Pilgrim Church. She earned the Ph.D. from Southern Baptist Theological Seminary, Th.M. and M.Div. from Princeton Theological Seminary and B.A. from Douglass College. She has written numerous articles, essays, and books including *The Goddess Revival, God through the Looking Glass, Beyond the Curse,* and *The Prayer Life of Jesus.* She has worked with Hispanic Americans as a social worker, English as a second language teacher, and Bible teacher.

Individualized instruction is what all astute educators talk about, but few do. When our son began kindergarten no one had told us that preschool was a prerequisite. Within weeks he was behind. He was being taught to read phonetically, at a fast pace (since it really was a review for most students). In phonetics a word is broken into its parts and then joined together again. My husband asked my son if he wanted to learn to read. And he nodded, "Yes." So, my husband took out Laubach's literacy manuals, which he had been using for adults. In two weeks our son learned how to read. Laubach uses the whole word approach. A word such as "bird" is placed next to a picture of a bird: "*b*—bird, *b*—bird." The student repeats the sound *b*, the word "bird," and thereby learns to read. Even at a fast pace our son learned.

That is individualized instruction. It is not merely instruction done by an individual to an individual, but even more, an individual teacher using an instructional method that especially suits an individual student's learning style. The *content* still remains the same. In this case, literacy, the ability to read. The style or *method* of teaching varies.

God uses individualized instruction with humans also. God decides, "It is not good for Adam to be alone, I will make for him a helper that corresponds to him" (Gen. 2:18). However, what does God then do? Create the helper? No, God brings the animals and birds he had created to Adam so that in the intimate process of naming them Adam could learn whether any of them could be appropriate corresponding (literally, "as if in front") helpers for him. None of them, Adam discovers, will be satisfactory (Gen. 2:20). However, when God creates a woman from Adam's very side, like him in every way, Adam decides she really is that equal helper he had sought, explaining why a wife can be a more than worthwhile reward for leaving parents (Gen. 2:23–24). God had already decided what Adam needed before Adam ever expressed such a need. However, God created an educational process for Adam that would help Adam perceive his need and appreciate its fulfillment. In the same way, God teaches humans about God's self. God acts. Sometimes those actions are individualized. God interprets, especially with the listener in mind.

In this chapter we will highlight what we can learn about God from the first chapter of Genesis and from what the Bible presents as God's own verbal self-revelations.

What Creation Teaches about God

The primary method God employs to communicate to humans is by action: "In the beginning when God began to create the heavens and the earth, the earth was nothing and empty" (Gen. 1:1–2). The human learns about God by inductive observation. Nothing existed before God made it exist. Therefore, everything is under God's control. "The Spirit of God hovered over the face of the earth" (Gen. 1:2). "Hovered over" is a metaphor here. It is used literally for mother birds who "hover over" their young (Deut. 32:11).

A second method God uses to communicate to humans is figurative language. Why cannot God be more literally described? God has no form. God is a Spirit. Moses explicitly explains to the Israelites:

> Since you saw no form when the LORD spoke to you at Horeb out of the fire, take care and watch yourselves closely, so that you do not act corruptly by making an idol for yourselves, in the form of any figure—the likeness of male or female, the likeness of any animal that is on the earth, the likeness of any winged bird that flies in the air, the likeness of anything that creeps on the ground, the likeness of any fish that is in the water under the earth. And when you look up to the heavens and see the sun, the moon, and the stars, all the host of the heaven, do not be led astray and bow down to them and serve them. (Deut. 4:15–19)

No human, animal, or inanimate thing has God's form. Jesus reiterates in New Testament times that God is *spirit* (John 4:24). Therefore, to learn about God we humans need to observe the results of God's work in the world (in other words, God's action) and use analogies to describe God from God's formed creations. To paraphrase Jesus' teachings to Nicodemus, we can observe the working of God's Spirit but we cannot see the Spirit (John 3:8).

Even when God takes on form at the incarnation (John 1:1, 14), the form itself, the human body, is never described as "God." Jesus is the image of the invisible God.[1] Jesus was in the form *(morphē)* of God before the incarnation. In other words, Jesus before the incarnation, looked on the outside what he was on the inside. At the incarnation, Jesus took on the form *(morphē)* of a slave (Phil. 2:6–7). The metaphor "slave" fully describes God's loving, others-oriented character, dying even on a criminal's cross so that humans could approach God. Jesus also was born in human likeness (*homoiōma, schēma;* Phil. 2:7–8). The outward form was fully human. But unlike other humans, Jesus never sinned (Rom. 8:3; 2 Cor. 5:21). Jesus was fully God and fully human. But, being human is not a full reflection of God.

Thus, when God's Spirit "hovers over" the "face" of the earth, we learn that God's relation to creation was an intimate, loving one as a mother hen protecting her chicks, a metaphor God when on earth will repeat (Luke 13:34). God is not a mother hen or an eagle. God has no form. But God is like a hen or an eagle in some ways, being caring and protecting. God is also unlike a hen or an eagle. Their intelligence is limited; God's is not. Their care and protection is more biological than a conscious desire. All metaphors and similes are like *and* unlike the concept they claim to explain.[2]

"Then God said, 'Let there be light'; and there was light" (Gen. 1:3). God's word is powerful. Christians differ over whether creations like light came instantaneously or over time. But, the key deduction from this act is that God's creative ability flows successfully and powerfully from intention.

From action now God moves to contemplation and appreciation: "And God saw that the light was good" (Gen. 1:4). Everything God creates is good. Therefore, we humans can deduce that God is good. "From their fruits, you will know them," Jesus said about humans (Matt. 7:20). What a person really believes is demonstrated by *action*, not merely *words* (James 2:22–26). Those people who say "Jesus is Lord" but do not treat Jesus as a Lord they must obey, are not, in God's sight, Christians at all (Matt. 7:21–23). Similarly, from God's actions we can deduce God's character. Thus, David the psalmist sings and exhorts others: "Give thanks to the LORD, because God is *good;* for forever is his love" (1 Chron. 16:34).

God Communicates through Verbal Self-Revelations

The Bible also has a third method of revelation: interpretive words, descriptive adjectives and nouns. Sometimes actions can be misinterpreted. When I was a community organizer among Hispanic Americans in New Jersey, at one get-together the director of Adult Education, the director of the Young Women's Christian Association (who was Jewish), and a prominent Hispanic woman came to compliment me on my work as an organizer. (Believe me, genuine compliments are rare in any profession!) I knew then that if my actions remained uninterpreted, I would simply get credit as a "good person." I replied, in much fear and trembling, "The reason I am a good community organizer is because I am a Christian." That statement caused a pause in the conversation, but then one of the women replied, "Because I have seen your actions, I take seriously your claims."

So God too interprets God's actions. That is the focus of this chapter. But, as I mentioned, God's interpretations, although always true to God's character or "content," are also individualized toward the person(s) listening. God also accepts and affirms any descriptive adjectives by humans which are accurate. God's character is constant and eternal. But all of God's character is not fully explained in every revelational moment. However, no revelational moment gives an untrue description of God.

24

God of Seeing

The first name for God recorded in the Bible is given by a human, a woman, a slave of color. When Hagar runs away into the wilderness from Sarai's harsh treatment of her, God sends an angel to communicate to her God's concern and promise. She responds by calling God "a God of seeing," for God had seen her and she had seen God's messenger and yet remained alive (Gen. 16:13). The name she gave God was an accurate one. Therefore, it was acceptable to God.

Similarly, today different people of different nations may give God different names, which is an appropriate action as long as they refer to the same God. Giving the God of the Bible the same name as other gods is not acceptable, because those other names refer to other gods.

What self-descriptions in words does God use? The twelve self-descriptions of this chapter are keys to interpreting God's actions and God's character. In my study of the Bible I have found God's self-revelations to refer to God's various attributes and actions and to individual persons and places. The attributes often interpret specific actions.

God Almighty

For instance, the Bible's first recorded adjectival self-revelation given by God, "I am God Almighty" (Gen. 17:1), precedes a command and a promise that God will make. It occurs after a lengthy relationship between Abraham and God. Abraham is already ninety-nine years old. Possibly Abraham knew about God as a child when his father Terah decided to go to Canaan (Gen. 11:31). Abraham was himself called to go to Canaan when he was seventy-five (Gen. 12:4). Thus, as far as we know, Abraham had known God for at least twenty-four years before the adjective "almighty" was disclosed by God to Abraham. Self-revelation is not required of God. It is a response of love to love. As the apostle Paul, paraphrasing Isaiah 64:4, writes: "What eye has not seen and ear has not heard and upon a human heart has not arisen, that (very thing) God has prepared for those loving him" (1 Cor. 2:9).

Because God is "almighty," Abraham therefore should daily walk conscious of God's presence ("walk before my face") and should be "whole, complete, perfect," fully mature (Gen. 17:1). "Almighty" *(shaday)* may come from *shad*, "female breast" (e.g., Lam. 4:3) or *shod*, "violence, havoc, devastation" (e.g., Isa. 22:4).[3] If the former, God thereby is saying to Abraham, I am personally concerned in your well-being as a mother to her young. Remember my love and concern. I want you to mature fully from child to mature human. If the latter, God thereby is saying to Abraham, be conscious of my personal presence and become fully mature. I have the power to help you and to punish you. Power is especially important with the promise God will make: "And I will make my covenant between me and you, and I will multiply you with all might" (Gen. 17:2). Before God promises Abraham he would be the ancestor of many nations, God uses the self-description, "all power-ful." Or possibly, only a God who is like a nursing mother could enable Abraham to be the first of many. God also uses the same adjective "almighty" when communicating to Jacob and again the title holds the promise for an ancestor of many. Jacob is also commanded to "be fruit-ful and multiply" because "a nation and a company of nations shall come from you, and kings shall spring from you" (Gen. 35:11). God as "almighty" has the power of parentage.[4]

God I Will Be

The second recorded adjectival description by God comes as an answer to Moses' request. After God observes the suffering of Abraham's descendants at the hands of the jealous Egyptians, God responds in compassion and chooses to deliver them by sending Moses to Pharaoh (Exod. 3:7–10). When Moses responds in terror at the idea, God allays his fears by telling him "I will be with you" (Exod. 3:12). Is Moses simply trying to deflect God again when he tells God that of all things, the Egyptians would most want to learn God's name? Never-theless, the name God gives Moses is "I will be" (Exod. 3:14).

I always read this with a smile. I see it as God's humor. What kind of name is this—"I will be"? Nevertheless, even amidst the gentle humor are many profound points. "I will be" at least is a reminder to Moses that God promised "I *will be* with you." The God who answered the Israelites' cry will be with them in their distress and with Moses in his deliverance. Moses learns that at any time the people can call on their God because God *will be* with them (Deut. 4:7; Ps. 145:18). The Jewish Paul too explains thousands of years later to the Gentiles of his time that God always *will be* with them because in God "we are living and we are moving and we are being" (Acts 17:28). Jesus highlights this name also during his lifetime, declaring, "I myself am the bread of life," "I myself am the light of the world," "I myself am the gate of the sheep,"

"I myself am the good shepherd," "I myself am the resurrection and the life," "I myself am the way and the truth and the life," "I myself am the true vine."[5] When Jesus tells his fellow Jews, "before Abraham was born, I myself existed" (John 8:58), his listeners knew he was claiming identity with God and they sought to stone him as a blasphemer (John 8:59).

God uses the verb "I will be" as a reminder of God's promise to Moses. It is also a way to suggest God's great potential for the future. Jews and Christians believe in the God who "will be," the God who is always in the process of acting. ("I will be" is in the imperfect tense.) What new thing will God do (Isa. 43:19)? God is the hope for the future. God is "the first" and "the last" (Isa. 44:6).

The vowel points for the verb of being seem to be the basis for God's unpronounceable name YHWH (Exod. 3:15; 6:3), suggesting a certain mystery to God's nature. Of whatever God revealed to Moses, the Masorite editors of the Old Testament wrote down only the consonants. They wrote the vowels for another Hebrew word, *adonai,* or "Lord." The vowel points we now have do not go with the consonants as written in the Hebrew. Therefore, this God of the future will be doing a work we humans may not fully expect. God's mysterious name reminds us of God's own mysterious and unique nature.

God of Your Ancestor

God does not simply leave this self-revelation as "I will be." God also tells Moses that this God, who is about to deliver them from their suffering, is known to them: "The LORD, the God of your ancestors," "the God of Abraham, Isaac, and Jacob" (Exod. 3:16). Another technique God has used in communication is reminding the listener of God's relationship to the listener's relative. To Isaac, God becomes "the God of your father Abraham" (Gen. 26:24). To Jacob, God becomes "the God of Abraham" and "the God of Isaac" (Gen. 28:13). God reminds Jacob of God's relationship with his father again before Jacob ventures to Egypt (Gen. 46:3). And when Moses meets God at the burning-but-not-burning-up bush, God now tags on the name of Jacob: "I am the God of your father, the God of Abraham, the God of Isaac, and the God of Jacob" (Exod. 3:6). "I am the God who has already established a covenant relationship with your father." "I am not unknown to you." Eventually God is simply described as the God of the Hebrews or of Israel.[6]

If God so chooses to define God's self by referring back to a previous covenant-maker, would we also today be amiss to call God by the name of our familial or racial ancestors, and then tag on our name too? When we renew the covenant our mother and/or father has made with God, then God becomes our God too, even as Ruth tells Naomi, her mother-in-law: "Your God will be my God" (Ruth 1:16). That is why the God of Abraham, Isaac, and Jacob can also be the God of Hagar and Ruth and of "all flesh" (Jer. 32:27). God can be the God of "all flesh" because all are invited to be specific members of God's covenant (Rom. 3:29).

God of Bethel

That personal interconnection is established by God not only by referring to an earlier parent or ancestor, but also to a place that has specific significance for an individual. When Jacob is escaping Esau, God appears to him in a dream. In response, Jacob pledges that this Lord will be his God under certain conditions (Gen. 28:12, 20–21). God reminds Jacob of his pledge later in a dream, defining God's self by referring to the place where God had made those pledges: "I am the God of Bethel" ("Bethel" means "House of God," Gen. 31:13). This title does not mean God is limited to the place Bethel. Rather, God simply reminds Jacob of the place where he had "anointed a pillar" and where he had "made a vow" (Gen. 31:13).

God the Healer

God chooses titles that have significance to people. God also chooses titles that remind people of actions God has done. When the Israelites could not drink the polluted water at Marah and the Lord shows them how to clean it, God then uses the description "I am the LORD who heals you" (Exod. 15:26). The self-description was also a reminder that they would not receive illnesses as punishment for disobedience if they obeyed God's statutes. To reinforce this lesson, after this event God led the Israelites to Elim, which overabounded in fresh spring water (Exod. 15:27).

God Who Delivered from Slavery

Even the law God gives the Israelites is preceded by a reminder of God's actions: "I am the LORD your God who led you out from the land of Egypt from the house of slavery" (Exod. 20:2). Obedience to the law is then, by implication, a loving response to God's caring and powerful acts. Because God is so special, the Israelites need no other deities (Exod. 20:2–3; Deut. 5:6–7). Because God led them out from an oppressive people, the Israelites are themselves not to oppress other people with dishonest or oppressive business practices.[7] They can live peacefully and comfortably and be successful in battle if they continue to obey God.[8]

God of Hosts

Who first coins the phrase "the Lord of hosts" is unclear. "Hosts" literally are army troops.[9] The verb *saba'* signifies "wage war, serve."[10] As a term for God it first occurs in the narrative of 1 Samuel (1:3). It seems to be a term especially associated with the ark of the covenant, in particular the mercy seat between the two cherubim (Exod. 25:22; 2 Sam. 6:2). Since God had used the ark of the covenant as a symbol of God's presence in several striking victories (Josh. 3:3, 11, 14–17, Jordan River; Josh. 6:6, Jericho's wall; 1 Sam. 5:6–12, tumors among the Philistines), the ark also came to be associated by the Israelites as a symbol of God's victory in war (1 Sam. 4:3–4). And indeed cherubim or angels were (and are) God's warriors (2 Kings 6:17). Hannah calls God the "Lord of hosts" when she wants a child, one reason being to vanquish her enemy Peninnah.[11] Samuel uses the term when he comes to anoint Saul and charge him to wage war against the Amalekites (1 Sam. 15:2). David shouts out at Goliath that David will be victorious because he is supported by "the Lord of hosts, the God of the armies of Israel" (1 Sam. 17:45). Nathan also uses this term for God when addressing David, reminding David that all his military victories were due to God (2 Sam. 7:8–9). Thus, the Lord of hosts seems to be a title that not only reminds people of God's previous actions, but also promises God's future actions.

God the Creator

God uses terms that highlight specific connections and also more general relationships. When Jeremiah is called to speak to the rulers of Edom, Moab, Ammon, Tyre, and Sidon, God begins by using the more specific "the Lord of hosts" and "the God of Israel," but then goes on to add the more general actions: "I have made the earth, humanity and the animals that are upon the face of the earth with great power and outstretched arm" (Jer. 27:5). God reminds the listeners of this more general covenant established by the act of creation.[12] Then God goes on to declare that neither Israelites nor surrounding neighbors will be able to stop the approaching victory of people from afar, the Babylonians (Jer. 27:6). This description of God in more universal terms then becomes a basis for a more universal decree.

God alludes again to creation as a means by which to highlight God's omnipresence: "Do I not fill heaven and earth?" (Jer. 23:24). Therefore, since God not only created the world, but also sustains the world, no one can lie in God's name without God's knowledge (Jer. 23:24–25). Jesus also reminds his disciples that the Father is "Lord of heaven and earth" and therefore powerful and sovereign enough to choose to whom God's revelation will be given (Luke 10:21).[13]

God Is Jealous

God not only reminds people of *God's* past and potential actions, God also chooses attributes to highlight to remind people of actions *humans* should take. The Israelites should not make covenants with other deities not only because these other deities did not save them from the Egyptians, but also because "the LORD, 'Jealous' is his name, a jealous God he is" (Exod. 34:14). The Lord's covenantal relationships are unique.[14] God is not a "bigamist."

God Is Compassionate

As one reads in the early chapters of the Bible, God's self-revelations appear to build upon each other, which shows that God is slowly educating humans, especially the Israelites who are to reach out to others (Exod. 19:6). In Exodus 20, God uses God's mysterious name (YHWH, 20:2), when reminding the people of their deliverance from Egypt and explaining that God is monogamous, and therefore will punish those who disobey the covenant but reward those who obey it (20:5–6). However, when Moses asks God if he could learn more about God, God pronounces God's mysterious name and elaborates on the self-description already given earlier in Exodus 20: "LORD (YHWH) God, compassionate and merciful, slow to be displeased and greatly loving and faithful" (Exod. 34:6).

In this series of adjectives lies the heart of God's character. They summarize the adjectival self-descriptions already mentioned. "Lord" alludes to the God who "will be," the God who has created the world and is now sustaining the world and is in the process of new, mysterious acts, powerful and omnipresent. Since this God is spirit and not form, only *qualities* describe this God's essence, not shape.

What are those qualities? All five qualities are synonyms. First, God is compassionate. *Rahamim* is the plural of "womb," *raham.* God has a motherly compassion. This term alludes back to God "almighty." The Aramaic suggests "be soft, gentle."[15] God's first quality is a motherly one. Like a nursing mother whose very body reminds her of a nursing child (Isa. 49:15), God too never forgets or abandons or destroys the people who have made a covenant with God (Deut. 4:31). Because God is compassionate, God forgives repentant people (2 Chron. 30:9). Because God is compassionate, God gives food to those who keep the covenant (Neh. 9:19–21). In the Old Testament the term in the plural is used mainly of God, except for Psalm 112:4 where it refers to generous and just people who help others even at night.

A similar image is used by Jesus to express compassion. *Splagchnon,* especially in the plural, are the inward parts of a mammal, especially the heart, lungs, liver, kidneys, and womb.[16] Jesus exemplifies compassion *(splagchneuō)* when he sees the widow of Nain mourn her only son, the crowds harassed and helpless like sheep without a shepherd, and the blind men who ask to see.[17] In every case the "gut-level" feeling is followed by action. Jesus tells the widow not to weep and he acts to allay her situation by commanding the son to arise (Luke 7:13–15). Jesus tells the disciples to pray for more workers and then appoints some to go out (Matt. 9:38–10:1). Jesus touches the blind men and causes them to regain sight (Matt. 20:34).[18]

The second quality listed in Exodus 34:6 is a synonym of the first quality: *hannun.* This noun in the Bible is used only of God. It appears to refer to active concern for those who are in severe physical or economic distress. When God heard and freed the Hebrews from slavery, God demonstrated "grace" or "mercy." When God listens to the poor because the rich have taken their garment overnight as a pledge for interest, leaving the poor with nothing to warm themselves in their sleep, that is "mercy" or "graciousness" (Exod. 22:27 [26]). When God preserves the life of the person near death, that too is "mercy" (Ps. 116:5–6).

The third quality is a different way to express compassion. God takes a long time before becoming angry or displeased. God was angry with

Moses when Moses did not trust God to help him speak (Exod. 4:13–14). God chose Aaron to replace him anyway. God was angry with the Israelites who complained of manna and their travels even after all the marvelous miracles God had done to free them (Num. 11:1, 10). Fire ensued. When Miriam and Aaron criticized Moses' marriage and leadership, God was angry with them (Num. 12:9). Leprosy ensued. When Balaam attempted to deceive the Hebrews, God was angry (Num. 22:22). An angel blocked the donkey's advance. When some of the Israelites began to have adulterous relationships and worship the Moabite gods, God became angry with them (Num. 25:3). Those people had to die. When the Israelites were too terrified to enter Canaan, God was angry with them (Num. 32:9–10). They had to wander for forty years.

In other words, God is not pleased with lack of trust, lack of appreciation, criticism, deceit, and infidelity. But God's punishment does not always last forever (Exod. 32:14; Micah 7:18–20). The fire stopped. The leprosy disappeared. The wandering ended. God's punishment comes only after a while, after clear and persistent warnings. As the apostle Peter explains, the Lord is patient: "one day from the Lord is like a thousand years, and a thousand years are like one day" because God does not want any to perish, but all to come to repentance (2 Peter 3:8–9). God takes a long time before punishing, but eventually God will punish if a person does not stop unloving and unjust acts.[19]

The last two qualities are very frequent in the Old Testament and in themselves summarize the entire list: "greatly loving and truthful" (Exod. 34:6). Jesus' glory, glory uniquely coming from the Father, "only-begotten," was "full of grace and truth" (John 1:14). *Hesed* may refer to love, kindness, goodness, benevolence, grace, and beauty.[20] It is a broad word that includes leading and guiding people (Exod. 15:13), helping someone in difficult circumstances,[21] keeping one's word not to kill a family (1 Sam. 20:14–15), never giving up on someone recalcitrant (Jer. 31:3–4), forgiving people's sins,[22] and remaining with someone when times are difficult (Ruth 1:8). Someone who has this kind of love is completely trustworthy and generous.[23] No other deity has God's "steadfast love" (2 Chron. 6:14). God's "steadfast love endures forever."[24]

'Emeth includes the love and support of a nursing mother and the trustworthiness of a loving parent. It includes "firmness, faithfulness, truth, reliability, stability." The verb *'aman* means "confirm, support."[25] When a woman takes care of a nursing child, that is "faithfulness" (Num.

11:12; Ruth 4:16). When a person can rely on someone for honest wages and to keep their word, that is "faithfulness" or "honesty."[26] When a vine is tame and healthy, that too has "integrity" or "truth" (Jer. 2:21). When evil is punished, that too is "firmness" (Ps. 54:6 [7]). This "truth" is "a shield and a buckler," a protective and offensive weapon which lasts forever (Pss. 91:4; 117:2). *'Emeth* is the quality of faithfulness and firmness which leads a child from infancy to complete maturity.[27]

God has *ḥesed* and *'emeth* when God is personal, individually communicating, monogamous, jealous, treating each person as unique, reminding people of covenants and victories, and a healer.

This same list of qualities describing God occurs again and again throughout the Old Testament. Jonah knew God would forgive the Ninevites if they repented (Jonah 4:2), but he wanted them destroyed. Joel too promised God would not punish his listeners if they repented with all their heart (Joel 2:13). God helps, does not always accuse, forgives, has compassion like a father's, and takes care even of sinners.[28]

A synonym for compassion is "comfort" *(naḥam)*. God too is the one "comforting" or "soothing" (Isa. 51:12). Comfort can simply refer to answered prayer or reward.[29] It is the opposite of anger or punishment.[30] Frequently, it refers to soothing, as a mother soothes a distressed child or as a brother or relative soothes fearful family members. God too soothes, removes fears, and protects because God is both loving and powerful, and is not deceitful.[31] Comfort may also refer to family and friends who soothe someone who is mourning a deceased loved one.[32]

Exodus 34:6 is the core of God's revelation to Moses. It has an addendum. This same God "preserves love to thousands, bearing away sin and faithlessness and transgression, yet punishing the people not yet punished, visiting a sin of parents to children and to children of children to the third and to the fourth generation" (Exod. 34:7). Jeremiah rephrases this sentence. God "visits the sin of parents to a bosom (or lap) of children after them" (Jer. 32:18). Few readers would question the first clause: God "preserves love to thousands." God's love is great. Here the great number of people afflicted are highlighted. God can be loving because repentant people's sins are taken away from them. They become pure and innocent. Yet in contrast, as suggested by God's anger and truth, those who are not pure and innocent will be judged.

Whenever some people read the second half of the sentence they become disturbed. How can a just and loving God punish the *children* of sinners? Is that not unfair? First of all, God clearly and explicitly tells Moses that "You shall not put to death parents for their children and children shall not be put to death for the parents, people shall be put to death for their own crimes" (Deut. 24:16). God also reminds Jeremiah and Ezekiel that only the person who sins shall die.[33] In other words, children of sinful parents are not excluded from God's loving protection and presence simply because of parental sin.

Second, rather, the emphasis in Exodus 34 is a warning to parents. "Parent, your sin has collective ramifications. When you sin it affects your children for four generations." Jeremiah's imagery is provocative. It is as if a parent were to have a radioactive possession that at death is then thrown onto a child's lap. When a parent sins, that affects the child's upbringing and those practices are passed down through the generations. God apparently puts a protective guard after four generations. But this addendum reminds Moses that breaking God's covenant affects the innocent too.

Exodus 34:6–7 also has a major impact in the New Testament. Jesus' mission was "to seek and to save the lost" (Luke 19:10). Jesus has authority to forgive sins (Mark 2:10). Jesus came to earth "to serve and to give his life a ransom for many" (Mark 10:45). "I am gentle and lowly in heart" (Matt. 11:29). No wonder John can declare: "God is love" (1 John 4:16). And few humans could ever have guessed that God's love would be so great that God would come in the person of Jesus to die as a final scapegoat for all transgressors.[34]

God Is Holy

God brought the Hebrews out of Egypt because of a great love and compassion. But the Hebrews too had to remember that they were not simply running *away*; they were also running *to*. They must become like the God who led them, and unlike the humans who oppressed them. They are not to eat animals that defile "for I am the LORD your God, therefore purify yourselves and be pure because pure I am" (Lev. 11:44–45).[35] God is "pure" or "holy" *(qadash)*, set apart, consecrated. Because God is holy, the Israelites must honor their parents, keep the sabbath rests, not worship or consult idols, do offerings according to God's instruction, leave food for the poor, have integrity in work, be just, and not slander.[36] Because God is special, we humans need to follow certain laws to be special or set apart too. Some of these laws no longer are necessary for believers: laws about food and the sacrificing of animals and the keeping of certain festivals.[37] However, God still remains holy and God's people also are to be holy, even though the specific laws may vary, as Jesus, the Holy One on earth, prayed that his followers "in the world" not be "from the world."[38] The larger principle of loving one's neighbor as oneself remains valid.[39]

Because God is holy, God has no evil side (1 John 1:5). No one can ever be tempted to do evil by this God because "every good gift and every perfect present is from above coming down from the Parent of lights, from whom there is no movement of turning shadow" (James 1:17).[40]

God Is One

God is monogamous, not only because God is loving and faithful, but also because God is one God. Moses wants the Israelites to learn and teach this truth: "Hear Israel, LORD is God, LORD is one" (Deut. 6:4). "Lord" is the Tetragrammaton, the four consonants, YHWH. Who is the Lord is defined by two words: "God" and "one." The Hebrew for "God" is *'ĕlôhîm*. It is an abstract plural noun. The plural ending indicates an intensification of the characteristics. Whatever makes God to be God is present here. God is also "one," not many gods (1 Cor. 8:4–6). God is one; therefore, only God deserves our total allegiance (Deut. 6:5). The abstract plural *'ĕlôhîm* and "one" allow for the possibility of three Persons in One.[41] God has always had one name (Matt. 28:19). But this one name has three Persons. Thus, when God created humans in God's image they too have one name ("Human" or *Adam*) but two genders or persons, male and female (Gen. 1:26–27; 5:1–2). The church also, Christ's body, is *one* church (Eph. 2:14) in which every individual is important. Marriage between two people makes them *one* flesh (Eph. 5:31). God's oneness is a truth that affects many areas of life.[42]

Conclusion

Many of the attributes God has revealed are summarized in Moses' talk to the Israelites before they enter the land of Israel:

"For the LORD your God is God of the gods and Lord of the lords, the Mighty, the Great, the Strong, and the Wonderful, who is not partial and does not take bribes, executing justice for orphan and widow and loving every stranger, giving each one food and clothing" (Deut. 10:17–18).

"Your God, the one present with you, is a great and awesome God" (Deut. 7:21). This God with all these marvelous qualities is "great," "mighty," "old," and someone to fear or reverence. Here is God's mysterious, holy name. God is unique. This God is "almighty," a powerful Parent, Creator of the world and active in everyday events and places. But what does God do with this power? Because of God's compassion, grace, love, and faithfulness, God uses this great power to be just, to make sure those humans with less power, the parentless child, the single mother, and the foreigner, are treated justly and provided with their necessities.

Therefore, God's people too are to love the stranger (Deut. 10:19) and take care of the widow and orphan (Exod. 22:21–24).[43] God is the God who made everything and everyone and reminds the Hebrews that they too were strangers once. With a strong heritage and support, James can conclude that "pure and undefiled worship to the God and Creator is to care for orphans and widows in their trouble, to keep oneself unstained from the world" (James 1:27). That is because our God is a compassionate God who uses power individually and concretely, employing an angelic host and a community of followers, to respond with deliverance and wholeness and education to those under oppression, to those who are obedient.

But how has this great God been revealed in the United States? What have true Christians, as opposed to alleged Christians, communicated about God?

TWO

God of Power versus God of Love: The United States of America

William David Spencer

William David Spencer holds a Th.D. in theology and literature from Boston University School of Theology, Th.M. and M.Div. from Princeton Theological Seminary, and B.A. from Rutgers University. Born and reared in New Jersey, he serves as adjunct professor of theology with Gordon-Conwell Theological Seminary and pastor of encouragement with Pilgrim Church. Now a writer, he has served in urban and campus ministry, literacy, and education. He has published many articles, chapters, and books including *The Goddess Revival, God through the Looking Glass, Mysterium and Mystery, The Prayer Life of Jesus*, and *Chanting Down Babylon*.

Luke, the evangelist and Gospel writer, records that one day Jesus was accosted by someone out of a crowd complaining that his brother had stolen his family inheritance from him. Jesus warned, "Look out! Be on guard against all kinds of greediness" (Luke 12:15). Then sizing up the crowd as needing a lesson in sharing, he gave them an illustration about a plantation owner whose estate produced a bumper crop. Confronted with his abundance and all the options and responsibilities wealth levies on the rich, this plantocrat chose to build bigger barns in which to hoard his wealth rather than share it out with others. Enraged, God, the ultimate owner of all land, takes a most deadly and thorough reprisal, causing the owner to lose his abundance, his estate, his very life. His poverty of spirit is revealed behind the false façade of material abundance.

Following this illustration, Jesus points out a similar choice to his disciples (Luke 12:29–31). Will they be like greedy pagans *(ethnos)* or trusting believers? Believers share their abundance with others, demonstrating trust that God will continue to share with them what they need (Luke 12:32–34).

When one examines the arrival of Europeans to establish the Americas, one sees graphically a choice between greed or trust presented to them and with it an ensuing struggle of philosophies and practices between the spiritual descendants of this greedy landowner and those of Jesus' disciples.

In Jesus' explanation, his handful of sharing disciples were contrasted with a vast array of unbelieving nations grasping and fighting with one another. The sides were similarly vastly unbalanced in the early invasion of the Americas, illustrated by Columbus's initial crew, salting but two priests in among three shiploads of sailors. When settlers were soon sent, the odds increased. Unable to get many decent, sane people to go to distant lands feared to be inhabited by monstrosities and cannibals, the earliest settlers were drawn from "delinquent men and women" who had been convicted of murder, assault, and other crimes. The inducement to taking this risk was strong since the death penalty could be revoked in exchange for two years of service. Lesser sentences were relieved in one year. In addition, exiles condemned to work in the mines were now being sent to the West Indies.[1]

Therefore, for the majority, rather than seeing God as one who believes wealth should be distributed evenly, a God of love, most of these earliest explorers and settlers projected God in the image of Jesus' greedy landowner. The primary attribute of God in their perspective was that of God's power, God's omnipotence. Eventually, their imperial theology would turn the Americas from a vestige of Eden's garden to a grinding sweatshop of greed, enslavement, pollution, and degradation in the service, not of God, but of money. Had the majority choice for God's primary attribute from the beginning been that of love, rather than of power, the history of the Americas and of the United States would have been very different, as would the United States' present national state, its role in the world, and the requirement before it to ensure its place in the future. But, as the operating view of God of so many was through the characteristic of power, those who saw themselves called by such a God also saw themselves as invested with a portion of that absolute power to subdue the land and its inhabitants as "Providence" so willed.

However, against these, from the beginning of European involvement in the Americas, a minority of true, sharing believers struggled valiantly, knowing that God's absolute power is guided by God's absolute love, until now that minority has altered the majority opinion. Today the constitutional United States of America ideal is to balance power with love, making one intercooperative, sharing nation of a multicultural citizenry. Such an ideal more truly reflects the nature of God, seeks to redress the errors of United States history, and can forge the present into a future that all United States residents can share in the context of a global community of nations. Accurate theology is indeed essential for producing healthy practice.

In this chapter we will examine the Americas' relationship with God by following the biblical model of analyzing the history of nations theologically (as the Bible does Israel) within the context of God's self-revelation. Understanding that love is God's primary attribute and that divine omnipotence is guided by love, we will see how most Europeans who came to the Americas chose to emphasize power over love, precipitating calamity for the indigenous population. The deity they were following was fateful might, later articulated as Social Darwinism. We will also discover that a minority chose emphasizing love over power. Their position offers to help North America out of its present power-precipitated difficulties.

Divine Power Is Guided by Love

In the Scriptures, the omnipotence of God is clearly a characteristic that is tied into God's sovereignty.[2] Job confesses in 42:2, "I know that you can do all things, and that no purpose of yours can be thwarted."[3] The beleaguered Jeremiah, in the teeth of the Chaldeans setting up siegeworks recognizes, "Ah Lord GOD! It is you who made the heavens and the earth by your great power and by your outstretched arm! Nothing is too hard for you" (Jer. 32:17) and God agrees with him (Jer. 32:27).

Jesus taught, "for God all things are possible" (Matt. 19:26), a declaration the angel made to Mary about Jesus' own virgin birth in Luke 1:37. And the confession of God's omnipotence is the song of heaven, as Revelation 19:6 echoes it for us, "Hallelujah! For the Lord our God the Almighty reigns." But, interestingly, each one of these key passages deals primarily with God's omnipotence as it rescues people from eternal destruction, not simply brings destruction upon them.

When Job confesses God's omnipotence, God vindicates him in front of his friends. Jeremiah's lesson in God's almighty power concerns God's ability to restore the land to Judah after defeat and exile. Jesus spoke of God's omnipotence in assuring his disciples that God can save humans from eternal death, which was the message the angel was conveying when directing Mary to give her child the name "Jesus"—"the salvation of the Lord" (Luke 1:31). And, finally, that is the key message of Revelation 19:6. As in the case of Israel's conquest of Canaan, though, God does flex an almighty arm to defeat and subdue evil (Lev. 18:24–25). Still, God blends together "salvation and glory and power" when dealing with those being good, even when those good are being salvaged from among God's enemies, as was the harlot Rahab (Josh. 2; 6:17–23).

Love Is God's Primary Attribute

Exodus 34:6 recounts the first great confession God gave to Moses to accompany the recutting of the Ten Commandments, to replace the first set that Moses smashed in his anger at the apostasy of Israel. Descending in the mystical cloud of unknowing with which the perfect God is shrouded from the sight of fallen humans, God's booming voice declares:

> The LORD, the LORD,
> a God merciful and gracious,
> slow to anger,
> and abounding in steadfast love
> and faithfulness,
> keeping steadfast love for the
> thousandth generation,
> forgiving iniquity and
> transgression and sin,
> yet by no means clearing the
> guilty,

> but visiting the iniquity of the
> parents
> upon the children
> and the children's children,
> to the third and the fourth
> generation.

Here in this primal confession, to be learned by heart and taught through Israel's successive generations, is the interplay of both attributes of God. Here we find love in its most bounteous form, and power in its most ferocious.

The Lord, we are told, can be angered and can punish the guilty, not only in their lifetimes, but afterwards by allowing the ramifications of their evil to plague successive generations. Thus, the sad fact exists that generations of incest create idiot children and addictions to heroin can be passed on to fetuses in utero.

But, at the same time, power and punishment form only the second part of the confession, the shadow side of choosing against God rather than for God, the negative image that sets itself in contrast to the positive image. Before that sobering omnipotence is introduced, God gives an equally potent positive statement. And by the fact that it comes first, that positive statement is the primary attribute in operation. The Lord is first of all merciful and gracious. Able to be angered, yes, but not easily. God is slow to be angered, for God is primarily merciful and gracious. In fact, God abounds with *hesed,* the Hebrew word for love, kindness, benevolence, goodwill, favor, benefit, mercy, grace, piety, and beauty.[1] And this loving-kindness slows God's anger, remains faithfully blessing generations, and forgives the sins of all who seek forgiveness. In tempering God's anger and providing the escape of forgiveness, it provides a way for the repentant guilty and their children to avoid the terrors of the omnipotent judgment of God.

The sacrifice of God in Jesus Christ stands at the center of this mystery. God's love opens the way that sinners can escape God's anger and punishment by providing the means of forgiveness in the sacrifice of Jesus, whose death atones for that guilt. God's love does not set aside God's judgment; it satisfies it without cost to any human but Jesus, God's appointed one to die for human sin. All religions reflect this sacrifice, whether its reflection is as ferocious as the death of the male in goddess worship, the sacrifice of family members in African traditional religions, bog strangulations in Druidism, or as mildly symbolic as the sacrificial asceticism of Buddhism, purifying starvation in Hinduism, or the abstinence from various foods and from sexual intercourse demanded by various avatars. All religions that recognize the reality of sin recognize the need for atonement. The Good News of Christianity is that God's primary love took precedence among God's attributes and therefore, by example, it dictated that the true followers of God should make loving-kindness their operating principle as well.

The Sin of Those Who Chose Power over Love

The tragedy of the Americas is that this principle of the primacy of love was not initially put into practice. What was missing in the actions of so many from the beginning was this dual theology of power *with* love. Most Europeans who invaded refused to admit that God's power to punish is tempered by God's mercy and steadfast love, that God is slow to anger and quick to forgive. Instead, they set about their conquest as if they were Israel entering Canaan.

But, as Columbus's own evidence clearly shows, such a program as that of Israel in Canaan was *not* in operation on any level in the conquest of the Americas. The Amerindians were not in revolt against God, but welcomed the Bible's message, as we shall see, while the intention of these conquistadores was *by no means* the Christianizing of the land, but its subjugation and financial exploitation to enrich the adventurers individually and finance the wars of Spain.

That, then, was the key theological error used to justify the horrors inflicted by these conquerors on the Amerindians, and after them the African slaves shipped in to replace them: the refusal to admit that while all the attributes of God are true to God's character, love, as 1 John 4:8 tells us, is God's central operating hermeneutical characteristic. First John's scriptural revelation could have told us that God is wisdom, because God is omniscient. It could have told us that God is ubiquitous, because God is omnipresent. It could have told us that God is power, because, as we have seen from the Bible passages cited earlier, God is omnipotent. But, what it told us is that, in essence, God is love. Love determines the use of God's power, wisdom, judgment, and forgiveness.

The catastrophe of the Americas is that from the beginning "God is power" was the mistaken theological hermeneutic, or operating principle, that dictated the so-called Christian action of many, not this true biblical hermeneutic that "God is love." From this heretical misapplication came a most horrible conquest and a troubled aftermath. From the outset, while piously toting the name of God, most of the conquerors served money, mammon, as Jesus called it in Aramaic, and not the self-revealed God of the Bible. The racial warfare in United States cities, the climate of fear and violence that pervades this nation, the decline of its social institutions—particularly its fragmenting homes, weapon-filled schools, and disintegrating churches—fester in aftermath in direct relation to these primal sins visiting down the generations upon us, the descendants.

And, ultimately, philosophically, as we shall see, the principle in operation finally revealed itself as not biblical, but diametrically opposed to the biblical perspective: a line of thought that came to be termed philosophical Darwinism. Social Darwinism clearly articulated the sentiment that had actually been providing the impetus for violent action all along. The struggle among nations was theorized as natural. "Providence," that uninhabited deity, was the province of whomever was the most powerful. And gold was the only sacrament.

The Horrors of Choosing Power over Love

When King Ferdinand and Queen Isabella commissioned Columbus to sail on behalf of Spain to discover new lands, they were open about their intentions in their grant to him of April 30, 1492:

> For as much as you, *Christopher Columbus*, are going by our command, with some of our vessels and men, to discover and subdue some Islands and Continent in the ocean, and it is hoped that by God's assistance, some of the said Islands and Continent in the ocean will be discovered and conquered by your means and conduct, therefore it is but just and reasonable, that since you expose yourself to such danger to serve us, you should be rewarded for it.

The Old World Expected Power and Money

Clearly, Columbus was sent not as envoy, but as soldier with a mandate to conquer. Further, he was sent expecting to be rewarded. And the sending agency was clearly not God, whom they merely hoped would assist, but the King and Queen of Spain. They realized that they were striking a purely economic deal that would benefit them and

Columbus without thought for whom they might find in these unfortunate lands:

> And we being willing to honour and favour you for the reasons aforesaid; Our will is, That you, *Christopher Columbus*, after discovering and conquering the said Islands and Continent in the said ocean, or any of them, shall be our Admiral of the said Islands and Continent you shall so discover and conquer; and that you be our Admiral, Vice-Roy, and Governour in them, and that for the future, you may call and stile yourself, D[on] *Christopher Columbus*, and that your sons and successors in the said employment, may call themselves Dons, Admirals, Vice-Roys, and Governours of them.[5]

Vice, in addition to "Vice-Roy," is what Columbus bequeathed to his descendants as his share of this unhappy bargain. Although himself a professed Christian who forbade the trading of broken items in order to encourage Christianity in the Amerindians, Columbus still did not mistake his primary commission. On March 14, 1493, while enroute back to Spain, after his October 12, 1492 discovery and initial explorations, he reported:

> I reached the Indian Sea, where I discovered many islands, thickly peopled, of which I took possession without resistance in the name of our most illustrious monarch, by public proclamation and with unfurled banners.[6]

For Spain, Columbus annexed the Americas.

What Columbus found was a network of islands peopled by peace-loving Taino-Arawaks who worshiped a supreme deity, believed in heaven and hell, had a flood account, and were completely open to the gospel, seeing parallels between it and their belief in life after death. These had subsumed the predecessing Ciboneys and were mortally in terror of the ferocious cannibal Caribs working their way up from South America. They hailed Columbus and his crew as emissaries from heaven, an answer to their pleas for succor to Guamaonocon, the name they called the one Supreme God. How wrong they were.

Instead, Columbus on his part took advantage of this apocalyptic expectancy and used it to his advantage. As he reported to Ferdinand and Isabella:

> On my arrival at that sea (the Caribbean), I had taken some Indians by force from the first island that I came to (Hispañola, the present site of the Dominican Republic and Haiti), in order that they might learn our language and communicate to us what they knew respecting the country; which plan suc-

ceeded excellently and was a great advantage to us. . . . These men are still traveling with me, and although they have been with us now a long time, they continue to entertain the idea that I have descended from heaven; and on our arrival at any new place they published this, crying out immediately with a loud voice to the other Indians, "Come, come and look upon beings of a celestial race"; upon which both women and men, children and adults, young men and old, when they got rid of the fear they at first entertained, would come out in throngs, crowding the roads to see us, some bringing food, others drink, with astonishing affection and kindness.[7]

Had only Columbus and his crew returned that kindness and been the envoys of heaven which the Taino-Arawaks hailed them. But, "Gold was always the object of Spanish actions here,"[8] lamented the eyewitness Benedictine priest Bartolomé de las Casas, who watched those hopes dashed as the Indians' welcome turned to horror as Columbus and his followers subjected them to a slavery so heinous in attempting to scrape gold out of the land that they were exterminated nearly immediately.

The Repercussion of Choosing Power Was Destruction

Setting their home base on Hispañola, the conquerors swiftly began their program of destructive servitude. When several Amerindians, expecting payment for guiding some Spaniards, stole clothing from them as reimbursement, Columbus declared war. His followers threw themselves with great relish and great guile into the battle. Devising a strategy based on their theological misidentity by the Amerindians, the conquerors traveled from island to island inviting the inhabitants to return with them to heaven to visit departed loved ones. Instead of heaven, the beguiled were thrown into mines. When word got out or a population hesitated, the Europeans would drop the ruse and fling men, women, children, both young and old, into their ships' holds "like the basest of animals,"[9] according to one eyewitness. Stuffed below deck without air, light, food, or water, up to one-third would die between islands, being thrown overboard so plentifully that following ships could navigate their courses by steering along through the floating bodies. To break the villages' resistance, the Europeans would invite the chiefs (called caciques) and the elders to a council. When eighty leaders had filled the large village meeting hut, the conquerors would step outside on a ruse, bar the door, and set the hut aflame. At one point, blood-lusting Spaniards raided a village, stealing the women. When the men pursued and the conquerors saw they could not escape with their captives, they disemboweled all the women, holding the anguishing men at bay with their guns. Mounted conquistadores would test the sharpness of their swords on passing Amerindians and day by day the Taino-Arawak died by butchery, lechery, overwork, and despair.

The popular misconception that has come down to us in our history books that the Americas were conquered by "the cross and the sword" was a lie repudiated from the beginning. The first priest ordained in the West Indies, confidant of Columbus and unceasing foe of the enslavement and extermination of the Amerindians, charged: "The same falseness applies to the statement about indoctrination into the holy Catholic Faith, for, upon my oath, the truth is that in those days and many years later there was no more concern for their Christianization than if they had been horses or working beasts."[10] The conquistadores themselves dropped all semblance of religion: "Sin leads to sin, and for many years they lived unscrupulously, not observing Lent or other fasts."[11] When Dominican friars arrived and protested the abominable slavery, the settlers stormed their residence and demanded their removal. The conquerors also fell into a most loathsome form of idolatry, "planting crosses and inducing indians to worship them," so that Amerindians "can be made to worship a stick."[12] As a result, the Amerindians eventually dismissed Christianity as sheer lies. This marked a complete about-face from their initial response of hailing it as descended from heaven. As one early cacique on what is now Cuba told Columbus, "This ceremony (the mass) is very good, because it seems to me you are giving thanks to God by means of it."[13] Once the lie of the explorers' lives defamed the integrity of their religious words, Amerindian slaves would say when asked if they were Christian, "Yes, Sir, I am a bit Christian because I have learned to lie a bit; another day I will lie big, and I will be big Christian."[14] And daily the conquerors would reinforce this attitude by breaking treaties, enslaving villages, setting up thirteen gibbets on a scaffold, executing thirteen Amerindians at a time, jesting that they were dangling for Christ and the twelve apostles.

In grisly demonstration of the dark side of Jesus' warning in Matthew 25:31–46, Jesus was once again being crucified in the slaughter of the weak of the earth.

Reaping Power's Bitter Harvest

Surveying the hypocrisy-hidden slaughter of the Amerindians he was unable to prevent, Father Casas mourned:

> Endless testimonies . . . prove the mild and pacific temperament of the natives, as well as the fact that we surpassed them in arms so that, had we lived among them as Christians, we would have had no need of weapons, horses or fierce dogs to attract them to us. But our work was to exasperate, ravage, kill, mangle and destroy; small wonder, then, if they tried to kill one of us now and then.[15]

Although he admired Columbus's many fine qualities, Father Casas realized the responsibility for setting the policy of power that allowed such slaughter lay with the imperially commissioned Columbus. Despite any personal faith Columbus may have espoused, Father Casas observed, this pious "admiral and his Christians, as well as all those who followed after him in this land, worked on the assumption that the way to achieve their desires was first and foremost to instill fear in these people, to the extent of making the name Christian synonymous with terror."[16]

The true Christians who were contemporary with the conquerors, like Father Casas and the Dominican and Franciscan friars who fought with him against slavery, realized that "God did not want Christianity at that cost; God takes no pleasure in a good deed, no matter its magnitude, if sin against one's fellow man is the price of it, no matter how minuscule that sin may be."[17] Instead, they lectured, "When Christians merely pass through infidel territory—but even if they should stay—the safest rule is to set a good example of virtues, so that, as Our Redeemer says, the sight of it will prompt men to praise and glorify the God and Father of Christians: they would see that such believers can only worship a good and true God."[18]

When such is not done, these true fifteenth-century Christians recognized, the character of God is impugned:

> If God had not chosen to enlighten a few through the preaching of good friars and against all human power and knowledge, all Indians would think, like the majority, that our God is evil, unjust and abominable, since he sent such iniquitous men to afflict and destroy them by means never heard of before.[19]

Those who claim they are "Christians" but live waging war in the name of God are among those who Jesus damned in Matthew 7:21–23.

Casas explains: "The reader will find out about the state of eternal damnation in which those people live who procured and recommended preaching by means of war."[20] But the damnation with which they cursed themselves also passed as a legacy cursing the attitudes of their progeny, as we shall see presently.

When the Amerindians died, the conquistadores attempted to drag more Indians from the mainland, still following their policy of primary power. But here they encountered the fierce Caribs and other Amerindians who were inclined to resist. Exhausting the small gold available on the islands, they were now attempting to develop an agrarian economy out of the Americas, but still they kept up their legacy of force, kidnapping Africans from their homelands to take the place of servitude of the fallen Taino-Arawaks.

The English-Speaking Follow the Spanish Model

When the British swept over the West Indies and other countries began to claim islands, the policy established by the Spaniards remained.

Through 350 succeeding years of African enslavement, the British and then their descendants who became the citizens of the United States and the Caribbean islands maintained the relationship of slave to master, resisting, often persecuting, and sometimes executing Christian missionaries, elders, pastors who denounced slavery and called for a God of empowering love and justice, rather than a God simply of power.

After the continental United States was founded, among the most pernicious of these maintenance measures was what was called the "Fugitive Slave Act." As representative of the accumulating weight of the legacy of power, it reveals the continuing presence of a most imperious attitude toward human ownership persisting through the generations. Slavery had continued nonstop into the founding of the United States. It preserved and extended northward the perspective with which the Caribbean had been conquered, for the desire to conquer remained at the initial founding of the colonies that would eventually unite to become the United States.[21]

Holding self-serving charters, issued by their own monarchs, to take the land from the Amerindians, European settlers who traveled up into the North American mainland also received the power investiture to fight off other claims and the assurance that theirs was a mission from God in the name of Christianity. No wonder they felt the land and all the people in it had been issued to them to enjoy and dispose of as they saw fit.

By the time the Puritans settled New England, even they bought slaves to serve them. The bizarre history of the Salem witch trials commenced when a Barbadian slave, Tituba, said to be half Carib, half African, and owned by the Reverend Samuel Parris, began to share with Parris's daughters and friends her knowledge of obeah, the West Indian memory of the sorcery component of African traditional religion. If ministers had never owned slaves, the witchcraft trials may not have happened.

That slavery did not continue in the North may not be as much due to increasing virtue, as to the failure of huge crops like tobacco and cotton to flourish. That it became so entrenched in the South is directly economic. Free work is immediately profitable.

Manifest Destiny Was a Culminating Concept of Power

This legacy of imperial attitude, which claimed it had been divinely granted the right to own a land and its people, expanded in the microcosm with legislation like the "Fugitive Slave Act" of September 18, 1850, and in the macrocosm through the concept of "manifest destiny." These kinds of measures were created to ensure its hold would continue to reach and secure what it grasped. The new concept called "manifest destiny" ensured that all the land within reach would ultimately belong to the expanding states, while the Fugitive Slave Act ensured owners that no matter where slaves fled, they too would remain within the reach of masters' power. What this latter legislation did was to close previous safe lands to which slaves could escape. And not only did it strike down any territory as a safe haven for escaping slaves seeking freedom, but it prosecuted all persons who aided them and even fined the police from whom they escaped. Truly this legislation marked the depth of disregard for human welfare against which the growing minority had to struggle if they were ever to secure the United States of America as a "land of the free." And when Christians did protest, they were beaten or murdered, as the abolitionist Lovejoy who was shot down at his door by a Missouri mob, or the young Lane seminarian John G. Fee who was hounded from Kentucky and disinherited by his father for preaching emancipation, or the Kentucky farmer Van Zandt whose Ohio farm was seized and he himself imprisoned for aiding runaway slaves.[22]

How could so many in a nation justify this attitude century after century? If God is seen as having empowered some to rule and some to serve, that legacy frames the perimeters of one's doctrine. God had invested their foreparents with more power than the prior inhabitants, they reasoned, so they subdued, enslaved, and eventually eradicated them. In this tradition, one rules one's present slaves in the name of the God of overbearing power. Whether to Spanish, Portuguese, or British, this legacy passed on through each succeeding group that came and conquered the Americas, each contributing its part to the attitude that eventually produced measures like the Fugitive Slave Act and manifest destiny.

Yet while all this was happening, change was at work. It began in the struggle against slavery of Casas and his friars, was augmented by abolitionists through the years, and culminated in the heroics of greats like Harriet Tubman, the "Moses of her people." Decade by decade it gathered decisive strength. By the 1860s, half of the country had abandoned the legacy of slave-holding and were ready to end slavery. These United States citizens had become convinced enslaving others could not be God's will. And they were vindicated.

By the late 1800s, the true faceless deity served by the concepts of slavery and manifest destiny and by all the conquerors who preceded their articulation and contributed to their formulation became apparent.

Fateful Might: The True Name of the God of Power

Though Charles Darwin first published *The Origin of Species by Natural Selection, or The Preservation of Favoured Races in the Struggle for Life* in 1859, the full mushrooming impact was not felt until several decades later.

In the Caribbean islands, particularly on Jamaica, its stage had been set philosophically by such reinforcements to servitude as the infamous "Queen's Letter," sent from England and reported by Jamaica's Committee of Assembly on January 28, 1832. This document blighted the dream of equality in freedom, as it adjured "negroes" to work "not uncertainly or capriciously but steadily and continuously" for their "born Lords."[23]

While the attempt by planters to pin such a position on biblical proof texts was the subject of hot debate by Christian abolitionists, Darwinian thought provided an unequivocal basis on which to establish natural inequality by the argument of natural selection, marking a new slant of non-Christian philosophy of colonial rule.

In the United States it served the racist, expansionist mood of the 1890s. Manifest destiny was viewed, accordingly, not as the justification of greed, but as the natural response to faceless nature's urging to struggle, and to the stronger and the more fit to win and rule. The Americas' bloody history became proof of the validity of that philosophic position.

O'Sullivan Promotes Manifest Destiny

In 1845 John L. O'Sullivan, a newspaper editor and eventually a diplomat to Portugal, had first used the term "manifest destiny" in print when he wrote of "our manifest destiny to overspread the continent allotted by Providence for the free development of our yearly multiplying millions."[24]

O'Sullivan introduced the phrase "manifest destiny" to justify his call for annexing Texas from Mexico, employing it in an editorial in the July issue of his *United States Magazine and Democratic Review.* That worked so well he used the phrase again in December to prove the United States had a right to own the Oregon Territory as well. In O'Sullivan's view, "California will, probably, next fall away. . . . Imbecile and distracted, Mexico never can exert any real government authority over such a country." Further, he set his sights on "the British Canadas . . . soon to be followed by annexation; and destined to swell the still accumulating momentum of our progress."[25]

How could O'Sullivan write so blithely of coveting and stealing neighboring territories? He recognized no obligation to "weak" neighbors and did not see annexation as "unrighteous . . . military conquest" or "territorial aggrandizement at the expense of justice." Why not? Because God, "Providence," had intended this continent for the "advance guard of the irresistible army of Anglo-Saxon emigration . . . to pour down upon it."[26] Such an attitude encouraged national pugnacity.

Manifest Destiny Has Vocal Advocates

By 1895 a young Teddy Roosevelt, watching President Cleveland's quarrel with Great Britain over Venezuela, chafed, "Personally I rather hope the fight will come soon. The clamor of the peace faction has convinced me that the country needs a war."[27] The eventual election of Teddy Roosevelt as president suggests the country agreed. Fitting the militantly evolutionary national mood, war professionals, like Alfred Thayer Mahan, wrote long treatises on warfare, explaining that nations *must* struggle against each other. If the United States did not, it would perish. In his book *The Influence of Sea Power upon History, 1668–1783*, Mahan presented colonization as a natural response of the stronger, commenting, "colonization, as of all other growths, it is true that it is most healthy when it is most natural."[28] "Natural" became the key word to excuse all imperialism.

Who was fitted by nature to do this colonization? "The Anglo Saxon believes himself to be the child of destiny,"[29] explained Rena M. Atchison in the exclusionary book *Un-American Immigration: Its Present Effects and Future Perils* in 1894. Unrestricted immigration of other races, the article explained, would only tear that destiny down. Other races apparently existed to serve.

The legacy of supposed divine or natural power investiture, of subjecting others and of handing on that error to succeeding generations invaded the twentieth century, creating the climate of estrangement and of contention that molests contemporary North America. If today the United States chokes on the fumes of its own industrial sacrificial fires to mammon, it is only keeping stoked the first fires of the conquerors, burning villages and smelting the ore scraped out by the hands of the original inhabitants. Through these fumes the United States is taking a belated look out today at the rest of the world, seeking to preserve fresh water, air, and virgin forests somewhere. But the rest of the world, kept closely informed by the United States' internationally broadcast television transmissions and exported films of its life of technological comfort and leisure, wants the same results and is willing to pay similar costs in subjecting the land that mammon, the god of power, exacts.

The ripping out of the rain forest in the Amazon is an example of Brazilian farmers looking at the industrialization of North America and wanting similar material rewards. The killing of Christian Colombian farmers who will not grow cocaine and reap the large profit in drugs from the multibillion-dollar North American market is the telos of profit=power=destiny. What the drug lords want is the same thing the conquerors wanted: gold at any cost. They are among the true heirs of the legacy of profit by violence in the service of money. The ethnic gangs who war for possession of each set of city blocks in the United States' urban centers follow the doctrine of manifest destiny in microcosm. They continue a struggle for supremacy as the fittest in that they are the best armed in their neighborhoods. As at the beginning, the power of control and its tribute wealth is a compelling motive. Mammon is served when a society is predicated on human greed. If God is primarily viewed through power, then imperial actions, both macrocosmic in collective action and microcosmic in individual action, follow that commanding characteristic of the cruel and faceless deity. They imitate the deity of unbridled power.

The Blessing of Those Who Choose to Serve Love over Power

On the other side, in every nation around the earth in which sin abounds God's grace also abounds mightily. And grace has abounded powerfully in the Americas.

Individuals Choose Love

Out from among the conquistadores, God called a young adventurer to give up his slaves and join the Dominican order as a priest. In company with these fervent believers, Bartolomé de las Casas preached potent, scathing sermons against slavery, eventually being named official protector of the Amerindians by the king. From the true Christianity of Casas and his fellow priests and converts come remarkable reports of grace in action as exemplified by Enrique, a Taino chieftain who organized surviving Amerindians from many islands into a skillful army that held off Spain. A true Christian who said his prayers as he circled his camp each night, Enrique became a model of merciful warfare, restraining his warriors, sparing the lives of his captives at the price of promising not to fight against his people again. To all, Amerindian and conqueror alike, he demonstrated true Christian love and power.[30]

The legacy of Casas and Enrique and their Christian contemporaries carried down through the long hard years of majority slavery, producing giants like Betsey Stockton, daughter of a slave mother, who became a pioneer educator of the poor and the first unmarried woman missionary sent out from North America, and George Liele, a Virginia-born slave whose powerful preaching enabled many in the United States into God's kingdom and, after he was set free, in the West Indies as well.[31] Protests to abolish slavery continued from true Christians. As early as February 1688, the Mennonites attacked the recent instituting of slavery in Virginia, declaring themselves "Against the Traffic of Mensbody." Through the abolitionist movement, burgeoning Christianity gathered increasing strength until its mercy finally overpowered the economic advantage of slavery to bring hard-won freedom to all United States residents.

From the establishing of what would become in time a new nation, the names of great believers who protested the sin of the status quo and pointed a better way reads like a who's who in United States' history.[32] The Reverend Samuel Willard and the Boston clergy opposed the extremes of the Salem witch trials and Governor Benjamin Fletcher made New York a refuge for the accused, through such efforts largely keeping contained to the Salem area the madness that sent nineteen people, including protesting fellow clergy, to their deaths. Orator Frederick Douglass, author Harriet Beecher Stowe, activist Sojourner Truth, and legislator Abraham Lincoln led the abolition movement to victory. The great Wahpeton (Santee) Sioux physician Ohiyesa (Dr. Charles Eastman), as well as renowned missionary David Brainerd, advocated for the Amerindian cause.

These followed such stalwart Spanish missionary pioneers as Antonio de Montesinos, a Dominican renowned for championing Indian rights, and Eusebio Kino, who baptized four thousand Indians, while introducing stock raising and doing extensive social and spiritual ministry. French missionaries followed Paul Le Jeune's dynamic leadership of the Jesuits to extremes of humane service. Jean de Brébeuf identified so closely with the Huron that he created a grammar and lexicon for them and eventually died beside them when they were annihilated by the western Iroquois. When John Eliot and the British missionaries arrived, they worked on the premise that the Indians had a right to their share of the land, though every concession they tried to secure was violated by the imperialists. Though in many ways these champions failed to deflect suffering, exploitation, and disenfranchisement from the continental Amerindians, still one can give a sizable portion of credit to these advocates that the United States' Native Americans were not ruthlessly eliminated as were their counterparts on some of the islands of the Caribbean. Simply, more missionaries, more true Christians, were at work on the continent than initially in the islands. Further, Christians like William Penn, the Quakers, and the Mennonites stood out against all war, not just that against the Amerindians.

On another front, women like the brilliant Anne Hutchinson and prayer warrior Esther Edwards Stoddard set a legacy of learning and piety that eventually resulted in inspiring women's education, emancipation, and leadership in such purgative movements as those for abolition of slavery, women's suffrage, temperance, civil and children's rights.

Through the great awakenings, revivals, the rise of the Sunday school, and the application of the gospel to urban social problems, this burgeoning minority has produced today's socially and spiritually thriving United States churches and such globally effective parachurch organizations as World Vision and Church World Service. Today God's remnant in North America has grown into a strong, active spiritual and moral force that runs through all levels of the people of the United States. The legacy of the true gospel of Jesus Christ has levied a powerful mandate of mutual respect, love, freedom, and equality in distributing wealth and power that permeates the ideals of the United States of America.

Today the United States remains in a state of decision considering which legacy it will follow: the way of self-serving, abusive power or the way of others-oriented, supportive love. While this chapter was being revised, a fascist bombing of a government building in Oklahoma killed many in the name of vengeance on the second anniversary of the slaughter of the Branch Davidians in Waco, Texas. The heirs of the conquistadores and of Casas still battle over which God this nation will serve: violence or the loving Christ.

Policies That Choose Love

Today, however, the majority of United States' citizens, and under their direction the government, are no longer simply accepting the perspective of change by violence of the Americas' first criminal conquerors as a mode for operation. Rather than a two-layer culture of conquered and conquerors, the United States today is a pluralistic nation, remarkable for its spirit of volunteerism and its use of its budget to help other nations. As of 1995, an estimated 19,767,316 foreign-born people are welcomed to live in the United States, nearly one-quarter of these being added since 1985. Together with all North Americans these nearly 20 million look back out toward helping the world.

Since World War II, the United States has disbursed almost $310 billion around the world, $14 billion in 1993 alone. Within the United States in 1993 the greatest single expenditure was not the military, as many suppose, but social security benefits, taking care of the elderly, a figure that exceeded the military budget by over $13 billion.

While the administration of justice was allotted $15 billion and the general government operating budget $13 billion, income security received a whopping $207.3 billion, the lion's share of the budget. Itemized under this fund: public assistance given to families with dependent children; food and nutrition assistance programs; food donation programs; food to Puerto Rico, our associated state, and to our territories; home energy subsidies; homeless persons housing, as well as housing subsidies to keep many from becoming homeless; Amerindian relief; low-income home cooling costs and weatherizing; maintenance assistance to the disabled, repatriates, and refugees; Medicaid to the elderly; nurse midwife services; aid to veterans' homes; and work incentive programs.[33]

A further $315.7 billion was divided between Medicare, health, education, and veterans' benefits, with more going to community development, and general science, and energy, looking to the future.

While the United States' government budget reflected its population's interest in providing good lives for citizens here, it also reflected its concern for the living conditions of the citizens of other nations.

Since William F. Lederer and Eugene Burdick's *The Ugly American* opened eyes to abuse in the distribution of foreign aid in the 1960s, citizens have become aware of almost legendary abuses in the use of the United States aid budget at home and abroad. But, judging by *intention,* the North American public reflects a vastly different attitude from the first European conquerors who began the Europomorphizing of the Americas. United States citizens "vote" with their tax dollars and clearly those are intended to help rather than hurt, subvert, or control other nations.

In 1995, for example, foreign aid was officially extended by the United States through such organizations as the African Development Foundation, established as a nonprofit government corporation to "support the self-help efforts of poor people in African countries." Also receiving funds was the Inter-American Foundation "to support the self-help efforts of poor people in Latin America and the Caribbean." This organization was established as a direct response to the report of abuse. According to its intention, "the Foundation was established because of congressional concern that traditional programs of development assistance were not reaching poor people. Instead of working through governments, the Foundation responds directly to the initiatives of the poor by supporting local and private organizations."[34]

Added to these, the United States' Peace Corps fields thousands of volunteers throughout Latin America, Africa, the Near East, Asia, the Pacific islands, central and eastern Europe, providing workers in education, agriculture, health, small business development, urban development, and the environment. These days this assistance has expanded into the former Union of Soviet Socialist Republics as well as out through the United States in the worldwide schools program. Hollywood, in the name of entertainment, loves to posit the CIA as riddled through all these organizations, and no doubt involvement exists. But the good faith of the volunteers themselves and the United States citizens who support them stands as a testimony to how far North America has come in growing beyond the limited and self-centered vision of its first invaders.

Finally, looking toward the future, the United States' foreign aid sponsors the United States International Development Corporation Agency, an international policy planning program for developing countries. This agency is particularly concerned with looking out for the interests of developing countries when the United States sets policies and plans how best United States bilateral assistance can be implemented.

Over and above the way United States citizens have developed the government's giving, a plethora of United States-based private sector volunteer organizations extend helping hands to assist people all over this country and throughout every country of the world.

Leading this "pitch in and help" attitude of the United States are, and have always been, the churches. As a single example, in the Presbyterian Church (USA) alone, as of November 1994, a representative poll revealed that 95 percent of lay elders, 82 percent of pastors, and

75 percent of lay members, the vast majority of the church, do completely donated volunteer work. In 1993, $133 million was forwarded beyond the expenses of individual congregations to support "regional, national, and international church projects" by this denomination alone[35] and the United States is filled with sacrificially giving denominations and individual churches of all varieties.

A nation that began by being taken and stratified has now homogenized the heirs of both slaves and masters into one giving people. And these have mobilized themselves into action.

This is where the witness of those who follow the example of Father Casas and the first missionaries can speak so powerfully. North America needs fully, on every level, to abandon the god of self-absorbed, abusive power. Let us Christians, through proclaiming the cross of Jesus Christ, lead everybody in the United States consciously to meet and serve the true, omnipotently caring God. Through obedience to Jesus Christ and his Father's law of love, the dream of Bartolemé de las Casas, of Eusebio Kino, of Esther Edwards Stoddard, of Betsey Stockton, of Harriet Beecher Stowe, of Frederick Douglass, and of Martin Luther King and Billy Graham in our own age, of all North America's roster of heroes and heroines can come true today.

Choosing to Serve the God of Love

In June 1969 the National Commission of the Causes and Prevention of Violence, established by President Lyndon Johnson to understand the violence that had recently disrupted North American cities and claimed the life of Senator Robert Kennedy, received its report. The findings reached a parallel and independent conclusion to that of this chapter, without exploring the full theology implicit in the Americas' legacy of violence. Rather than among the causes, it viewed expansionist theologies successively as an "impediment to understanding":

> A fourth impediment to understanding our violent past has been the powerful strain of optimistic parochialism that has variously equated the growth of the American nation with the New Jerusalem, Manifest Destiny, and ineluctably progressive Darwinian evolution.[36]

However, rather than merely ethnocentric blinders on the eyes of those who conquered North America, as we have seen, these variations on a single divine theme were instead theo-philosophical road maps for action that, handed down through generations, have kept the United States traveling on a path of racial war and lethal economic inequity. If we are threatened at arriving as a nation at the gates of internecine urban civil warfare, the threshold of the hell of the god who values power above all, should anyone be surprised? It is the ultimate destiny of all who live by the sword.

Individual and Collective Decisions Are Needed

Now is the time to tear up that map and lead this nation on another route. Envision every North American beginning to act on the characteristic that God is love. What if not just some, not just the government in foreign aid on behalf of the rest, but *all* United States citizens and residents began today to deploy the wealth received and the resources at hand to help others and serve God's reign, living modestly on a reasonable income, simply getting what is needed and not all that is wanted, and sharing the rest in graduated tithing, increasing the percentage of giving in proportion to what is earned?

Immediately we would greatly diminish the amount of evil, exploitation, and violence in which we have permitted ourselves or our businesses to participate. Our mutual goal would be to assist everyone on the globe to reach the standard of living we enjoy. We would invest in organizations involved in securing gainful occupation for the starving, and in those bolster the diminishing unpolluted natural resources from which we should all draw. The kinds of concerns we would have would alter. We would all be concerned with obtaining profit in a symbiotic mode beneficial to each country. Since we were investing personally in others we would be more severe in combating graft and making certain our investments reached the people we wished to help. How would other countries respond? When gold was recently discovered in the Dominican Republic, a number of foreign businesses vied to win the government's contract. The Dominican government, after weighing out the offers, decided to pass over the usual, powerful foreign companies whose past records had revealed more exploitation than benefit and selected a smaller company from Puerto Rico that had in the past shown concern for improving the lot of the Dominican people. United States' businesses learned a lesson from that decision. Simply paying off government officials does not ensure lasting business relationships with a country. Prestige is built more solidly with a symbiotic program that benefits both investors and hosts. Corporations, as well as individuals, open themselves up to receiving the corresponding blessings of the God of love. "Commit your work to the LORD," counsels Proverbs 16:3, "and your plans will be established."

If we set out to forge each individual and national policy on the model of the love of God, what would the Americas look like? A reflection of Eden could return that would satisfy many postmillennial dreams for the entrance to heaven on earth. Love, not simply power, would dictate how we all act toward one another and toward the earth. The God we serve would be the true God who tempers anger with mercy and guides all by love—the true God revealed in the Scriptures. And serving this God, true followers would struggle not to subdue flesh and blood, but would cooperate to eliminate evil, exploitation, and violence in emulation of the loving intention of God to rescue people from sin and oppression.

Today North America faces a unique opportunity to change. The United States of America is a country in radical change. The "Two-Thirds-Worldizing" of the United States' urban centers, the new economic and social mobility of minorities (reflected in such neologisms as "Buppie" [the Black Upwardly Mobile]), the transculturation of our popular culture and economy through the influx of Japanese computer chips, Filipino shoe wear, world music, Thai cuisine, Chinese-American news anchors, Mexican knit wear, and so on reveal a nation becoming more a global reflection than an Anglo-Saxon imperial power seat. Rich in resources, still young and strong, the multicultural United States of America has a unique opportunity to raise its theo-cultural consciousness to a new understanding of its duty to God and to its neighbors, an opportunity shared in North America by the Dominion of Canada as it works out its own symbiosis between United Kingdom, French, and Amerindian extracted citizens.

As Israel, the United States Has the Opportunity to Decide

Second Chronicles tells us that when Solomon, gifted by God with wisdom, finished the temple he had built in God's honor and the parallel house he built to enjoy himself, God appeared to him with this instruction: "If my people who are called by my name humble themselves, pray, seek my face, and turn from their wicked ways, then I will hear from heaven, and will forgive their sin and heal their land. Now my eyes will be open and my ears attentive to the prayer that is made in this place" (2 Chron. 7:14–15). If the United States feels its days of glory slipping away, its institutions weakening, its prestige tarnishing, its respect, power, positive self-image all on the wane, perhaps the eyes and ears of God are turning away in unrequited love and sorrow for its lost opportunities to extend love to others.

Neither Solomon individually nor Israel collectively heeded God's warning. That nation was divided, suffering defeat and exile. Each nation around the globe is offered a chance to repent—that is, turn around on the path of primary power and move instead along the path of love—and be established by the omnipotent God who values love above all. The Bible tells us God evaluates each nation and decides which to sustain afloat and which to scuttle and raise up again with a new crew aboard (e.g., Luke 1:52).

If the entire United States in its third century chooses to abandon the false image of God as primarily power and the oppressive lifestyle engendered by that god and chooses instead to serve the God of love in loving actions to others, it would not suffer the fate of the rich landowner in Jesus' parable with which I opened the chapter. Rather, the United States could find itself thriving again in the empowerment of God's forgiveness that would lift the curse of its violent legacy off its current and future generations. It would experience a new millennium of inner harmony and outer respect and symbiotic cooperation with other nations seeking the same God of love.[37]

Toward this end, Christians should issue a serious call for individual and corporate loving actions, cessation of exploitation and provocation for the sake of financial profit, in short, a thorough national housecleaning of the accumulated dust of past imperialistic sins and their aftermath of majority guilt and minority estrangement. People who feel they have ownership in an enterprise respect that enterprise and work for its good. People who do not feel this ownership attempt to tear it down. Salvaging a nation is the responsibility of every citizen, every resident, and the intention of the loving God whose will is that none should perish (2 Peter 3:9).

This is the God that the United States and its hemispheric neighbor Canada, and southern neighbors Brazil and others, need to serve if the West is not to be reduced to the world's polluted dung heap in the next millennium. Every nation and every individual needs to serve the God whose love, not power, is primary.

The following chapter explores the nature of this love and shows that the present cultural danger in the United States of America is to define love in a relativistic, pluralistic fashion and not a biblical one, thereby producing a response that would fall short of the ideal corrective of God's just love that is outlined here.

The Complementarity of God's Love and God's Righteousness: The United States of America

Gretchen Gaebelein Hull

Gretchen Gaebelein Hull, lecturer, writer, and stateswoman, is also an elder in the Presbyterian Church U.S.A. She has a B.A., magna cum laude, from Bryn Mawr College, graduate work in philosophy from Columbia University, and a Litt. D. from Houghton College. She is author of *Equal to Serve* and contributing author to *The Women's Study New Testament, Applying the Scriptures,* and many other books and articles. She is editor of *Priscilla Papers.*

In 1776, the Declaration of Independence of the Thirteen American Colonies from British sovereignty boldly stated:

We hold these truths to be self-evident that all men are created equal, that they are endowed by their Creator with certain unalienable Rights, that among these are Life, Liberty, and the pursuit of Happiness.

These cherished words are at the heart of the United States' national self-identity, and yet putting these words into practice has been far from easy. In 1790, the ink was scarcely dry on the hard-won Constitution of the United States when people perceived that more specific language was needed to guarantee certain individual rights. And so, only a year and a half later, in December 1791, the States ratified the first ten constitutional amendments, popularly known as the Bill of Rights. More amendments followed as the new nation sought to delineate appropriate guidelines for life in a free society.

For example, while in late eighteenth-century usage the word "men" supposedly included all human beings, the reality was that none of these "self-evident truths" about "unalienable Rights" (including the precious right to vote) applied equally to the black slave population, Native Americans, or women. Granted, certain legislative measures have helped ameliorate these inequities, such as the Emancipation Proclamation freeing the slaves (effective January 1, 1863), the Thirteenth Amendment abolishing the institution of slavery altogether (1865), and the Nineteenth Amendment finally granting women the right to vote (1920). Nevertheless, over two hundred years after its founding, the United States of America is still struggling with how best to provide each citizen equal opportunity to "Life, Liberty, and the pursuit of Happiness." Sadly, for many Americans there is nothing fictional about George Orwell's biting satire: "All animals are equal but some animals are more equal than others."[1]

One of the very positive results of the United States' civil rights movements of the 1950s and 1960s was sensitizing the overwhelmingly white population majority to how carelessly and unjustly those controlling political, economic, and social power can treat minorities. One of the most far-reaching actions alerting the United States to the evils of racial prejudice was Rosa Parks' courageous refusal in 1955 to sit in the back of the bus behind whites any longer.[2] When confronted with the continuing anguish of fellow citizens still denied even the most basic rights and privileges of citizenship, persons of good will vowed to work actively toward redressing past wrongs and creating a new climate in which injustice can be swiftly recognized and fairly dealt with, regardless of race, class, or gender.[3]

Facing Diversity

However, as the twenty-first century commences, implementing fair play for an increasingly diverse population seems harder rather than easier. One can hardly open a newspaper in the United States today without reading about disagreements over issues such as affirmative action, equal economic opportunity, and equitable application of social welfare benefits.

Unlike the country's earliest years, when the population reflected a predominantly white Anglo-Saxon and northern European background, today the United States is home to citizens drawn from a wide variety of geographic locales and ethnic origins. In addition, although the majority of Americans may still reflect a Judeo-Christian religious heritage and may personally be comfortable with biblical standards of behavior, newer immigrants represent an array of religious traditions.[4]

Racially and spiritually, the United States of America has become much more multicultural than many persons would like to admit.[5] Even at the most basic level of whether English should be the official language, Americans do not agree as to how to accommodate the nation's increasing diversity. Further, tensions inherent in a pluralistic society appear only likely to intensify; the United States Census Bureau predicts that by A.D. 2050 the non-Hispanic white majority will have shrunk to barely half the population total.[6]

Facing this pluralism head-on, most Americans hope to avoid the sort of ethnic strife that has yielded such bitter fruit in the Balkans, and they resolve to do their best to avoid the paralyzing religious strife of Northern Ireland and the Middle East. United States citizens determine that America will handle diversity peacefully, saying: "We must recognize that we are all sisters and brothers under the skin."

Drawing on memories of that Judeo-Christian heritage, the popular thinking is: "After all, everyone is a child of God, and since God loves everyone let's all try to get along together." Therefore, in order to avoid any appearance of intolerance, conventional wisdom concludes that in the interests of social harmony it is best to eliminate religious references from public discourse. If, in the words of an author who greatly influenced contemporary culture, "I'm OK—You're OK,"[7] then invoking one's religious tradition might signal to those outside that tradition "You're not OK." Thus James M. Wall observes: "It is politically correct to claim a religious cover, but politically incorrect to testify that we are acting on our religious claims."[8]

And so in turn-of-the-twenty-first-century America many persons have become almost obsessed with upholding the separation of church and state. Although this separation was primarily designed to protect the church from domination by the state, as the First Amendment makes clear,[9] today conventional wisdom is that separation of church and state should mean protecting our pluralistic society from even the most minimal interaction with the church in order to avoid any hint that one group's religious beliefs might be used to oppress another's. The result of such thinking means that when grappling with even the knottiest social problems, we uniformly agree to proceed (in the words of Dietrich Bonhoeffer) "as if God were not there."[10]

Ironically, the evangelical wing of the church may inadvertently have contributed to this removal of God from public discourse. Evangelicalism has so stressed the need for a *personal* decision to accept Christ as *personal* Savior that some persons have concluded that religious belief should be a purely private matter. Many members of mainline Protestant denominations have built on such *de facto* privatization of God in order to promote the notion that sharing one's faith outside of one's own religious community is intrusive and discourteous. However, if the gospel message is so internalized by God's people that any mention of God is lost to society at large, the actual result will be almost as effective as openly declaring "God is dead."

Analyzing the Cultural Problem

Paradoxically, this reasoning leads to a situation where in one breath God's love of all humanity is invoked as rationale for affirming everyone's equal worth and dignity, but in the next breath God's love becomes the rationale for immediately removing mention of God from public life lest we unlovingly appear to discriminate against another person's faith tradition. The practical effect of such a culturally based manipulation of God's love has been for many people to conclude that biblical standards can no longer be used as social guidelines in a pluralistic society.

This conclusion fails to see that God's love is not a solitary attribute. Although we may well consider God's love to be God's primary attribute, nevertheless God's love is one of many other attributes—including God's righteousness.[11] Furthermore, because God is one God, all God's attributes are complementary and cooperative. The psalmist observes poetically that in God's economy: "Steadfast love and faithfulness will meet; righteousness and peace will kiss each other" (Ps. 85:10). God's love cannot be divorced from God's righteousness. Rather, God's love for humanity operates in conjunction with God's righteousness because true love wants only what is best, right, and fair for the loved one, and rejects anything that hurts or mars God's good creation.[12] Thus, the psalmist further declares of God: "Righteousness and justice are the foundation of your throne; steadfast love and faithfulness go before you" (Ps. 89:14). The apostle Paul puts it that through God's saving, loving grace in Christ all who are in Christ are new creations reconciled to the holy God so that "in him we might become the righteousness of God" (2 Cor. 5:17–21). As Oswald Chambers concludes about the intertwined claims of God's righteous love: "If God's nature is holy, His love must be holy love, seeking to embrace everything until we become holy."[13]

My thesis is that an overemphasis on the accepting nature of God's everlasting, steadfast love without any corresponding recognition of the imperatives of God's righteousness will fail to bring about social harmony. God's love demands that we affirm the worth and dignity of all human beings equally, but only a society upholding God's righteousness will provide the just and compassionate setting within which that affirmation can be most truly made.

The deficiency of using God's love as rationale for eliminating biblical standards will become evident as we examine how the United States culture has sought to cope with the absence of mention of God by looking to the legal system as a neutral vehicle for providing and transmitting moral guidance. We will also explore problems arising within Christian theology when love is emphasized apart from righteousness. Finally, we will present God's loving righteousness as the only lasting means of bringing wholeness to a pluralistic society.

Attempting to Substitute Human Law for God's Law

In everyday life, the cultural emphasis on loving toleration has led many people to conclude that all persons' religious beliefs have equal validity, and therefore that "All roads lead to God."[14] Any other conclusion is perceived to be bigotry.[15] But this thinking also means concluding that not only each person's religion, but also their resulting value systems and lifestyle choices, should be affirmed as well. Thus, in its attempt to be completely tolerant, the contemporary United

States culture not only buys into that "I'm OK—You're OK" philosophy but also into the sentimental notion that "Love means not ever having to say you're sorry."[16]

Yet, as a practical matter, even the most devout civil libertarians realize that "anything goes" is not a prescription for social harmony but for social chaos.[17] Instinctively people do understand that at some point society must take into account the good of the many; certain individual behaviors are harmful and must be restrained. To use obvious examples, drug dealers, rapists, and serial killers are *not* "OK."

Most people also realize that a healthy society needs a means of resolving issues of guilt and providing for restitution. In order to heal individual and communal hurts, the truly loving response may indeed involve publicly saying: "I'm sorry."

But when religion is ruled out of the social equation so as to avoid favoring one religious belief over another, to what will secular society look for appropriate guidelines for communal behavior? What vehicle will be adequate to transmit those guidelines to future generations? It seems apparent that the moral void left when God's laws are displaced is being filled by appealing to human law. Increasingly, in the United States the legal system is perceived to be an acceptable neutral means of providing and upholding the moral guidelines necessary to insure a just and stable society.

Analyzing the ethos of the contemporary United States culture, Harvard law professor Mary Ann Glendon writes: "In countries like ours . . . law often takes on the role of the carrier of values. It reveals who we are and what kind of society we want to be."[18]

Therefore, unlike earlier generations in America for whom the law was the servant of moral values, the expectation now is that the law *by itself* will be able to provide those values. People think: "If we can only manage to appoint or elect persons of good will to craft and enact the right laws, and then get the courts to enforce those laws, social wounds will be healed."

Evidence of this shift in thinking can be seen in twentieth-century America's heavy dependence on the legal system as the chief means of bringing about social order. As Julius B. Poppinga, past president of the Christian Legal Society, observes:

> The great expectations of American culture lie with the law. Americans may not *understand* the law. We may dread *encounters* with the law. We may not always *obey* the law. But nevertheless, when faced with a problem of human

behavior, our immediate reaction is, "There ought to be a law". . . . As the moral and ethical void in our society spreads and grows, it is the law that is expected to fill it with some sense of accountability and responsibility.[19]

And so, instead of considering the legislative process simply an agent helping to promote a harmonious society by operating in support of biblical values already instilled by church, family, and school, today many people have slid into thinking that the right laws *by themselves* will be able to instill the moral values needed to heal societal dysfunctions such as hard-core poverty, crime, and the epidemic of teenage pregnancy. As columnist Russell Baker sarcastically comments:

> Americans are confessing something they ought to be ashamed of. That is, that they are incapable of self-control. Worse, that they want government to step in and control their behavior for them. . . . "Pass a law" is the plea being heard. . . . "Pass a law that will make us stop our rotten behavior."[20]

Sadly, such dependency on the law places an unrealistic burden on the human capacity to create righteousness. The age-old proverb still holds: No one can legislate morality. No law in and of itself can be expected to instill personal moral standards; simply enacting or enforcing laws is no substitute for developing one's personal moral value system.

Similarly, an unrealistic expectation has also been placed on the criminal justice system as the best vehicle for dealing with guilt and expiation. Consider how frequently the media reports crime victims looking to a jury verdict to bring "closure" to their personal pain, or how we read of a released prisoner saying: "The books are closed; I've done my time." However, all too often court verdicts do not bring closure to social wounds, nor is society all that accepting of the ex-offender.

New York Times reporter Seth Mydans describes this syndrome as "Looking to the Courts for Catharsis."[21] In a 1993 account of the sensational trials involving police brutality and mob rioting in Los Angeles, Mydans depicted "a city that continues to seek, and fails to find, a catharsis in the legal system." Mydans also quoted UCLA law professor Peter Aranella's analysis of the futility of such a search. Aranella concluded:

> We have come to look at our criminal justice system as more than a mechanism to decide guilt or innocence but also as a mechanism to somehow

resolve fundamental rifts in the community. People naively expect that a trial can somehow give them justice, but that is literally impossible because people in the community have different substantive expectations of what justice demands. . . . We could have endless trials, and it still wouldn't change the tragic place we're in.[22]

Mydans' own conviction was: "The problems of Los Angeles cannot be solved by anything so simple as a verdict."

Just as the legislative process cannot create righteousness, neither can the criminal justice system provide atonement, moral restitution, or final emotional and spiritual closure for instances of injustice. To expect court verdicts to heal social anguish places an unrealistic burden on the human capacity to heal unrighteousness.

Thus, the attempt to separate America's Judeo-Christian heritage from public discourse has not had the desired unifying and healing effect. Although the initial hope appears to have been to use the legal system as neutral ground from which to debate social issues, neutral ground is not necessarily common ground. Professor Aranella comes to the heart of the matter with his trenchant observation that people have different expectations of what justice involves.[23] In order to arrive at a consensus about appropriate behavior, there has to be some sort of common frame of reference. Without any unifying moral authority, individuals may decide to become their own authorities. One Washington, D.C. attorney said bluntly: "To be perfectly honest, some laws seem to apply to me, some I disregard. . . . I don't need the Pope, the press, or some lowly cop telling me how to live my life."[24] Thus, subscribing to that cultural philosophy of "I'm OK—You're OK" may well mean that when people's moral judgments differ, they will feel entitled to conclude: "Our word is as good as yours."

Turn-of-the-century America has also been heavily influenced by the distinctively American proverb, "Different strokes for different folks." Although initially designed simply as a colloquial affirmation of cultural diversity, today this popular slogan can be broadened to include the notion that everyone's moral choices are equally valid. In her careful analysis of "Different strokes for different folks," author Alyce M. McKenzie highlights the dangers inherent in trying to cite this proverb in order "to reduce all truth claims to matters of personal preference." She further observes: "Lacking a theological compass, [people] may bloat the proverb from partial truth into a universal moral relativism and lose the ability to distinguish between choices among toasters, cars, lifestyles, and faith claims."[25]

The Need for a Higher Authority

A. W. Tozer states: "Because we are the handiwork of God, it follows that all our problems and their solutions are theological. Some knowledge of what kind of God it is that operates the universe is indispensable to a sound philosophy of life and a sane outlook on the world scene."[26]

Significantly, the initial language of the United States founders did recognize an authority higher than human law in its declaration that human beings "are endowed by their Creator with certain unalienable Rights. . . ." Unfortunately, those who (in the name of God's love) would remove mention of even a remote "Creator" from public discourse today fail to see that without God as authoritative guarantor no guarantee exists of the very rights they so zealously defend.[27]

For example, Article 1 of the United Nations' *Universal Declaration of Human Rights* proclaims: "All human beings are born free and equal in dignity and rights. They are endowed with reason and conscience and should act towards one another in the spirit of brotherhood."[28] But by eliminating any reference to a Higher Power, in the final analysis this declaration is unenforceable. It is all very well to assume that "persons of good will" will be self-enforcing, but what happens when an individual or nation has no interest in good will? Human rights accords are, ultimately, only as good as the self-interest of the parties involved, because even the pressure of world opinion is an inadequate lever to force compliance if a powerful nation refuses to honor the terms of such an agreement.[29] To whom can an oppressed individual or an oppressed nation appeal if there is no common Higher Power guaranteeing human freedom worldwide, no common measure of the phrase "equal dignity and rights," not to mention no common Source endowing human beings with reason and conscience to begin with?

As Thomas Jefferson asked over two centuries ago: "Can the liberties of a nation be thought secure when we have removed their only firm basis, a conviction in the minds of the people that these liberties are the gift of God? That they will not be violated but with his wrath?"[30]

So, in contrast to the present-day attempt to remove God as higher authority, the founders of the United States did indeed build on a common understanding that ours is a created world rather than the product of spontaneous generation, and that the Creator can be appealed to as unchanging originator and guarantor of human liberty. The Declaration of Independence affirmed the people's right to "the separate and equal station to which the Laws of Nature and Nature's God entitle them."

However, what is problematic is whether even that most broad wording of the Declaration of Independence could be agreed upon today. In the current politically correct climate, one is hard pressed to imagine the United States Congress passing a bill using language acknowledging a "Creator," or the United States Supreme Court opining on the grounds of God's prior claims rather than legal precedent. Indeed, the intense pressure to erect a higher and higher wall between church and state makes it difficult for many contemporary citizens to think of themselves in even bare-bones deist terms as "One nation under God." Instead, it seems as if their motto should be "One nation under the laws of the land."

Unfortunately, with no common national frame of reference with regard to the ultimate source of governmental authority, society can be reduced to that level of "My ideas of justice and morality are as good as yours." The present national polarization regarding abortion policy reveals such an impasse. Both "pro-choice" and "pro-life" proponents claim the moral high ground, the former championing women's rights and the latter upholding the rights of the unborn child. Given the politicized nature of the debate, any speedy or harmonious resolution of the abortion issue seems unlikely, as each position claims to be the most moral.[31] Further, such presumption to higher authority is nowhere more apparent than when government power shifts from one political party to another, and basic concepts of what constitutes appropriate social welfare policies can change dramatically.

In addition, the time-honored United States virtue of rugged individualism can also work against achieving moral consensus in the community at large. Bitter divisions over issues concerning what constitutes free speech or over the need for gun control illustrate how difficult it is to balance individual freedom and corporate welfare.[32]

Granted, even the most intense political debate may be necessary and even healthy in a free society. Nevertheless, a society will have difficulty arriving at a harmonious resolution of conflicts between individual liberty and the good of the many without some common ground upon which to base that resolution. Ironically, United States culture increasingly looks to that supposedly "neutral" human law as the necessary common ground, failing to recognize that only upholding God's loving and righteous law will bring about the good of all.

My conclusion is that removing all mention of God from efforts to find common ground on which to balance individual freedom and social order leads to instability rather than stability. Justifying such removal as done in the name of loving toleration of a plurality of beliefs does not change the result. Only recognizing the biblical God as the source of human governmental authority (in line with Genesis 9:1–17 and Romans 13:1–7) provides the necessary common ground. As theologian Carl F. H. Henry puts it:

> Biblical theism alone provides adequate intellectual struts for . . . human rights, whereas nontheistic views render such rights merely postulatory and problematical. . . . The evangelical view is that human rights are grounded in the revealed will of God, that religious liberty and political liberty are alike based on the Bible.[33]

Shifting human governments with their different philosophies of government can never replace the governmental principles of Creator God, whose throne is founded on everlasting righteousness and justice, and who implements that justice faithfully and with steadfast love (Pss. 89:14; 111:3; 2 Peter 3:13).

Cultural Pressure on the Church

The Christian community is not insulated from the intense contemporary cultural pressure to abandon allegiance to biblical authority. All branches of the church are urged to compromise core beliefs about God's transcendence, sovereignty, holiness, and righteousness in order to endorse the cultural ideal that "Love is all that matters."[34] One immediate result of giving in to that pressure is that once God's love has been isolated from God's other attributes, it is all too easy to slide into thinking that if God is love, then "Love" is god.[35]

In the name of "Love," the secular culture presses the church to join with the culture in accepting a wide diversity of lifestyle choices. Self-love cloaked as God's love has become such a dominant cultural theme that, even in the church, many persons now feel entitled to an ethic

73

that validates their behavior, rather than asking: What is the biblical ethic, and what does that mean for my everyday life?

For example, speaking of his desire to find a new spiritual home that would accept his lifestyle choice, one man commented: "I made a commitment that I would never again join a church that said who I am is not O.K."[36] Further, *The New York Times* reported on the search of some couples to find "a church for themselves and their children that provided a moral center without moralizing."[37] Such people fail to see that a Christian "moral center" will of necessity engage in moral discourse, including exploring what Scripture teaches about which lifestyles are or are not "O.K." Yet it can be commonly thought that whether or not someone is a "nice" person is more important than whether or not that person's behavior reflects biblical morality (which, it is implied, is sadly outdated in the modern world, and thus in need of revision).[38] People ask: "If a person is thoroughly decent, how is that inconsistent with basic Christianity?"[39] The flaw in such reasoning is that basic Christianity is not a matter of being "nice" or "thoroughly decent" but of becoming a new creation in Christ Jesus, with a new call to strive first for the kingdom of God and God's righteousness rather than self-actualization (Matt. 6:33; 2 Cor. 5:14–17).

Furthermore, once again the question of ultimate authority arises: If biblical morality is abandoned by the church, what authority will define who is or is not "thoroughly decent"? One person's decency may be another person's indecency, and vice versa.

Yet the current cultural touchstone for whether an individual or a denomination is deemed "Christian," not only by society at large but also by many people in the Christian community itself, appears to be whether or not the individual or group is perceived to be "loving," with love defined in terms of that aforementioned complete acceptance of everyone's beliefs and lifestyle choices.[40] In the name of the god of "Love," that intense cultural pressure is brought to bear on the church, urging the church to accept the validity of every behavior which secular society accepts; otherwise the church is not deemed loving, and therefore not Christian either.

Such a touchstone very quickly proves unreliable. It soon becomes apparent that, because the definition of what constitutes "loving" is culturally defined, that definition is not absolute. "Loving" will shift to include or exclude whomever a particular cultural group includes or excludes. As already noted, no one in the contemporary United States culture would "lovingly accept" the lifestyle choice of a mass murderer. But what a difference a different culture makes! Consider these words from the mother of a Palestinian suicide bomber who killed twenty-five passengers (and himself) on a Jerusalem bus: "We have to accept that he is a martyr and thank God."[41]

In a culture that expects instant gratification and sound bite solutions to complex problems, careful thought about these important issues can be increasingly bypassed. Religion reporter Peter Steinfels observes that, regardless of the specific issue involved, "there is a dividing line not just between those who agree or disagree with their church's teachings but also between those who reach their conclusions by conscientiously weighing such teachings and those who simply follow the public mood or the pull of their own emotions."[42]

All too few people today are willing to resist cultural pressure long enough to step back and ask some very necessary questions. First: Does secular society mirror the biblical definition of love? Second: If the biblical definition is different, why should Christians individually or corporately be termed unloving simply because they seek to mirror a different paradigm than that of their culture? And third: What right has secular society to demand that the church change to conform to society's definition of love? The United States still upholds religious freedom. To pressure Christians who disagree with the conventional secular wisdom to embrace that wisdom when by so doing the Christians must abandon allegiance to God's wisdom is unreasonable.[43]

In contrast to the popular notion that in a pluralistic society the legal system is the most appropriate carrier of values, God's Word must be the primary carrier of values for the Christian. No matter how long human laws have been in existence, or how widely accepted they may be, even at their very best those human laws will still be only reflections of the primary values we find in God's Word. Further, Christians are ultimately accountable to a higher authority than the law of the state (Acts 4:19–20; 5:29). We will one day answer to a higher court than the United States Supreme Court: the judgment seat of Christ (Rom. 14:10–12).

Seen in that light, persons in the church who are tempted to give in to the temptation to overemphasize the accepting nature of God's love and underemphasize the moral imperatives of God's righteousness might do well to consider Dietrich Bonhoeffer's warning of the dangers inherent in "a concept of what is 'Christian' which has been won not from the truth of Scripture but from the verdict of human examination." In contrast, he himself affirmed: "All that matters is whether or not one opts for Christ, not Christian opinion." And his sad conclusion was: "The weakness of liberal theology was that it conceded to the world the right to determine Christ's place in the world."[44]

The Attempt to Divide God

Giving in to that worldly pressure, however, many Christians have thought it appropriate to approach Scripture selectively and to amend or even ignore any biblical teaching about God's call to righteousness that might seem offensive and discriminatory to persons of differing beliefs in a pluralistic society.

Joseph Fletcher's 1966 book *Situation Ethics: The New Morality* has played an influential role in promoting the church's accommodation to the culture. Although Fletcher is careful to emphasize that his key principle is New Testament *agape* love,[45] his thesis separates love from all other values by asserting: "Only love is a constant; everything else is a variable."[46] While initially sounding not only altruistic but even scripturally orthodox, Fletcher's refusal "to give any principle less than love more than tentative consideration"[47] precludes a biblically holistic approach to moral choices. Whether or not to factor God's other attributes (such as mercy, holiness, or righteousness) into the moral decision-making process is now reduced to a matter of personal preference. Love becomes an isolated and subjectively determined value, rather than a full-orbed biblical principle.

One by-product of choosing love over righteousness has been virtually to ignore the Old Testament with its supposed depiction of a stern, unloving God and to concentrate primarily on portions of the New Testament that supposedly present a more gracious God of love. From such proponents we hear much talk of the love of *Christ,* suggesting that Christ's love is somehow different from any love that might be shown by the remote almighty God of the Old Testament. In common parlance, Jesus is presented as a kinder, gentler Deity, one who in some way may choose to "wink at" human foibles like a loving older brother might compassionately gloss over the peccadilloes of weaker siblings.[48]

Thus, in some circles we hear people say: "We're New Testament Christians," the implication being that a choice exists between giving allegiance to the stern, righteous Judge of the Old Testament or to the kinder, gentler New Testament Savior. And obviously, given such a choice, who would not find the Good Shepherd more approachable than the Lord God of hosts? The problem, of course, is that this is a false choice. God cannot be divided.[49]

The Unitary Nature of God

A. W. Tozer points out: "All of God does all that God does; He does not divide Himself to perform a work, but works in the total unity of His being."[50] Therefore, God's love, including God's love revealed in the Second Person of the Trinity, cannot be different in nature from the love shown by another Person of the Trinity. Recalling that Jesus himself said, "The Father and I are one" (John 10:30), we see a unity of the divine nature that does not admit of that nature being expressed in contradictory ways. God's love never varies, regardless of whether that love is revealed through or expressed by Father, Son, or Holy Spirit, and God's righteousness does not vary either.

The totality of Scripture does not support any notion that there is a grim Old Testament God who sets up old-fashioned standards of righteousness, and a softer New Testament manifestation of Deity who (solely in the interests of being loving) somehow waters down the command: "You shall be holy, for I the LORD your God am holy" (Lev. 19:2).[51]

In the mystery of common grace, God does indeed offer good gifts to all people (Matt. 5:45; Acts 10:34), and God in Christ lovingly welcomes into the kingdom of God all who believe (John 1:12; 3:16; 6:37). But such divine graciousness is not to be confused with a blanket acceptance by God of all persons' thoughts and actions. Notably, in the Beatitudes Jesus calls "blessed" those persons who hunger and thirst after righteousness, and those who are pure in heart (Matt. 5:6–8). Nowhere in Christ's teaching or in the rest of the New Testament do we find that love gives room for license, or that Jesus had a lesser concern for righteousness than the concern expressed in the Hebrew Scriptures. Jesus upheld the highest standards of moral purity, never suggesting that divine love "winks at" personal or corporate unrighteousness.

So although there is that intense cultural pressure on the Christian community to emphasize God's love without taking into consideration the other attributes of God, even to the extent of making "being loving" a solitary goal, Scripture presents a balanced, integrated, unitary view of God and God's attributes. God is love, but God is also holy, and—in complementarity with God's holiness—Scripture declares that righteousness and justice are the very foundation of God's throne (Ps. 89:14). Any overemphasis on God's love without justice will produce theological distortion. Divine love and divine righteousness are not competing attributes, but complementary revelations of the unitary nature of the Triune God.

Further evidence of the unitary nature of the Persons of the Godhead is that the Holy Spirit is not only loving Comforter but also the one who convicts the world of sin and righteousness and judgment (John 16:7–11).

Tough Love

Anyone who promotes the notion that there is a softer, more tolerant "New Testament religion" must be confronted with the unified testimony of God's love and God's righteousness as revealed in the person and work of Christ.[52] The righteous love displayed by Christ is never mere sentimentality but what could reverently be termed "tough love." Yes, Christ lovingly assures humanity that "anyone who comes to me I will never drive away" (John 6:37). But then Christ goes on to challenge all who come to him to seek a heart righteousness that is far deeper than mere external law keeping (Matt. 5:12–48). Jesus' concrete, practical examples of this righteousness call his disciples to show love for others by being pure in heart and transparent in integrity, never being manipulative or showing vengeful retaliation. Loving as Christ loves involves doing everything possible to resist all unrighteousness that mars God's good creation, and to combat all that hurts human beings created in the image of God. Jesus Christ is the one who said that if anyone hurts a little child it would be better if that person were weighted with a millstone and thrown into the sea (Luke 17:1–2).

This book explores the various attributes of God most apprehensible or evidently operant in a variety of cultures today. But the authors unite in warning that no matter what the peer pressure, God's people dare not selectively pick and choose among God's attributes, including those attributes revealed in the Second Person of the Trinity, but must keep the complementarity of God's attributes in balance.

One attribute may be a particular window into God's nature from a particular culture's standpoint, but it leads into all the other omnipresent attributes of God's full character. Therefore, proclaiming the whole gospel mandates following Jesus' example of upholding both love and righteousness.

For example, early in John's Gospel, Jesus deals with a crippled man at the pool of Bethesda (John 5:2–14). After Jesus graciously heals this man, Jesus warns, "See, you have been made well! Do not sin any more, so that nothing worse happens to you." In contrast to the encounter in John 9:1–3, Jesus' words in John 5 strongly imply that the man's disability had resulted from a moral problem.[53]

Using our imaginations, we can put this incident into contemporary terms. An alcoholic might have a crippling accident when driving while intoxicated. Jesus might graciously heal that person, but also warn, "Do not sin any more, so that nothing worse happens to you." What might "worse" be? If the alcoholic persisted in driving under the influence of alcohol he might himself end up dead, or—worse yet—involve others in his abusive behavior by maiming or killing innocent parties. Admittedly, if the alcoholic's friends were honest with themselves, none of these friends (including Christian friends) could adopt a "holier than thou" attitude because they would know in their hearts that their actions, such as exceeding the speed limit or driving when sleepy, were also potentially tragic. But, nevertheless, they would not be truly loving friends to the alcoholic if they failed to warn, "Do not sin any more. You must never drink and drive again, so that nothing worse happens to you." Only heeding the whole counsel of God with its twin imperatives of love and righteousness would protect both the individual and the others in the community.[54]

The Oldest Temptation

When we ponder the temptation to bypass being righteous in favor of being "loving," we may be helped by remembering that in Scripture righteousness does not denote some sort of sanctimonious, holier-than-thou attitude, nor does biblical righteousness mean dry legalism. Biblical righteousness joins hands with self-giving love, a love that is never a passively disengaged sentimentality but an active confrontation of any unrighteousness that brings dishonor on God's name and mars God's good creation. Thus biblical righteousness involves not only moral purity, but also reconciliation of broken relationships, and an abiding concern that God's covenant people apply the wonder of God's saving love to help heal all injustice in the surrounding culture.[55]

Yet how pressured the church is today to speak only of God's redemptive love and conveniently ignore God's call to righteous living! People rationalize this selectivity by telling themselves: "Certainly God did not mean to set such impossibly outdated and unworkable moral standards." As Joseph Fletcher asks:

> Are we not entitled to say that, depending on the situation, those who break the Seventh Commandment of the old law, even whores, *could* be doing a good thing—*if* it is for love's sake, for the neighbor's sake? In short, is there any real "law" of universal weight? The situationist thinks not.[56]

As they conform to their "I'm OK—You're OK" cultural value system, the proverb of choice becomes "Different strokes for different folks" rather than "Trust in the Lord with all your heart, and do not rely on your own insight" (Prov. 3:5). As a result, cultural analysts James Patterson and Peter Kim state: "Everyone is making up their own personal moral codes—their own Ten Commandments."[57] As evidence, Patterson and Kim cite polls showing 74 percent of their respondents condone stealing "from those who won't really miss it," 64 percent condone lying "so long as it doesn't cause any real damage," and 53 percent see nothing wrong with being unfaithful to their spouses because "after all, given the chance, he or she will do the same."[58]

Such persons have fallen prey to that oldest of all temptations: not taking God's Word seriously, including God's Word as it comes to us through Christ, the Incarnate Word. Recall the scene in Genesis 3:1, where the serpent says to the woman: "Did God say, 'You shall not eat from any tree in the garden'?" The serpent's further words (v. 5) unmistakably foreshadow all those so-called reasonable voices in our modern culture, voices that say: "Did God really say all that in the Bible? Did God really mean to set parameters on your human actions? Surely not. Surely you too can be like God, and set your own standards." Yes, from the beginning of time humanity has been all too easily seduced into asking: "Has God really said this particular word?" Some persons would go even further, by denying that God has spoken any Word at all. For them, the Bible becomes one of many relative teachings. As Houston Smith puts it: "The enduring religions at their best contain the distilled wisdom of the *human race.*"[59] By such means, people evade obedience to God's standards, tragically misunderstanding that God's call to righteousness is not to make humanity miserable but to make humanity whole.

The Healing Power of Righteousness

Persisting in this misunderstanding, many Americans now look to the secular legal system as both carrier of values and agent of reconciliation for a diverse society. However, outward obedience to the letter of the law is no substitute for inward commitment to the spirit of even human law. As Deborah Tannen of Georgetown University observes:

> Prisons used to be called "penitentiaries" because inmates were expected not only to serve their time but also to repent. Nowadays many offenders seem to regard prison sentences as contractual: I served my time, I paid my debt. No apologies.[60]

Such legal contracts between society and the offender can neither create personal morality nor absolve guilt. Yet Julius B. Poppinga notes: "Our society is assigning an ever-expanding role to the courts, reflecting the broadening demands upon the law to achieve what is perceived to be the common good."[61]

Unfortunately, however, the current United States cultural belief that law is our primary carrier of values, and thus that the legal system can eventually heal social ills, places an impossible burden on a human-made system that can only serve morality, not create morality. Similarly with the political arena in which those laws are first proposed: No matter what good intentions our political leaders may have, to expect social salvation from laws formulated by persons of good will places an unrealistic hope in the righteousness of mere human good will. Being a person of good will on the natural level alone will always be inadequate. As writer P. D. James wryly comments: "Human kindness is like a defective tap: the first gush is impressive, but the stream soon dries up."[62]

We human beings need far more than natural good will. We need a new will. Concern for issues of justice must be transformed into convictions of a new heart that the just God alone can give. Although the human legal system may indeed prevent social chaos, Walter J. Burghardt of Woodstock Theological Center points out:

> But the Judeo-Christian tradition offers us hope. It declares that justice as humans perceive it—you get what you deserve—is good, but not good enough. . . . God's Word takes our human justice for granted but rises above it. Biblical justice is fidelity. Fidelity to relationships, to responsibilities that stem from a covenant with God. . . . not to give in proportion to merit, but a self-giving over and above the demands of sheerly human ethics. Love as Jesus loved—even unto crucifixion.[63]

Any persons who have not yet seen the necessity of accepting God's offer of re-creation must face up to the fact that on the practical level good intentions alone have failed. Nationally and internationally, social problems remain entrenched, not diminishing.[64] That defective tap *must* be replaced, and a new stream of resolve *must* come from the never-ending reservoir of strength and love and justice that only God has the power and authority to provide. Even the combined human good will of the many United Nations member states can never replace the revealed will of the biblical God who offers both love and righteousness as complementary agents of reconciliation in a fallen world.

The Good News is that God loves humanity too much to let human beings settle for finite palliatives that may produce momentary deadening of personal or societal pain but afford no lasting cure for the causes of that pain. God the Great Physician never prescribes placebos or numbing sedatives. Our Creator knows that fallen humanity needs far more than some superficial, sentimental "love" that—solely in the name of toleration—accepts human brokenness with all its resulting guilt and shame. Once again, it is a theological distortion to emphasize secularized "love" at the expense of failing to proclaim the biblical prescription for God's healing process: repentance, renewal, and a return to righteousness.[65] Only this prescription deals with unrighteousness head-on, adequately addresses guilt and shame, and provides opportunity both individually and corporately to enter into the gift of new life in Christ.[66]

Melvin Hugen and Cornelius Plantinga give this insight into God's design for spiritual health:

> Incarnation, atonement, resurrection, and ascension—the going down and the coming up of the Son of God—open the way not only for the forgive-

ness of our sins, but also for the lifting of our shame. For these are ingredients in the accepting grace of God and in the invitation to union with God's Son.

If the Christian gospel springs from the states and events of Christ, and if it addresses our shame and our guilt, then we ought to minister the gospel accordingly. . . . In fact, remarkably enough, confession of sin may be too simple. Many a problem drinker would much rather say "I drank too much last night and got way out of line; Please forgive me" than [say] "My name is Sam, and I'm an alcoholic." For this last declaration goes to who he is and not simply to what he has done; it goes to his shame, and not just to his guilt. . . . The truth is that he needs not just the God who forgives, but also the God who heals; not just the Good Pardoner, but also the Great Physician. He needs the care and support that have been shaped to fit what actually ails him.[67]

God freely offers that care and support to all who turn to God in believing faith. The wonder of God's love is that the one who created us always stands ready to recreate, to heal all that has estranged us from our Creator and from each other, for our Redeemer and Sustainer knows that the abundant life is only possible when what is broken has been made whole. Therefore, as God promises through the prophet Malachi: "For you who revere my name the sun of righteousness shall rise, with healing in its wings" (Mal. 4:2).

Exploring God's Answers to the Needs of a Pluralistic World

God's complementary attributes of love and righteousness not only bring individual healing but can also provide healing for the deepest social conflicts arising in a pluralistic society. God's loving offer of new life in Christ provides inner spiritual healing; God's caring righteousness provides the vehicle for outer social transformation. Therefore, God's people will most faithfully image both God's love and God's righteousness when they uphold God's complementary priorities of evangelism and social concern.[68] In essence, we are called to the same unity of purpose as exhibited by the God in whose image we were originally created. As Richard Foster explains:

Jesus lived in singleness of purpose with God so perfectly that he could say without embellishment that he did nothing of his own accord (John 5:19). Jesus' words were the words of the Father, his deeds the deeds of the Father. And, astonishingly, Jesus calls us in our small way to enter this unity of purpose.[69]

83

Jesus calls us to abide in his love by bringing forth good works that honor the Father (Matt. 5:13–16; John 15:1–10). As we seek to obey Jesus' new commandment to love others as he has loved us (John 13:34–35), Jesus' clear expectation is that this mutual abiding will reveal God's love to others in visible ways.[70] Thus the apostle Paul enjoins: "Bear one another's burdens, and in this way you will fulfill the law of Christ" (Gal. 6:2). The First Letter of John further declares: "We know love by this, that he laid down his life for us—and we ought to lay down our lives for one another" (1 John 3:16).

Such a call to sacrificial servanthood will not be popular in a culture that exalts rugged individualism as the best measure of freedom in a pluralistic society. Heavily influenced by conventional wisdom such as "I'm OK—You're OK" and "Different strokes for different folks," many Americans can feel entitled to "do their own thing" without much thought to the impact of their actions on the larger social body. But, as Darrell Jadok of Muhlenberg College wisely cautions: "Whole individuals are nourished and sustained by the wholeness found in community. Contrary to what many Americans assume, strong individuals are the product of a strong community. . . ."[71] Significantly, God places individuals within the faith community (1 Cor. 12:12–13; Eph. 4:4–6) and then calls that community to be a witness to the secular community (John 17:15; Acts 1:8). Therefore, in both personal and corporate life, we must be guided by God's Word given through the prophet Micah (6:8):

> He has told you, O mortal, what is good;
> and what does the LORD require of you
> but to do justice, and to love kindness,
> and to walk humbly with your God?

Furthermore, as we follow these guidelines, we find that God thinks globally and so must God's people. Although individual Christians will not be able to lend support to every justice issue, nevertheless each instance of injustice demands the collective attention of God's people. Collectively, God calls us to look beyond both personal and national self-interest, to put aside political preference (and even allegiance to cherished religious traditions), and instead to uphold biblical standards of love and righteousness. As historian Tom Sine states bluntly:

> Those who try to fuse faith in Christ with faith in the American way will always end by subordinating the gospel of Jesus Christ and his church to civil

> religion—which is quite simply idolatrous. . . . [O]ur identity as Christians is distinct from our identity as citizens of America and . . . we do harm if we confuse the two. We should not be raising barriers between ourselves and other members of the body of Christ who live in other national and cultural contexts.[72]

Much more than being good United States citizens, or people preserving a certain cultural heritage such as Western civilization (laudable as those goals may be), much more we are called to be *God's* people.[73]

Therefore, I am discouraged to hear "God bless America" invoked in a manner that would exclude America's perceived enemies from any manifestation of God's blessings.[74] As George MacDonald points out, such an invocation has the effect of making God merely "a partisan of your ambitions."[75] I am equally discouraged to realize that this invocation can be made with little recognition of the common humanity of one's political enemies and God's compassion for them (Jonah 4:11).[76]

No group, least of all one that acknowledges a Judeo-Christian heritage, has a manifest destiny to control, manipulate, or harm another people group. Instead, theologian Carl F. H. Henry points out: "The rise of the Euroamerican middle class is a remarkable exception in history, not a norm, and it imposes special stewardship responsibilities upon Western civilization, especially in respect to the world missionary enterprise and humanitarian needs."[77] Rather, the temporal destiny of God's women and men is: "Like good stewards of the manifold grace of God, serve one another with whatever gift each of you has received" (1 Peter 4:10). Furthermore, the measure of good stewards is that they are found faithful, as they serve the good of the many rather than serving personal or even national self-gratification (1 Cor. 4:2; 11:33). God is not "ours" but "everyone's" and God inclusively declares:

> But let justice roll down like waters,
> and righteousness like an everflowing stream. (Amos 5:24)

In particular, we must resist an unloving parochial and nationalistic mind-set (even among some in the Christian community) that might hinder sharing our vast personal and national resources with those in need.[78]

Inescapably, however, those who claim to love God must love what God loves, and the psalmist tells us that God loves righteousness and justice (Ps. 33:5). Therefore, as theologian Ronald J. Sider notes: "One crucial test of whether Christian political activity is free of ideological bias from both left and right will be whether it emphasizes both freedom and justice in equal measure."[79] Thus, irrespective of temporal citizenship, God's people are in truth citizens of a heavenly kingdom and must be in the forefront of upholding kingdom values by combating both personal and institutional unrighteousness wherever in the world those occur.

God's Word never separates God's love for all humanity from God's ideal that all of humanity be fairly and justly treated. Deuteronomy 10:17–19 declares:

> For the LORD your God is God of gods and Lord of lords, the great God, mighty and awesome, who is not partial and takes no bribe, who executes justice for the orphan and the widow, and who loves the strangers, providing them food and clothing. You shall also love the stranger. . .

The totality of Scripture gives unified witness to God's priority of applied righteousness. The Book of Proverbs (21:3) tells us that "to do righteousness . . . is more acceptable to the LORD than sacrifice" and then continues more specifically (31:8–9):

> Speak out for those who cannot speak,
> for the rights of all the destitute.
> Speak out, judge righteously,
> defend the rights of the poor and needy.

The prophet Zechariah records: "Thus says the LORD of hosts: Render true judgments, show kindness and mercy to one another; . . . and do not devise evil in your hearts against one another" (7:9–10). The Book of James unites loving compassion with holiness, teaching: "Religion that is pure and undefiled before God, the Father, is this: to care for orphans and widows in their distress, and to keep oneself unstained by the world" (1:27). And Jesus sums up: "In everything do to others as you would have them do to you; for this is the law and the prophets" (Matt. 7:12).

Thus, when people who are deeply frustrated by social inequities exclaim: "There ought to be a law!" God's people must joyfully respond: "There already is a law, the law of self-giving love." We must witness to the fact that this law springs from God's steadfast love and healing righteousness, operates in the complementary areas of evangelism and social concern, and when obeyed brings about reconciliation among all peoples. Furthermore, this law of self-giving love is backed by the authority of the unchanging Lord and Savior who alone has the power to bring equitable resolution of the stresses and strains present in a pluralistic society. Thus, looking forward to the final day when God's great love will at last bring perfect righteousness to displace all unrighteousness, Isaiah triumphantly proclaims:

> For when your judgments are in the earth,
> the inhabitants of the world learn righteousness. . . .
> The effect of righteousness will be peace,
> and the result of righteousness, quietness and trust forever.
> (Isa. 26:9b; 32:17)

The Highest Pursuit

Despite obvious imperfections in United States society, the world community still looks to the United States of America as the universal symbol of democracy. Both present United States citizens and those who aspire to citizenship cherish that original ideal stated in the Declaration of Independence that human beings are created equal, and are endowed by God with certain rights, including life, liberty, and the pursuit of happiness.

God's people, however, have a different pursuit of a higher goal. Speaking in the context of the need for basic human rights to food, clothing, and shelter, Jesus challenged his disciples: "But strive first for the kingdom of God and his righteousness, and all these things will be given to you as well" (Matt. 6:33). For those today who seek God's kingdom values above all cultural values, admittedly the search for righteousness will begin in the privacy of the individual heart, but that search must eventually be acted out in relation to other people. Striving to put God's kingdom righteousness above our own needs will mean following the example of Christ who "came not to be served but to serve, and to give his life a ransom for many" (Mark 10:45). Obeying God's law of self-giving love will mean striving above all else to bring God's healing righteousness to bear in the lives of others; only then will our own needs also be most truly met.

Incarnational servanthood harnessed in pursuit of God's righteousness will be as countercultural at the end of the twentieth century as it was at the beginning of the century, when President Theodore Roosevelt challenged the nation: "In the long fight for righteousness the watchword for all of us is spend and be spent."[80] Yet who among God's people would want to settle for anything less than striving with all our heart and soul and might to serve our great God who promises through the prophet Jeremiah:

> For surely I know the plans I have for you, says the LORD, plans for your welfare and not for harm, to give you a future with hope. (29:11)

United States parochialism has often made assimilating difficult for those aspiring to be citizens of the United States of America. In the next chapter we will look at the problem of assimilation, as experienced by many Hispanic Americans, as they find themselves caught between nations.

Four

God the Stranger:
An Intercultural Hispanic American
Perspective

Aída Besançon Spencer

Aída Besançon Spencer, born and reared in Santo Domingo, Dominican Republic, is professor of New Testament at Gordon-Conwell Theological Seminary and pastor of organization with Pilgrim Church. She earned the Ph.D. from Southern Baptist Theological Seminary, Th.M. and M.Div. from Princeton Theological Seminary, and B.A. from Douglass College. She has written numerous articles, essays, and books including *The Goddess Revival, God through the Looking Glass, Beyond the Curse,* and *The Prayer Life of Jesus.* She has worked with Hispanic Americans as a social worker, English as a second language teacher, and Bible teacher.

I gave the sermon first to Anglo Americans—middle class (and upper?)—North Americans of European descent. It was an ordination service. The newly ordained minister afterwards came to me looking baffled and sad: "I didn't understand it." After many years, I gave it again in Santo Domingo before an international church, and at the end I was swamped with appreciation. My mother wanted me to mail a copy to all our relatives. One elder said, "Where have you been?" And some parents said to me, almost in tears, "Our boys raised here in

Santo Domingo so much needed to hear that!" A message that is completely baffling or a life raft to a drowning person—I, too, had the same experience when Jesus preached it.

This chapter will begin with Jesus' warning to his potential disciples in Luke 9:58–62 that he has no country. Jesus' words encapsulate the situation of people who are intercultural. I am writing from the perspective of someone born in a Hispanic country, Dominican Republic, but who was reared after ten years of age in New Jersey. Even in the Dominican Republic I was a "stranger," since my mother was from Puerto Rico and my father was from the Netherlands. So, we will see in what way Jesus had no "home," and in the Old Testament how God is a stranger who watches over strangers and all Israelites and even all humans are strangers. What are the positive aspects of being intercultural? What are the negative aspects? How can "different" be wrong?

Jesus Had No Country

I remember the first time I ever read Luke 9:58. I was in high school. I had always been brought to church by my mother and thus I knew enough to find Christianity attractive and the person of Jesus intriguing. However, I began to wonder during those adolescent searches for meaning whether Christianity were really historically true. So I decided to open up my Bible to Jesus' words. This is a literal rendering of the message I read:

> The foxes—dens, they have,
> and the birds of the heaven—places to encamp,
> but the Heir of humanity does not have
> where he may lay down his head. (Luke 9:58)

What a strange thing to say! Why did Jesus talk what seems nonsense? Not until this decade of my life have I begun to understand these words. As a matter of fact, the significance came to me in a flash, and when it did, I suddenly knew that this passage spoke to the very core of my being.

Context of Luke 9:58

Luke organized his Gospel to answer two questions: Who is Jesus? (1:5–9:43a) and, What is entailed in following Jesus? (9:43b–24:53).

God dwelled among us so that we humans might get to know God better, learn what life is all about, and become reconciled to God. Luke records that while Jesus was on earth, he demonstrated his authority, power, identity, and concern for needy people (Luke 4:18) by the healings he did, the conversations he had, and the time he spent with people. The crowds, thereby, learned, as they grew in size, that Jesus indeed was God Incarnate: "All were shocked at God's majesty" (Luke 9:43).

But the crowds did not like the message he told them next: "The Heir of humanity is about to be delivered into human hands" (Luke 9:44) and "The one being least among you, this one is the greatest" (Luke 9:48). How could their Messiah, who would eradicate all their political, physical, and spiritual problems, get arrested and use children as his model for greatness?

The fascination of the crowd began to dwindle then. One village in Samaria did not welcome Jesus now because, literally, "his face was going to Jerusalem" (Luke 9:53). The idea of a crucified Messiah was not so appealing (Luke 9:51). Jerusalem is the place where prophets are killed because those in power, religious leaders, do not always like the message God sends (Luke 13:33). Truth is not always welcomed.

Thus, Jesus was warning the potential disciple, who so blithely proclaimed, "I will follow you wherever you may go" (Luke 9:57), "Watch out! I have no country! I have no home! I have no place to call my own—where I feel fully welcomed. I cannot even rest my weary head. Do you still want to follow me?" Jesus' metaphorical language declares that he does not have even a *temporary* home: "The foxes—dens, they have, and the birds of the heaven—places to encamp, but the Heir of humanity does not have where he may lay down his head."

Background to Imagery of Luke 9:58

Many foxes do not have permanent homes. They have only temporary homes. They do not even dig out their dens. Instead, foxes use abandoned underground dens made by other animals, such as rabbits and porcupines. Some in Jerusalem even live in deserted ruins. A reddish gray fox lives in the deserts of the Middle East. The red fox uses the den only to bear cubs. It lives alone and sleeps in the open even during bitter cold. Its tail keeps it warm. Nevertheless, foxes do have their own hunting territories in which other foxes are not permitted to settle.[1]

Jesus compares himself to an animal that has at most very temporary places of residence: dens. Jesus does not even have that.

Birds, too, have temporary nests in which to bear and raise their young. Some birds remain in an area only for months before they migrate on. For example, in autumn and spring, in Israel new birds appear daily.[2] They need places to "encamp," or "pitch their tents."

Jesus' verb in Luke 9:58 ("encamp," *kataskēnoō*) is reminiscent of John's description of Jesus: "And the Word became flesh and *pitched its tent (skēnoō)* among us and we beheld its glory, glory as of an only begotten from the Father, full of grace and truth" (John 1:14). Both verbs are built on the root idea of "pitching a tent" *(skēnoō)*.[3] When God became incarnate, God dwelled in close proximity to humans. God "pitched a tent," alluding to the Old Testament tabernacle, and God's shekinah glory. However, even though humans, thereby, marveled at God's "majesty" (Luke 9:43) or God's "glory" (John 1:14) when following God entailed any cost, many no longer were so receptive. Jesus "was in the world, even the world through him was created, yet the world did not recognize him. To his own he came, and his own did not welcome him" (John 1:10–11).

Unlike the fox, Jesus did not sojourn; unlike the bird, Jesus did not build. We should not take these words literally. Jesus' mother, Mary, and his siblings looked perfectly interested in providing a place for Jesus to stay.[4] Rather, Jesus explains, in hyperbolic fashion, that he has no earthly security that provides his ultimate identity. He has no home, residence, nationality, or country that is his ultimate priority.

Background of Luke 9:59–62

Having no "den," "nest," or place to rest one's head refers primarily to not having a home or residence. The second potential disciple has a more narrow sense of home. He politely ("permit me," *epitrepō*) requests: "Having gone away, first to bury my father" (Luke 9:59). "Home" is the place of obligation to one's parents. The third potential disciple also politely asks: "to say good-bye to the ones in my home" (Luke 9:61). "Home" is the place of loving concern.

When the literal priesthood was in full force, as it was in Jesus' time, it required priority over family at certain times. When a priest was about to offer a sacrifice at the temple (he had already been consecrated), if he suddenly heard that one of his parents had died, he could not leave: "He shall not go where there is a dead body; he shall not defile himself even for his father or mother" (Lev. 21:11). In other words, Jesus implied that following him is as urgent and as high a priority as a priest about to sacrifice in the temple: "Allow the dead to bury their own dead" (Luke 9:60). Duty to family, as important as it is, is less important than obeying God. People cannot have their affections in two places. (See also Luke 9:50.) Jesus responds also with imagery from farming: "No one having put the hand to the plow and having looked back is worthy of God's reign" (Luke 9:62). If you plow while simultaneously turning around, your foot is going to get caught and cut in the plow or you are going to plow in a circle. In other words, if you claim to be a Christian, you need to obey Christ, and, if you do, you can never fully identify with any human family or home. Jesus has no turf. A home is a man's castle. It is also a woman's castle. When one rests one's head, one relaxes, one sleeps. As the psalmists say: The Lord "gives sleep to his beloved" (127:2) and "I lie down and sleep; I wake again, for the Lord sustains me" (3:5; 4:8).[5] Jesus, however, is intending to go to Jerusalem where he expects to be killed, fatally betrayed in a deceitful manner. He cannot close his eyes, trusting the humans around him. Even his family does not believe in his claims (at this time) (Mark 3:21; Acts 1:14).

Psychologists have learned that "turf," or having a space to call one's own, is one of the most elemental human psychological needs. Territory is more fundamental than sexuality. "Turf is really the self."[6] But Jesus' message, then and now, is: you cannot simply marvel at God's majesty, as God takes care of you; you also need to receive your core security in God, by becoming a citizen of God's reign and by promoting God's desires in your life. If we follow Jesus "wherever he may go," we will find ourselves in the country between countries.

When I first came to New Jersey in sixth grade, I remember standing outside during one recess, when a girl, with a smirk, asked me where I came from. I said, "Dominican Republic." She laughed, looking at the others, and demanded, "And where is that?" I was baffled at first, but then it dawned on me that she was not asking me content questions, but rather she was ridiculing me because I was different. But, different is "different," not inferior or superior, or am I wrong?

Many United States Hispanic Americans Have Difficulty with Identity

I am not the only Hispanic American who feels caught without a country. For example, Daniel Rodríquez-Díaz explains: "In the Latino communities, as in the African-American, Asian, and Native American, the matter of *identity* burns in the heart of all."[7] After an extensive study of Hispanics in North America and Puerto Rico, Justo L. González concludes that:

> The mood and the basic imagery of Hispanics in this country are those of a people in exile. Many are exiles in the literal, everyday sense. For some reason, they have left their native lands and come to this land. Some are political exiles. . . . Others are economic refugees. . . . Others are "ideological refugees." The image projected by this country was such that they became convinced that the values of this society were better than those in their own native societies, and that therefore they would be more at home here. . . .
>
> Then there are many others who are not exiles in the sense that they left the land of their birth to come to this nation. They were born here. And so were their parents and grandparents. But they too are strangers in the deeper sense of living in a land not their own. Although they are U.S. citizens by birth, they are often seen and treated as less than full citizens, and therefore they are strangers living in a native land that remains foreign.[8]

Rodríquez-Díaz adds that in the United States: "There are degrees of acceptance of Latino identity. The degree of acceptance varies according to color and social status. The darker the skin and the lower in the socioeconomic ladder, the stronger the social/cultural differentiations."[9] The more different you look, the more likely you will not be accepted. But, how about when you are not even accepted among those who are rejected? You cannot embrace the majority culture because it is not yours, nor are you accepted by the minority culture either because you are *inter*cultural or you *look* like the majority culture.

That is the country between countries. In Europe, you can find such a land. It has no houses, no trees. It is a barren strip with barbed wire and guards between two countries. That is the country Jesus calls *all* disciples to enter. Do you want to go there? And for Hispanic Americans, and other intercultural people, that is not so far to go. You already feel alienated. You already feel identity-less. The step is not so far. We can identify with our Lord Jesus in this small way. Our intercultural background is an aid, an analogy, for understanding God's reign, which owes allegiance to no earthly country. Jesus' words in Luke 9:58–62 are different ways of explaining the "cost" entailed in following Jesus (Luke 9:23–25). Good news costs.

An intercultural background is an aid to understanding Christ's exhortations, but it is not identical to following them. I, as an intercultural person, had no choice. I did not choose to be between cultures. Jesus, in contrast, chose to take on a life without moorings. Furthermore, Jesus' alienation was a choice he made for the sake of others (Luke 9:51–53). My suffering was self-centered.

Hospitality Is Important

Jesus has no home. Therefore, he becomes the stranger: "A stranger, I was, and you gathered me in" (Matt. 25:35). "You welcomed me." "You received me as a guest." Welcoming the stranger has been God's antidote to alienation, treating the stranger as family. Consequently, being loving to strangers is a consistent theme in the New and Old Testaments. Every person in need might be "Jesus" or Jesus' messenger (Heb. 13:2). "Love of strangers" is one word in Greek because such a love is so important *(philoxenia, philoxenos,* Rom. 12:13; 1 Peter 4:9). Hospitality, or the care of strangers, is a requirement for church leadership (1 Tim. 3:2; 5:10; Titus 1:8). Hospitality is even more important than fasting (Isa. 58:6–7).

Hospitality is a major concern for Latin Americans: "When did we see you hungry and we gave you food, or thirsty and we gave you something to drink?" (Matt. 25:37). The giving and acceptance of hospitality seems to me to be more habitual among Hispanic Americans than Anglo Americans. Whenever people came to our home, my parents would offer them something to drink. I do not ever remember my mother not wanting to feed any visitor. She spent countless hours showing me how to prepare for guests.

The apostle Paul says even about enemies: "If your enemies are hungry, feed them; if thirsty, give them something to drink; for by doing this, burning coals on their heads you will heap" (Rom. 12:20). My father used to travel around the Dominican Republic checking on unpaid bills for the Curaçao Trading Company. Instead of being harassed, he returned filled beyond saturation, replenished by Dominican coffee, eatables, and potassium-rich bananas. Even now, my husband and I follow in Jesus' model by using the "comestible experience" as a significant time and way to serve others. My Dutch side appreciates the efficient use of time.) My Hispanic side loves to offer guests a gift and, in turn, receive a gift (when I eat at others' homes).

These experiences are not unique. After collecting several essays from different Hispanic Christian perspectives (Catholic, Pentecostal, Methodist, and Baptist), Justo González summarizes that a key description of "Latino worship is a fiesta." He adds that "Our people need that sense of family in order to survive in an alien world; they need to celebrate God's future in the midst of an oppressive and alienating present."[10] Allan Figueroa Deck concurs: "Worship and prayer are concerned with the entire feast, the music, the party, the dance, and most certainly the food."[11] Hospitality, celebration of the Christian family, takes seriously love for Christ now and also love for one another in the messianic banquet to come (Matt. 26:29).

Even as far back as Columbus's time, the Taino Indians in Hispañola loved to give and receive, too. Christopher Columbus wrote in his journal that he and his soldiers gave the Taino Indians:

> some red caps and some glass beads. . . . At this they were greatly pleased and became so entirely our friends that it was a wonder to see. Afterwards they came swimming to the ships' boats, where we were, and brought us parrots and cotton thread in balls, and spears and many other things, and we exchanged for them other things, such as small glass beads and hawks' bells, which we gave to them. In fact, they took all and gave all, such as they had, with good will.[12]

Ana María Pineda adds that the Taino heritage was not simply hospitality, but also artistic. Mural art and poetry is an important part of "the diverse Hispanic/Latino neighborhoods in the United States."[13] When we would worship at the Presbyterian Church in Caparra Heights, Puerto Rico, the church poet would always write and recite a poem for every special occasion. In the United States, one of the recent major "crimes" is youth "tagging" or writing on public property. In one television program I saw, I was surprised how many of the "taggers" had Spanish surnames. Could this crime simply be a cultural gift without opportunity to flourish? Instead of painting over the graffiti, should not instead these deviant artists be made to make something beautiful?

coerced?

All Are Strangers

God as the stranger who is concerned for strangers is also a consistent Old Testament theme.

Positive Old Testament Models

God appears as a visitor in a group of three who is welcomed by Abraham and Sarah by the oaks of Mamre (Gen. 18:1–22). Two key additional ideas underlie the strong empathy for strangers among the Hebrews. First, the Hebrews must always remember they were once all aliens. Abraham and Sarah were foreigners in Canaan among the Hittites.[14] Moreover, all the Israelites were aliens, even slaves, in Egypt.[15] Second, all humans are also aliens. In Genesis 1 we learn that God created the world; therefore, it belongs to God. "The land is mine," says the Lord, "with me you are but aliens and tenants" (Lev. 25:23). Or, as David prays: "For all things come from you, . . . For we are aliens and transients before you, as were all our ancestors; our days on the earth are like a shadow" (1 Chron. 29:14–15) or "Hear my prayer, O LORD, . . . For I am your passing guest, an alien, like all my forebears" (Ps. 39:12, see also Ps. 119:19). David certainly spent much of his life outside of Israel waiting for the actualization of his ruling anointment (e.g. 1 Sam. 16:13; 19:18; 21:10–22:5). Thus, identification with intercultural people runs from Jesus' preaching back to the earliest biblical records.

Consequently, one of the major listings of God's attributes centers around strangers and other potentially oppressed people, orphans and widows. When Moses calls the people to obey God from the depths of their hearts, he reminds them:

> For the LORD your God is the one who is God of the gods and Lord of the lords, the Mighty, the Great, the Strong, and the Wonderful, who is not partial and does not take bribes, executing justice for orphan and widow and loving every stranger, giving each one food and clothing. (Deut. 10:17–18)

When one is a newcomer, one is potentially vulnerable. The first-century Stoic philosopher Epictetus explains that a person who travels:

> is considered to be a helpless person and exposed to those who wish to harm him. For this reason when we travel, then especially do we say that we are lonely when we fall among robbers, for it is not the sight of a human creature which removes us from solitude, but the sight of one who is faithful and modest and helpful to us. (*Discourses* III.13)

Think of Esther. When Mordecai tells his niece that a decree had been signed to destroy the Jewish nation in Ahasuerus's kingdom, Esther replies:

All the king's servants and the people of the king's provinces know that if any man or woman goes to the king inside the inner court without being called, there is but one law—all alike are to be put to death. (Esther 4:11)

The Jewish nation was vulnerable at this time. An intercultural person like Esther was needed to step in before the conquering leaders in its behalf. She became even more vulnerable in the process.

When one is vulnerable, one needs a powerful advocate. God is such a powerful advocate. Power, in itself, is never wrong. The moral question is: How does one use one's power? God uses power for dispensing impartial justice.

Rodríquez-Díaz has mentioned how color of skin can be one means of discrimination. God, in contrast, is described as the being who "receives no face." This imagery was so important to Christian writers that they coined a new term, *prosōpolēmptēs*, "face receiver," to indicate that God does not care about nationality, wealth, or power as reasons for affirmation.[16]

Positive Models Which Should be Followed

God's character is not simply to be admired. It is also to be copied. Therefore, immediately after God is described as partial to strangers, the believers are exhorted: "You shall also love the stranger, for you were strangers in the land of Egypt" (Deut. 10:19). The psalmist alludes to Deuteronomy 10 and celebrates it:

> [The Lord] executes justice for the oppressed;
> . . . gives food to the hungry.
> The LORD sets the prisoners free;
> the LORD opens the eyes of the blind.
> The LORD lifts up those who are bowed down;
> the LORD loves the righteous.
> The LORD watches over the strangers;
> he upholds the orphan and the widow,
> but the way of the wicked he brings to ruin.
> (Ps. 146:7–9)

Many Old Testament laws were written to benefit the alien. The third-year tithe had to be shared with the newcomers in the landowners' midst, as well as the Levites, orphans, and widows (Deut. 14:28–29; 26:12–15). Any harvest not gathered at the first gathering was to be left for the poor and the alien. The first fruits and festival of weeks and Sabbath harvests were also to be shared with foreigners.[17] Pay was never to be withheld from the alien (Deut. 24:14). Even refuge cities were to be available for foreigners (Num. 35:15). Justice and benevolence were always to be extended to the newcomers, because all Hebrews were once, and still were, newcomers: "You shall not deprive a resident alien or an orphan of justice; . . . Remember that you were a slave in Egypt and the LORD your God redeemed you from there; therefore I command you to do this" (Deut. 24:17–18). If justice and benevolence were extended to the stranger, then the Israelites would be blessed (Deut. 14:28–29). But if it were not extended, the Israelites would themselves be punished (Deut. 27:19). And, indeed, injustice toward foreigners is one of the reasons God allowed the Hebrew nation to be taken into exile.[18]

The stranger is the silent presence at the covenant celebration,[19] warmly invited to bring a burnt offering to the one living God,[20] included in the weekly and seven-year Sabbath rests and important celebrations.[21] If the men were circumcised, they could eat the Passover.[22] On the whole, the Pentateuch had one law for native Israelite and for foreigner.[23] The foreigner, too, could not commit idolatry, blasphemy, drink blood, or do unclean acts.[24] In other words, the Pentateuchal laws reiterated in practice that the antidote for the newcomer is to be welcomed as family, because the Israelites, too, were once newcomers.

Examples of Intercultural People

So, too, I have found that being intercultural, especially partially Hispanic in the United States setting, has helped me to be more sensitive to injustice.[25] Also, being reared in several cultures has helped me understand that true law may not be limited to one nation's understanding of it.

Moses is a wonderful example of an intercultural person. His parents, both Hebrew Levites, to save his life had to give Moses away to their very oppressors. Nursed by his mother, watched over by his sister Miriam, Moses was reared by an Egyptian. And, as a young adult, when he saw an Egyptian beating a Hebrew, he was impelled to intervene (Exod. 2:1–12). However, when he again tried to intervene between two Hebrews, one challenged his authority: "Who made you a ruler and judge over us? Do you mean to kill me as you killed the Egyptian?" (Exod. 2:13–14). When Moses flees into Midian, he ends up marrying Zipporah, having now as well an interracial marriage.[26] And, consequently, he names his child Gershom, signifying: "I have been an alien residing in a foreign land" (Exod. 2:21–22). I have also wondered if Moses might have had "bilingual learning disability,"[27] having in the great computer of his brain several languages: Hebrew, Egyptian, and, possibly, the language of Midian: "I have never been eloquent, neither in the past nor even now that you have spoken to your servant; but I am slow of speech and slow of tongue" (Exod. 4:10). "Slow of speech" is literally "heavy of mouth." When a person knows at least two languages well, sometimes it takes a while for the right word from the right language to come to the fore of one's consciousness.

If being intercultural may make one more sensitive to justice and truth, it can also be incapacitating if fear of rejection cripples one's action. Even though in my home we spoke two languages, English and Spanish, I never became as fully adept at either as I could have been if I had been reared speaking only one language. My Spanish mother used to speak to me in Spanish[28] and my Dutch father used to speak to me in English. Even though Spanish was the first language I learned, my parents also taught me English and Dutch until one day when I stopped speaking altogether, like a car that had flooded. When a psychologist found out I was being taught three languages at once, he said to begin with one, and so I began to speak again. Though in a Spanish country, I was sent to an English-speaking school, and after a while my English abilities superseded my Spanish. But, the remarkable thing is that slowly, even in Dominican Republic, I became embarrassed to speak Spanish before my non-Hispanic friends. Remembering back these many years, I cannot recall how I ever learned such a sense of shame, but I did. And the more ashamed, the less I spoke, until my abilities in Spanish decreased even more. And, when I matured to the point that I wanted to improve my Spanish, I was too embarrassed to practice. Fear of rejection can be crippling. If Moses had gone ahead and spoken directly to the Egyptians, would Aaron, his spokesperson, ever have been consumed with his own power and allowed others to convince him to lead in making a substitute idol with its corresponding immorality?[29]

Different Can Also Be Wrong

If the Bible is so forthright on its acceptance of foreigners, how then could anyone misunderstand its message and become parochial and separatist? Several different Hebrew words may be translated "foreigner" including *ger*, "dweller," *zur*, "stranger," and *necar*, "foreigner." *Zur* especially has the basic sense of "strange," meaning "unholy," idolatrous, wrong, not according to God's directions. In the Pentateuch, *zur* or "alien" could simply refer to Hebrews who were not priests (Exod. 29:33) or people outside one's own family (Deut. 25:5). But, *zur* largely has negative connotations before Davidic times. For example, "Now Aaron's sons, Nadab and Abihu, each took his censer, put fire in it, and laid incense on it; and they offered unholy fire before the LORD, such as he had not commanded them" (Lev. 10:1). This sense of "strange," in other words, "unholy," became one significance of "stranger," as in "dishonor has covered our face, for aliens have come into the holy places of the LORD's house" (Jer. 51:51).

Thus, "strange" in the Bible may not simply refer to "different" (although it does, as in Isa. 28:21), it also may be "strange," a "different" that is wrong. *Necar* too can refer to "foreign gods," as in: "The LORD said to Moses, 'Soon you will lie down with your ancestors. Then this people will begin to prostitute themselves to the foreign gods in their midst, the gods of the land into which they are going; they will forsake me, breaking my covenant that I have made with them'" (Deut. 31:16).

The intercultural person may feel fear because of potential rejection and, as well, may cause fear in the native. One appropriate fear native believers may feel is the possibility of outsiders bringing different but wrong ideas and practices. *Anomie* has become a common sociological term in English (entering from the French *anomia*, "without law") meaning "lack of purpose, identity, or ethical values in a person or in a society; disorganization, rootlessness."[30] Anomie includes normlessness, confusion of norms, isolation, social maladjustment, meaninglessness, marginality. It is a state of deregulation or normlessness.

Anomia was originally a Greek term. In the New Testament, it is the opposite of righteousness and doing the will of God.[31] It is a synonym for sin (1 John 3:4). Infrequently, it also was used by Jews as a euphemism for Gentiles in a more neutral sense, as Peter uses it when he tells his Jewish listeners that they handed over Jesus to be killed by the Roman authorities (Acts 2:23; Rom. 2:12). Paul goes so far as to explain that he, a Jew, becomes like a Gentile ("lawless") to win Gentiles to the Good News (1 Cor. 9:21). Thus, the ancient Jews, like some people today, saw the foreigner as someone outside their laws. However, the greatest diatribes in the New Testament are given by Jesus not against lawless Gentiles, but rather against the religious leaders of his time and even against religious leaders to come. In other words, being intercultural was not at all the problem for Jesus. Rather, it was being inconsistent. Even prophesying in Jesus' name, casting out demons, and doing deeds of power would not ensure entrance into God's reign if these acts were not accompanied by doing God's will, because Satan can use wonders to delude people (Matt. 7:23; 2 Thess. 2:9). The scribes and Pharisees looked righteous, but inside they were full of hypocrisy and *lawlessness,* in other words, greed and self-indulgence. They did not understand priority of values, that the principles of justice, mercy, and faith are more important than any specifics on what exactly to tithe (Matt. 23:28).

Did Moses have a wrong kind of anomie when he killed the Egyptian? Did he lack ethical value or did he act from a godly value? When we worked in an ecumenical setting, one minister we knew left his family in Colombia and lived with us while he attended a training school in New Jersey. He became good friends with a woman, a recent convert, whose husband was an assassin for the Mafia and was serving time in prison. One day, this man and his female friend told us they were considering marriage. However, when his wife (in Colombia) wrote him that she was seriously ill, he returned home and we never heard from him again. Here is a case of someone who travels (in this case, for the first time in his life) and begins to act as if the God he knew in his native land was not the same God he now knows in this new land. Even though a professing Christian, he begins to act as if the ethics he had always practiced were no longer applicable, as if marriage vows were only applicable in one country, not wherever he travels. He became a person "without law."

Did Rahab have anomie? From the perspective of the ruler and ruling class of Jericho, Rahab did have anomie. She lacked cultural identity. She did not act as a resident of Jericho when she saved the lives of two Israelite spies in her home. But, she had a higher sense of identity, a higher law: "I know that the Lord has given you the land, and that dread of you has fallen on us, . . . The Lord your God is indeed God in heaven above and on earth below" (Josh. 2:8–11). For those of Jericho, Rahab was a traitor acting from anomie. For Israelites and Christians and God, Rahab was a great heroine, acting on the basis of God's higher laws.[32]

Thus, researchers who view anomie as largely negative, seeing anomie as an explanation of deviance, fail to understand its positive aspects because such researchers may be too embedded within their own cultures.[33]

Conclusion

Our task in this book has been to learn more about God by having people who love God and treat God's written revelation as authoritative and reliable reflect on God's attributes from their cultural situation. I wrote this chapter from the perspective of my personal story, as an intercultural person, in particular, an Hispanic American. I supported my own experience with those of other Christian Hispanic Americans. Particularly meaningful to me, and to other Hispanic Americans, is God's self-description as an impartial judge who is concerned for the stranger. God Incarnate, Jesus, continued this self-description by teaching he had no earthly security that provided his ultimate identity. Consequently, he identified himself as a stranger. God throughout history has been concerned for the needy stranger. The devout stranger was always welcomed in the covenant. The danger for the intercultural person is the possibility of forgetting that God is also omnipresently powerful and holy. Therefore, we need not fear and we must be holy wherever we go since God is not only a lover of strangers, but also a powerful and holy God.

God can also seem at times to be caught between cultures—celestial and terrestrial. The next chapter, expanding into a full Caribbean perspective, looks at the transcendent, but immanent, presence of God among us.

Transcendent but Not Remote:
The Caribbean

Dieumème Noëlliste

Dieumème Noëlliste serves as president of Jamaica Theological Seminary, Caribbean Graduate School of Theology, and Caribbean Evangelical Theological Association. He has a Ph.D. from Northwestern University, M.Div. from Trinity Evangelical Divinity School, and Th.B. from William Tyndale College. He has published numerous articles as well as monographs *Toward a Theology of Theological Education* and *Options in the Delivery of Education*. Born in Haiti, with first-hand experience of Afro-Caribbean religions, he is a Christian theologian, administrator, and evangelist.

A very encouraging phenomenon is occurring in Christianity at the moment. At last, the era of the concentration of theological reflection in only one sector of the world has come to an end. The rapid spread of the church in heretofore foreign areas is resulting in the decentralization of theological activity. Many regions of the world that used to depend totally on the outside world for their theological consumption are beginning to be served homegrown and locally produced theologies.

This is a welcome development. But it is at the same time a phenomenon that brings a challenge, which needs to be faced squarely. The challenge concerns the relationship of theology to culture. Of course, this issue is not new; it has been with us since the beginning of Christian thought. But the current trend toward the globalizing of the theological enterprise gives it heightened significance.

It is no secret that theology always bears the imprint of the socio-cultural milieu in which it is produced. And such cultural taint need not be seen as a liability of which theology needs to be relieved. Indeed, when wisely used, culture is an indispensable asset to the theological task. As Abbot Mulago has said, to formulate and communicate the Christian message to a people effectively, one must first of all pene-trate "the outlook, culture, and philosophy" of that people.[1] This has prompted another thinker to assert boldly: "A theology that does not take culture seriously is doomed to failure."[2]

But how is theology to take culture seriously *and* remain true to itself? The question has evoked several responses. It therefore merits more than a passing comment. We will examine it in some detail before pro-ceeding with our reflection on God in the Caribbean perspective, which will seek to show that, contrary to the Afro-Caribbean view, divine tran-scendence when rightly understood can comfortably accommodate divine presence.

Theology and Culture

One of the methods used to relate theology to culture has been sub-jugation. The history of Christian thought contains not a few instances where theology has been used to accommodate, legitimize, and defend the prevailing ideologies, moods, and practice of a given culture.[3] This kind of relationship has always produced a highly *ideological* theol-ogy, which muzzled Christian faith and seriously weakened its trans-forming power. If anything has been learned from two millennia of Christian thought, it must be the need to abandon this model.

In recent times another approach has been proposed. This time some suggest that theology should be totally fused with cultural analy-sis. Accepting the correctness of the ideology of religious pluralism with its claim that all religions are basically the same,[4] some theologians from the Two-Thirds World boldly advocate the exclusion from the the-ological task of anything that is specifically Christian, and the confin-ing of the theological activity to the articulation of the religious com-ponents of their culture.[5] This proposal is justified on the ground that indigenous religious ideas not only constitute an adequate basis for the formulation of a full-fledged theology, but in some cases they are superior to Christian ideas.[6]

This model decisively moves away from Christian theology in the direction of a thoroughgoing cultural theology. In so doing it poses a difficulty even for the theologian who places great premium on general revelation, but who is committed to the view that God's self-disclosure in Jesus Christ as attested in the biblical record is definitive and unsurpassable (John 1:18; Phil. 2:6–11; Col. 1:15–20; Heb. 1:1–3).

The difficulties identified in the aforementioned positions would seem to support the view that if Christian theology is to maintain its integrity, it must remain aloof of culture. In fact, some people think so. The holders of this position claim for theology a universality which presumably shields it from cultural taintedness. But if our contention is true, that all theology is in some sense culture laden, then any attempt at formulating a totally acultural theology is misguided.

Many who acknowledge the inescapability of contact between culture and theology advance that the best use theology can make of culture is that of facilitator in the process of the indigenization of Christian faith. In its effort to provide an autochthonous rootage for the faith, theology is asked to wrap the content of faith in the cultural form provided by the context.

Theology cannot do without cultural mediation. Hence, the appeal to theology to avail itself of the service of culture for the communication of the faith has much to commend it. However, the "form and content" approach may at the same time claim too much and too little. If, on the one hand, some hold that all the features of a culture are appropriate channels for the conveyance of the data of faith, then clearly their claim says too much. Many a cultural form is *not* a fit medium for the transmission of the content of faith. Can the Indian caste system, for example, play such a role? On the other hand, if some maintain that all the assistance theology can receive from culture is restricted to the provision of form alone, then their case is understated. Can culture not supply theology with some content as well? I think yes. If due weight is given to the fact of God's general revelation in the created order, then thinking that a given culture may contain elements that point to God and as such should be seen as legitimate data for theological reflection is not far-fetched at all. To say this is not to endorse the view of those who see in these elemental revelatory features an adequate basis on which a full-fledged theology can be constructed. It is simply a matter of acknowledging their true theological import.

If all the models considered above are deemed inadequate, what then are we left with? What if theology would engage culture in a continuing critical dialogue with the view to appropriating from it materials that are pertinent for Christian theological thought, but also correcting culture where it is at variance with revealed truths? Here theology is not merely asked to don an indigenous dress, it is challenged to integrate in its conceptualization those cultural elements that qualify as valid stuff of theological reflection. The approach requires that both the donning of the indigenous garb and the appropriation of the cultural data be guided by the revealed Word.

The approach being advocated here is not new. A growing number of theologians, who desire their reflection on Christian faith to avail itself of the service of culture while reserving the right to challenge it, are commending the model and are trying it out in their own work. For example, based on the conviction that in Africa a living Christian faith must interact with African culture, Merci Amba Oduyoye wrote a wide-ranging essay which shows the ways in which "Christian theology can be aided by African religious beliefs and practices."[7] While there is room for debate on some of her suggestions, there is no doubt that many of the themes she identifies can be integrated in theological reflection without endangering its Christian character.

In a similar vein, Kwame Bediako has argued for the sort of engagement between African culture and Christian faith that would result in the elucidation of the faith for the African world "without losing Jesus' uniqueness in that world."[8] Drawing on his own work and that of many of his African colleagues, Bediako has shown how promising the approach can be. He recognizes that it is a formidable challenge to achieve "relevance without syncretism,"[9] but he is convinced that it is a task that is required by the Christian gospel itself.

In the West, these views have been echoed in recent times by thinkers like William Dyrness, who has been emphasizing the need for a cross-cultural theology utilizing the interactional model of contextualization. Agreeing that "evangelical theology is primarily the interpretation of the Bible in context,"[10] Dyrness wants nothing less than a theology hammered out in the process of "a serious interaction between scripture and cultural realities"[11] and interchange between theologies from many different settings, representing different points of view.[12]

Perhaps there is no theological theme that lends itself more readily to the critical appropriation model being suggested here than the one being focused on in this present book: God. Biblical faith affirms that God is revealed both in the world and the Word (Ps. 19; John 1:1–18; Rom. 1; Heb. 1:1–3). Hence, in some way God is present in every context. Consequently, the world, which includes culture, should not be set aside totally when we reflect on God. But culture, as creation of humans, ought not to be equated with the divine revelation itself. Rather, it contains and offers an interpretation, a grasp, an apprehension of the divine disclosure embedded in it. As the creation of a fallen humanity, culture also partakes of fallenness. Hence the understanding of the divine being it contains is bound to be less than perfect. Indeed, Scripture teaches that the cultural conception can be a half truth or even a total distortion of the reality of God (Acts 17:22–31; Rom. 1:18–25). For this reason, while reflection on God must be open to the appropriation of the material of culture, it must, by the same token, reserve the right to challenge and correct the cultural viewpoint by the specially revealed Word when that becomes necessary.

Divine Transcendence in the Perspective of Afro-Caribbean Religions

What conception of God prevails in the Caribbean culture? How does it square with the datum of biblical revelation regarding the divine self-disclosure? How would that conception influence the way in which the Christian theologian who operates in that context thinks about God? These questions will occupy my attention for the balance of this chapter. But before focusing on them, I must take a necessary short detour.

African Religious Presence in the Caribbean

In his very fine study on the history of religions in the Caribbean, the Guyanese theologian Dale Bisnauth asserts that one of the results of the infamous slave trade was the substantial Africanization of the Caribbean. With the introduction of the odious commerce in human beings, the descendants of the African slaves were not only to become the most numerous of the several ethnic groups that were to people the region; but also the African presence was to affect profoundly "every facet of Caribbean life, including religion."[13]

The judgment is certainly correct, but the case could be stated more strongly. Rather than saying "including religion," Bisnauth could have said "especially religion," for it is difficult to think of an area of Caribbean life that has been more profoundly affected by the African cultural ethos than religion. The African religious presence in the Caribbean is pervasive. It is reflected in the establishment in the region of such predominantly African religious and semireligious cults as Cumina, Myalism, and Obeah. It is evident in the hybrid religious movements, which sprang throughout the region in the wake of the encounter of Christianity and African traditional faith. I am thinking of Haitian Vaudou; Trinidadian Shango; Cuban Santeria; and the Jamaican revivalist cults, such as Zionism, Pukkumina, and Kumina, to mention but a few. The presence is felt even in the established Christian churches—both Protestant and Catholic—through the pull and the attraction that African religious beliefs and practices exert on many of their members.

Bisnauth would certainly not object to this strengthening of his statement. He himself has argued convincingly that in the hostile and uneven encounter of Christianity and African traditional religion, ironically Christianity is what has been Africanized rather than African beliefs Christianized.[14]

The point of this brief detour is to venture the suggestion that if the impact of the African religious viewpoint on the Caribbean is that pervasive, then to focus on the movements that clearly reflect that influence in our attempt to identify a prevailing concept of God in the Caribbean culture would seem to be legitimate. What our investigation will yield will by no means be the only understanding of the divine reality in the region, but it should surely be a predominant one.

The Hierarchy of Divinities

When we examine the Caribbean religious cults, which preserve strong African cultural retentions, we observe a view of God which displays a highly hierarchical structure. These religious systems present us with a pantheon of divinities ordered according to the rank ascribed to categories of deities.

Three categories of divine beings are delineated or assumed in the Afro-Caribbean religious systems being focused on here. At the top of the pyramid is a supreme being who is believed to be the author and preserver of the created order. Called the *Gran Met La* or *le BonDieu* in Vaudou, Father or God Almighty in revivalism, the high god seems to remain nameless in Trinidadian Shango. His name does not seem to have survived the Middle Passage.[15] Below the supreme being are myriads of lesser gods with differing characteristics, personalities, functions, and predilections. Known as *loas* in Haitian Vaudou, "powers" in Trinidadian Shango, "trumping"[16] spirits in the revivalist cults of Jamaica, and "Saints" in Cuban Santeria, these divinities are said to pervade the cosmic order and are believed by some to serve as intermediaries between humans and the supreme being. The last category of deities is that of deified persons broadly referred to as ancestral spirits. Generally, this group consists of deceased members of a given religious cult who were highly regarded or feared while alive.[17]

A complete understanding of the view of God which prevails in the Afro-Caribbean religious systems would necessitate a close study—expositional and evaluative—of each one of the categories outlined above. This, however, would require a project of a much wider scope than the one being undertaken here. Consequently, our treatment will be limited to the upper tier of the Afro-Caribbean divine pyramid: the supreme god.

The Remote High God

In the eyes of the adherents of these religions, what matters, first and foremost, is not the metaphysical and ethical status of the deities they worship, but the benefit arising out of the relationship the gods maintain with humans. What devotees value is a God–human relation that yields experiential and pragmatic dividends. For the devotee the service of the gods has a twofold objective: possession by them and the enjoyment of an undisturbed existence.

Surprisingly, when viewed in the light of the relational yardstick, the supreme god does not seem to fare very well. In the understanding of devotees of Afro-Caribbean religions, the high god's relation to the creation, including humans, is minimal. Indeed, it is so minimal that we would be justified in describing their conception of God as *thoroughgoing transcendence.* Our contention is that although this particular apprehension of the divine being is not a total negation of revealed truth, and hence needs to be integrated in our articulation, nevertheless it does not represent an accurate portrayal of God as spoken of in Scripture and must therefore be corrected by the relevant data of special revelation. But before we do that we need to corroborate this judgment by highlighting a few salient ideas that form part of the Afro-Caribbean understanding of the supreme being.

In the first instance, the high god of the Afro-Caribbean religious system is a being who abides in solitariness, being shielded from interaction with human beings. By virtue of the position he occupies in the hierarchy of divinities, the supreme god is considered exalted and totally set apart. In his study of the revivalist cults of Jamaica, Joseph Moore found that in revivalism the high god "always stays in the high heavens."[18] Roles and functions performed by other divinities for the benefit of believers are deemed inappropriate for the supreme being. Whether the deities in question belong to the upper rung of the divine ladder makes no difference. Hence in revivalism Jesus and the Holy Spirit are said to be involved in one way or another in worship and other types of services offered by devotees. The high god, however, never condescends to such low ebb.[19]

From the foregoing follows a second idea which speaks of the utter transcendence of the supreme god: the virtual nonexistence of fellowship between that divine being and devotees. We know that possession by the gods is a central aspect of all Afro-Caribbean cults. As George Simpson observed, "From the point of view of the devotee, possession by a spirit is the height of religious experience."[20] In the state of possession the worshiper experiences the closest bond possible with the possessing god, taking on the god's personality and characteristics and mannerisms, and is taught by him or her. But scholars of these religions inform us that the high god does not possess devotees.[21]

That the aloofness is not to be charged to the divine side alone needs to be pointed out. Devotees themselves do not exhibit the same kind of interest in the supreme being that they show for the lesser deities. The formal worship of the high god seems lukewarm and in some cases virtually nonexistent. And even when the supreme being is addressed in prayer, this seems to be a nominal gesture or a hurried and perfunctory introduction to what really matters: transaction with the lower deities.[22]

Why this less than enthusiastic attitude vis-a-vis a being regarded as the highest of all beings? Some see it as a vestige of the influence of African and Indian religious beliefs. In neither of these systems is formal worship ascribed to the high god.[23] Each holds that as a god who is already kindly disposed toward humans, the supreme being does not need to be worshiped, propitiated, and prayed to.[24] For some scholars, however, precisely the utter transcendence of the high god is what explains the devotee's lukewarm attitude toward the supreme being. Because of the noninvolvement of the high god in the nitty-gritty business of an existence which requires constant supernatural assistance, devotees are obliged to put that unavailable god in the background and cultivate a much more intimate relationship with the deities who are readily accessible to them.[25]

A last idea that helps support our contention is that of the withdrawal of the high god from the world. Beside remaining in solitariness and sharing little or no fellowship with humans, the supreme god is believed to maintain a distance from the created order that is tantamount to a virtual absence from it. To be sure, like their African forebears, Afro-Caribbean religionists believe firmly that the world owes its existence and sustenance to the creative and preserving activities of God.[26] But for one reason or another, the supreme being withdrew from the world and presumably left it to the care of lesser but immanent deities who are said to mediate between God and humans.[27]

This idea of the delegation of the affairs of the world to deputy deities has led some thinkers to contend that to speak of the remoteness of God from the world in the Afro-Caribbean religious systems is not appropriate. God only "appears to be far away."[28] For "the lesser gods represent the myriad eyes of the supreme god watching over all and meeting [humans'] needs."[29]

But in response to this we can reply that even if the mediatorial role of the lesser gods is granted, we are still talking about a *mediated* presence. The presence of the lesser gods does not equate that of the high god. The Christian theologian must ask whether this notion satisfies the stipulations of biblical revelation.

Furthermore, underlying the contention is the notion that the metaphysical principle at work in the Afro-Caribbean religious system is that of diffused monotheism. George Mulrain opens his whole discussion of God in Vaudou with the statement: "Vaudou is a monotheistic religion."[30] But when one considers the ambiguity that characterizes the world of the lesser deities, this position faces a serious problem. Ethically, the deities that make up that world do not share the same status. Some are considered good and others evil. And yet the cults make use of both kinds.[31] Additionally, in Vaudou at least, a same deity *(loa)* can perform both good and bad deeds.[32] The question is: Who among these deities serves as the eyes of God in the world, and when does even a good deity function as God's deputy?

Difficulties like these have led many to question the viability of the deputization theory. Indeed, the Haitian anthropologist and theologian L. Hurbon has argued for its abandonment altogether—albeit on a different ground. Hurbon contends that in Vaudou the notion of intermediariness does not adequately explain the high god/lesser deity relation. He sees nothing less than a relation of "opposition between the *Gran Met La* and the *loas.*"[33] The two cannot coexist. The absence of the worship of the high god is a necessary correlation of the worship of the *loas.* God must be situated outside the system if their worship is to be at all possible: "The exclusion of God from the system of the loas is the genesis and the foundation of the putting in place of the system."[34] This is why Hurbon speaks of the nonplacing (French, *non position*)[35] of God in Vaudou. God is an empty box *(case vide).*

But why is the system unable to accommodate God? Hurbon's answer is anthropological. If God is allowed in the world, reality would become an "undifferentiated whole . . . impossible to manipulate"[36] since it would relate to one center only: God. God would dominate all, and reality would be flat and uniform. But with the "withdrawal and absence of God [from the world] differentiations, both in things and in society become possible."[37] Reality is then transformed into a field characterized by manifoldness, ambiguity, and unevenness. But it is in this universe of "ups and downs" that humans actualize themselves and fulfill their desires and aspirations. Hence, if humans must live, God must leave. And, if God is interested in the happiness of humans, God must remain withdrawn and remote. Hurbon explains: "God and [humans] cannot be imprisoned in the same totality."[38]

But the possibilities of self-actualization brought about by the absence of God cannot be realized by humans alone. To be a theatre of happiness and joy, the ambiguous world created by the flight of God needs to be adjusted and manipulated every now and then. And for this, humans need help; and the source of such assistance are the *loas.* The *loas* constitute a multiplicity of counterbalancing centers of reality, and are relied on by humans in their attempt to make sense of the real and in their desire to find meaning and fulfillment in it.[39]

Hurbon's anthropological explanation is not satisfactory in my view. We will interact with it later. But for our purpose here, his arguments are significant on two counts: they provide unassailable support for the concept of *thoroughgoing transcendence* and contend that it is not a concept that needs to be mitigated or apologized for, but one which is required by the system.

Obviously, Hurbon's argument related specifically to Haitian Vaudou. However, given the similarities that exist between the pantheons of Trinidadian Shango, Cuban Santeria, other Afro-Caribbean cults, and Vaudou itself,[40] if his overall contention were to resonate in these systems as well, we should not be surprised.

The Afro-Caribbean Understanding of Transcendence and Biblical Revelation

How is the Afro-Caribbean apprehension of the divine being to be assessed? What conception of God may be formulated for the Caribbean that would both do justice to this particular cultural understanding *and* preserve Christian uniqueness? To repeat the words of Bediako quoted earlier: How do we meet, in this particular case, the challenge to be relevant without being syncretistic?

If we take biblical revelation as our guide, we note several aspects that can be appropriated in the thoroughgoing transcendence notion. At several points it intersects with the revealed Word. This does not mean that the conceptualization is defects-free. Problems are inherent in it and these will be noted in the course of our interactive analysis. We need to note, however, that Christian theology *has* made use of notions of transcendence which, in thoroughgoingness, have come close or even surpassed the Afro-Caribbean understanding. Think for instance of Immanuel Kant's skeptical or agnostic transcendence, or of Karl Barth's dialectal model. Despite their defects these approaches were, and continue to be deemed, useful. We are not suggesting that precedence alone justifies the continuation of a practice. What we are contending is that, just as the formulations to which we alluded above, the Afro-Caribbean view intersects at some points with the revealed Word, and as such is useful.

The thoroughgoing transcendence concept and the biblical portrayal of God converge fully or partially at a minimum of three points.

God–World Distinction

Scripturally, the adherents of the Afro-Caribbean religious sects are on firm ground in their insistence that a clear distinction be maintained between the world and God. In agreement with the biblical writers, they credit the creation of the world to God and contend that Creator and created must stand apart one from the other. The biblical witness underscores this separateness in various ways. First, it states it *causally*. It mentions the word as one of the methods used by God to bring forth the world. God spoke and things came into being (Gen. 1). As Dyrness remarks, "creation by the word stresses God's transcendence."[41] It speaks of the primacy of God's will and the ease with which God works.[42]

Second, Scripture refers to this separateness *temporally*. To say that God relates to the world in Creator–created fashion is to speak of a temporal difference between the two. Logically, the Creator precedes the created. Scripture attributes preexistence and eternality to God, not the world. God not only exists *separately* from the world but also *before* the world. At various points Scripture refers to God's activity before the foundation of the world (John 17:5, 24; Eph. 1:4; 1 Peter 1:20).

Third, the Bible speaks of the separation *ontologically*. The being of God is self-caused; the being of the world is other-caused. God is necessary; the world is contingent. The two do not relate in a codependent mode. The world needs God for its sustenance, but God does not need the world for God's own. In this respect Hurbon is correct: "God and the world cannot be imprisoned in the same totality."[43]

God sustains the world through general providence and special intervention. It is worth mentioning that *thoroughgoing transcendence* allows for such special acts of God. Hurbon concedes that if the world order is about to fail, God stands ready to intervene.[44] This is a last resort kind of supernaturalism, but it is more in keeping with the biblical witness than the deistic stance which reduces God's involvement to the mechanistic workings of general providence only.

Last, Scripture expresses the truth *epistemologically*. Cognitively, the chasm between humans and God is unbridgeable. Using the lips of Isaiah, the prophet, God declares: "For my thoughts are not your thoughts, nor are your ways my ways, says the LORD. For as the heavens are higher than the earth, so are my ways higher than your ways and my thoughts than your thoughts" (Isa. 55:8–9).

Divine Majesty

As noted earlier, in the Afro-Caribbean understanding, God is not only *distinct* from the world; the divine being is also *over* the world. God's position is one of high exaltation. With this, Scripture basically agrees as well. The biblical writers portray the divine being as a majestic, sovereign, and highly lifted Lord. Under the impact of his glorious and awe-inspiring vision of God, the prophet Isaiah flatly declares, "The LORD is exalted, he dwells on high" (Isa. 33:5). Throughout Scripture God is referred to as the Almighty One to whom alone belongs absolute rule. In the Book of Revelation, chapter 4, John brings that out with great power. He describes the being he saw in his second vision as one who sits on a throne. The person of the heavenly being radiates a splendor that human thought cannot fully understand and human language cannot fully express. Now, to sit on a throne is clearly to rule, but more is implied than simple rule. The position of the throne in the magnificent scene that the apostle was privileged to see leaves no doubt that the enthroned being enjoys supreme majesty and rules with superseding sovereignty. The text makes clear that the being holds the reins of history and determines its course and destiny. "Come up here," the exalted Lord summons the baffled apostle, "and I will show you what *must* take place" (Rev. 4:1–2, italics mine). The purpose of the Majestic Ruler will be realized, for God's will cannot be forever frustrated.

In the biblical view, the majesty of God is something that evokes worship and praise. Hence, the creatures who surround the throne on which the exalted one sits lavish thunderous and unceasing praise on God (Rev. 4:8–11). And such response is by no means limited to heavenly beings. Recalling the sovereignty of God over the world, the psalmist issues this invitation to worship: "Clap your hands, all you peoples; shout to God with loud songs of joy" (Ps. 47:1). Why? Because "awesome is the LORD Most High, the great King over all the earth!" (Ps. 47:2 NIV).

Here the Afro-Caribbean view falters. We noted earlier that it makes little or no room for the worship of God. But the recognition of majesty and the ascription of worship are not mutually exclusive. In fact they go together. The acknowledgment of God's greatness ought to result in the spontaneous adoration of God. That relationship seems to work in a similar manner among humans: the higher the dignitary, the greater the reverence. As the highest being, God must receive the highest praise—indeed the only praise (Isa. 42:8).

In the realm of human affairs, too, the combination of greatness and goodness very often generates great admiration. The benevolent ruler is often revered. In light of this, the denial of worship to God based on the kind disposition of God toward the creation is baffling. One would expect the very opposite. We have here an attitude of ungratefulness and "taking for grantedness" which Scripture squarely rebukes (Rom. 1:21; James 4:13–17).

But a more fundamental parting of the ways must be noted at this juncture. In stark contrast to the Afro-Caribbean conceptualization, the biblical view rejects the notion that *majesty precludes condescension.* In the biblical understanding, human misconduct, though offensive to God, *does not* result in the permanent flight of God. Indeed, it shows us a God who never ceases to reach out to humans in their lostness.

Throughout the Scriptures, God's attitude toward humankind is one of gracious openness. God is portrayed as one who calls, seeks, invites, lures, restores, and uplifts. In allowing for God's intervention in the created order the Afro-Caribbean view avoids the deistic misconception of a totally closed universe. And that is good. But why limit God's intervening act to the very end? The view echoes biblical thought as well, in asserting that God will not allow the created order to collapse under the weight of evil. But the eschatological intervention of which it speaks is not the only one to which Scripture testifies. History is punctuated intermittently by God's intervening acts. These past acts are what inspire confidence in the certain fulfillment of the final one.

The Hiddenness of God

How available is God to humans? Does God remain in solitariness, cut off from interaction and communion with human beings as the Afro-Caribbean view maintains? Is God a hidden being inaccessible to mortals?

If we must speak of the hiddenness of God, biblically speaking, we must be clear that with God hiddenness is not to be thought of as a permanent and irreversible withdrawal of a deity who is forever angry with, and disinterested in, humanity, as seems to be the case in the thoroughgoing transcendence view.[45] True, Scripture does speak of a divine distancing from human reach, but such alienation seems to be attributed more to human deficiencies than to active divine concealment. For example, a hiddenness that stems from God's ontological status appears to exist. Awesome and translucent, the divine Being emits a brilliance that dazzles and repulses and frightens. God lives in inapproachable light. Hence, faced with the manifestations of God's awful presence, at the foot of Mount Sinai, the Israelites "trembled with fear, . . . stayed at a distance" and implored Moses: "You speak to us, and we will listen; but do not let God speak to us, or we will die" (Exod. 20:18–19). Even secondhand contact with the light that shines from the divine face seems unbearable to humans. After being in the presence of God on Mount Sinai, Moses' face acquired such an intense radiance that he had to veil himself when speaking to the people. They could not stand his bare face; "they were afraid to come near him" (Exod. 34:29–32). We must note, however, that the difficulty in this instance was with the inability of the people to stand in the divine presence. The prohibition did not come from God. And the inability cannot be said to be absolute, for at least one person, Moses, did bear the divine presence.

The Scriptures also speak of an ethical hiddenness. The perfect holiness of God tends to keep sinful humans at bay. When Isaiah got a glimpse of the utter holiness of God, he was immediately drawn to self-condemnation. "Woe is me!" he exclaimed, "I am lost, for I am a man of unclean lips, and I live among a people of unclean lips, yet my eyes have seen the King, the LORD of hosts!" (Isa. 6:5). But note that even here, God's lofty position and perfect status were no obstacles to the God–human intercourse. Indeed, the interaction between God and the prophet started with God's own initiative. O what condescension!

At times, however, God actively hides Godself from humans on the basis of their condition of fault. But these times are when the attitude of lowliness and the sense of unworthiness beautifully displayed in Isaiah's attitude are lacking. They are times when God is presumed upon, taken for granted and treated with utter contempt. Hence, to those who were strong in religious rituals but weak in the practice of justice, God declares: "When you stretch out your hands, I will hide my eyes from you; even though you make many prayers, I will not listen; your hands are full of blood" (Isa. 1:15). If contrition takes place, however, God's hiddenness ends at once and fellowship is restored, for to turn to the Lord is to experience free pardon (Isa. 55:6).

To the biblical writers, God's hiddenness is also epistemological. God is unknowable, unless God comes to us in self disclosure. In Job 11:7, Zophar puts this question to Job: "Can you fathom the mysteries of God? Can you probe the limits of the Almighty?" (NIV). Zophar's negative answer is implied in the way he puts the question. But Elihu is much more explicit, stating flatly later on: "The Almighty is beyond our reach" (37:23 NIV). Centuries later, Paul's reflection on the realization of God's redemptive purpose in Christ evoked an exclamation and prompted a query which speak volumes of the unsearchability of God:

> O the depth of the riches and wisdom and knowledge of God! How unsearchable are his judgments and how inscrutable his ways! For who has known the mind of the Lord? (Rom. 11:33–34)

A few lines ago, I stated that God is unknowable unless God is given to us in self-disclosure. This is the heart of the biblical view of God. God delights in self-disclosure. Hence, the hiddenness and transcendence of God do *not* preclude fellowship with humans. The construal of the Afro-Caribbean religions is way off the mark at this point. They seek to apprehend God anthropologically. Granted, for various reasons, humans may refrain to seek after God, but what if God chooses to seek after humans? If God were to do so, the transcendence would not be removed, but it would be softened and the God–human alienation would not remain forever.

I must recall here Hurbon's contention that the persistence of God–human estrangement is good for human beings because the absence of God is necessary for their self-actualization. Even if we grant that as persons, human beings have a role to play in their own becoming, we cannot fail to notice that Hurbon's logic breaks down at this point. He argues that with the removal of God, *paradise* has been lost forever. This means that *paradise* existed before God's exit from the world. But if the condition which preceded the removal of God is described as paradisiacal, it means that it was *ideal* for humans. Why must a less than ideal condition be seen as better for them? If in the former condition the divine presence had a salutary effect, why would the reintroduction of God in the postparadisiacal situation spoil life for people?

At this point, the Afro-Caribbean position is not only illogical; it flatly contradicts revealed truth, and must therefore be corrected and aided by it. Merci Amba Odoyuye has said that Christian theology can be aided by African beliefs and practices. The converse is also true, and in the specific case which has retained our attention, it is more so. Biblical revelation insists that the presence of God is essential for human

self-actualization. The Caribbean view needs this insight for both logical coherence and existential cash value.

Transcendent Presence

From the foregoing interactive analysis, we hope we have been clear
that in our view the main problem with the Afro-Caribbean concept
of God is that it does not pertain to transcendence per se, but to the
kind of transcendence that the view advocates. That God is transcendent to the world is accepted at once, but that God is absent and remote
from the world we find problematic. In our view it is essential that a
way be found that allows us to speak of transcendence without remoteness. We must be able to come up with a conceptualization that accommodates in a meaningful way both divine transcendence and divine
presence. We need a transcendence that neither fears contact with
immanence nor allows itself to be dissolved by immanence when the
two intersect. In other words, the ideal that we seek is a transcendence
that remains *transcendent* in its disclosure and self-giveness—a transcendent presence, if you please.

But how can we achieve this? How can we have transcendence without remoteness? To our mind this seems achievable if transcendence
is conceived ontologically rather than spatially, as the Caribbean view
has done. True, the Afro-Caribbean construal accepts the ontological
superiority of the supreme God, but it does not seem to see in that
superiority an adequate basis for the grounding of divine transcendence. For, as we have seen, it has chosen to lay stress on the *position*
of God vis-a-vis the world, rather than the *being* of God in relation to
the being of the world. Our contention is that the ontological status of
God by itself provides a sufficient anchorage for transcendence, thus
rendering superfluous the element of remoteness so prevalent in the
Afro-Caribbean understanding.

Transcendence is essentially a rise above the common, an edge over
the ordinary, an extension beyond the usual. In the case of humans,
the divide that separates the extraordinary from the ordinary, and the
uncommon from the common may be functional, performative, ethical, and cognitive, but never ontological. Regardless of achievements,
positions, and status, humans are ontologically equal. They share a
common ancestor and owe their beings and existence to a common

Creator and Sustainer (Acts 17:25–28). In the case of God, however, the gulf is wider—and infinitely wider. In addition to the areas already mentioned, the chasm encompasses the ontological domain, and there takes on a character that is unique, absolute, and ultimate. God possesses an ontological status that sets God apart from the created order and elevates God above that order. The excellency of God lies fundamentally in the surpassing character of God's being.

Nowhere is this more evident than in the revelation of the name by which God wishes to be known: *I am who I am* (Exod. 3:12; 6:3). As is well known, in biblical thought, a name is not a mere means of external identification, it is the revelation of the nature and character of the person. Hence, as God's name par excellence, the self-designation, *I am who I am*, describes the being of God in a most excellent way. The appellation marks God out as a self-existent, eternal, and changeless being. *I am who I am* implies that God is the ground of God's own existence.[46] It speaks of the immutability of the divine nature and purpose. It denotes the fact that God's character, commitment, and behavior always reflect perfect consistency and that these characteristics are exclusively God's. No other being can lay claim on them.

But, interestingly, the description that the divine name provides is, in the main, negative. The name contains more mystery than revelation. And this may well be its central value. While the verb forms in the Hebrew expression *('eh^eyeh 'easher 'eh^eyeh)* have been commonly rendered in the present tense ("I am who I am"), the best translation of the expression is the future tense: "I will be as I will be." Whatever this means, it should not be understood to convey the sense of becomingness in God. Rather, it speaks of the infinite and the inexhaustible character of God's being, and of the total freedom of God to reveal aspects of that being as God chooses. The enigmatic name reveals that, in stark contrast to all other beings, the being of God is unsearchable. More than any other being, God can be known only through self-disclosure. Where God is not self-given in this fashion, we must remain utterly speechless concerning God's nature. God is not only the being beyond whom no greater being can be conceived; God is a being who is not conceivable at all unless God allows Godself to be conceived in some fashion. Apart from God's gracious self-giving, God remains forever an unsurmountable challenge to human thought.

One of the ways in which the being of God is projected to humans is through the manifestation of the glory of God. The glory of God is the being of God partially revealed. And whenever it is revealed, what the divine glory confronts us with is precisely the loftiness and the greatness of the Person hidden behind the appellation *I AM:* "The glory is the visible and supernatural manifestation of the supreme and incomparable majesty of God."[47] It speaks of the weight or the substance that characterizes the divine being; it denotes the honor that stems from the manifestation of God's attributes, and it stresses the awe which such a disclosure evokes in those who contemplate it (cf. Ps. 96:5–9). The glory identifies the divine *I am* as the one who is unequalled in power and awesomeness. For the glory is not shareable with other beings (Isa. 42:8).

For the biblical writers this ontological superiority puts God in a class by Godself. For them God is unmatched and incomparable (Isa. 40:18, 25). He is utterly unique among all beings (1 Kings 8:27; Ps. 89:6–8). Indeed, they flatly claim that God alone has the right to be called God (2 Sam. 7:22). God is the *only* God; no other god exists at all or ever could exist (Isa. 43:8–13). Clearly, by virtue of God's ontological superiority, God is set apart as the Wholly Other—as one who is absolutely heterogeneous.

But granted that God enjoys this exclusive and unique ontological status, how does this establish our thesis that this status by itself constitutes an adequate ground for divine transcendence, thereby correcting the excess of the Afro-Caribbean construal with its insistence on the withdrawal and absence of God from the world? I believe that both experience and biblical revelation warrant the claim.

Experientially, we all know certain persons whose sheer status impresses us and creates a "distance" between them and us. Such an impression and "distance" may be created by their high moral character, the level of their achievements, the power of their intellect, their social status, and so on. And their impact on us is felt whether or not they are physically close to us. Indeed, that the impression is more powerfully experienced and the distancing more keenly felt in their presence than in their absence may be argued. When we examine the biblical data, this is what we find with respect to the divine being. Whether experienced in close proximity or from afar, the being of God projects a dignity, a gravity, and an awesomeness that overpowers and overwhelms. By itself it differentiates and elevates God far above the realm of creatureliness and exerts a dwarfing effect on humans.

When Isaiah saw the exalted Lord in his vision, he realized immediately he was in the presence of transcendence. But the exaltation itself was not what impressed the prophet and made him realize the great chasm that exists between God and humans. It was the sheer being of God's own self! It was the awareness that he had set eyes on a Person whose being combines perfect holiness, supreme majesty, and surpassing glory that startled the prophet and drove him to self-condemnation and humbleness. Note carefully his confession: "Woe is me! I am lost, for I am a man of unclean lips, and I live among a people of unclean lips; yet my eyes have seen the *King, the* LORD *of hosts!*" (Isa. 6:5 italics mine).

Isaiah is by no means alone in this. Many other biblical personalities had similar experiences. Before the manifestation of the glorious being of God they were all driven immediately to prostration. Ezekiel reports that "the appearance of the likeness of the glory of the LORD" made him fall face down (Ezek. 1:28). Daniel, Paul, and John all confessed that the sight of the brilliance of the light that shone from the being of the Lord sent them prone or to their knees and left them awestricken (Dan. 10:9–11; Acts 26:12–18; Rev. 1:16–17).

Clearly, to experience God takes nothing away from God's transcendence. For God, closeness does not amount to commonness. God's being inspires awe and evokes reverence even when God draws nigh. It erects a distance even when God is at hand. The sheer being of God reflects a radiance, exerts a power, projects a majesty, and emits a purity that alienates, frightens, and terrifies (Exod. 20:18–21; Luke 2:9; Acts 9:3–9). The splendor of God's being maintains a divine–human distancing that protects God from triviality and demeaning familiarity. Communion and intimacy with God are real and genuine experiences, but they never reduce God's awesome and awful dignity. In immanence God remains transcendent.

Moses' experience with God in the wake of Israel's apostasy at the foot of Mount Sinai makes this point with utmost clarity. The incident is well known. While Moses was on Mount Sinai with God, the people persuaded Aaron to erect a golden calf that they worshiped in the place of God. This gross sin of idolatry ignited the anger and indignation of the Lord who threatened to destroy the people. Through fervent and persistent intercession Moses sought the favor of the Lord on behalf of the guilty people (Exod. 32:7–11). The people repented and the harsh punitive action that God threatened to take against them was modified.

Not only would God spare them from destruction, but God also vowed to fulfill the promise made long ago to the patriarchs (Exod. 33:1–4).

God exercised mercy, but a problem remained. God informed Moses that the nation would no longer enjoy his unmediated presence for the balance of the journey. An angel would lead them instead for the rest of the trip. The people's sin had alienated God. Moses, however, would have none of it. He preferred to stay put rather than move without God. Moses was convinced that with all its abundance, the land of promise was worth precious little to the people without the divine presence (Exod. 33:2–3, 15–16). Contrary to the Afro-Caribbean understanding, God's presence does not interfere with human fulfillment. It promotes it, and is indeed essential to it. Moses was certain that it was God's presence which bestowed favor on the people and gave them the assurance of being God's people—and therefore unique among all peoples. And with this judgment the people agreed (Exod. 33:4, 16).

Convinced of the absolute essentiality of the divine presence, Moses not only insisted that God go with the people, he also asked for the manifestation of the presence of God in glory among the people. God acquiesced and gave him these reassuring words: "I will do the very thing that you have asked; . . . I will make all my goodness pass before you, and will proclaim before you the name 'The LORD'" (Exod. 33:17–19). God is absolute Goodness and forebearing Love. While offending his holiness and incurring his judgment, human misdeeds, however odious, do not cause God to withdraw from the world and abandon it to its own design. Graciously, divine self-disclosure occurs even in the tragedies and crises of history.

The presence that God promised to Moses was not "a mere sense of the numinous," but the "presence of a known, personal and distinctive Deity."[48] God was present in all of God's "weightiness" and "heaviness" (Hebrew, kabôd). However, the divine disclosure was not exhaustive. The condescension did not cancel out God's majestic transcendence. It did not overshadow God's greatness. God was in the midst of the people, but God was nevertheless distanced from the people by the utter awesomeness of God's being. Note carefully God's words to Moses: "My presence will go with you" but "you cannot see my face; for no one shall see me and live" (Exod. 33:14, 20). To protect Moses from the power of his awful and transcendent presence, God provided a separating shield and a safe hiding place for him. The divine instructions are telling:

There is a place near me where you may stand on a rock. When my glory passes by, I will put you in a cleft in the rock and cover you with my hand until I have passed by. Then I will remove my hand and you will see my back; but my face must not be seen. (Exod. 33:21 NIV)

Conclusion

In his discussion with the Athenian philosophers at the Areopagus (Acts 17), Paul took as his point of departure the view of God that he found in their own cultural context. In his discourse, Paul acknowledged their religiosity (Acts 17:22), affirmed their belief in God, and incorporated in his own theological articulation ideas about God indigenous to their culture (17:28). But Paul did not stop there. Drawing on special revelation, he went on to correct their view where it was found faulty, and to supplement it where it was found lacking (17:24–37). To be sure, judging by the response of his listeners, Paul's approach did not carry the day (17:32–34), but it did succeed both in engaging the culture and in preserving the integrity of theology as a Christian enterprise.

This is what I have sought to do in my own reflection on God in the preceding pages. Modern and contemporary Christian thought has shown a bias toward immanence.[49] Apart from the Barthian protest in the early decades of this century, immanence has triumphed since the reconstructions of Schleiermacher and Hegel. This has persisted despite the biblical credentials of transcendence. And in the realm of religious practice, if we judge by the irreverent casualness, the impatient hurriedness, and the lethargic spirit often evident in much of Christian worship, transcendence is denied in reality even where it is vehemently affirmed in theory. In light of this imbalance, the Afro-Caribbean focus on transcendence is relevant and needful for our time. If properly appropriated, it can help theology address its own shortcomings and lopsidedness.

But this acknowledgment of the appropriateness of the emphasis on transcendence does not mean a wholesale endorsement of the sort of transcendence advocated by the Afro-Caribbean religious system. The view has defects. In making the absence and remoteness of God the key element of its construct, the Afro-Caribbean understanding overstates the case, and hence stands in need of correction.

The concept of ontological transcendence provides that correction. It allows us to speak meaningfully of both the presence of God and the transcendence of God. And if the transcendent God can be present with humans, we have here the possibility of a God–human relationship of a much higher order than is allowed in the Afro-Caribbean religious system where close interaction between the high God and humans is minimal and even totally precluded. The notion of ontological transcendence does not merely correct the excess of the Afro-Caribbean view, it also fulfills in a much greater way the experiential objectives of that view.

The next chapter explores in detail the African roots of this concept of the unapproachable quality of the Supreme God that demands an intercessor.

Unapproachable God:
The High God of African
Traditional Religion

Tokunboh Adeyemo

Tokunboh Adeyemo, a Nigerian, is general secretary of the Association of
Evangelicals in Africa and chairman of the International Council of the World
Evangelical Fellowship. He graduated with high honors with a Th.D. from
Dallas Theological Seminary and M.Div. and Th.M. from Talbot Theological
Seminary. He has a B.Th. from Igbaja Theological Seminary in Nigeria. He
also has an honorary doctorate from Potchefstroom University, South Africa.
He has published many books including *Salvation in African Tradition, The
Making of a Servant of God,* and *Is Africa Cursed?*

O nce upon a time," says Chief Oyetunde of Ibadan, Nigeria,
"the gods lived very close to man. It was so close that men
could travel freely back and forth between earth and heaven
without any restriction. However, one day man got drunk and, in his
stupor, began to insult the ancestors and the Creator. He went even
further to rub his dirty hands on the sky which was regarded as the face
of the gods. The gods were insulted and offended, and in their anger,
they decided to relocate their abode far removed from man. Consequently, a big chasm evolved between heaven and earth, and access
to the gods, especially the Supreme God, became a problem."[1]

In one form or another, this story of a "paradise lost" is widespread among many African peoples in their creation mythology. In any epistemological consideration in which the doctrine of direct or special revelation cannot be attested, what people think of the world around them becomes crucial to their faith. "Our world view is like the umpire at a ball game," declared Bruce Waltke. "He seems unimportant and you are hardly aware of him, but in reality he decides the ball game."[2] Down through the ages cosmology has served not only as an explanatory device and a guide to conduct, but also as an action system. It is a profound statement that "as a person thinks, so he is" (Prov. 23:7 KJV). To understand an African's perception of God it is extremely important to know his worldview.

African Worldview

Writing of the Igbo people of eastern Nigeria, Uchendu said: "The Igbo world, in all its aspects—material, spiritual, and socio-cultural—is made intelligible to Igbo by their cosmology, which explains how everything came into being."[3] In a nonscientific sense, the African world is twofold: the world of humans and the world of the spirits.

The World of Humanity

Central to the thinking of the traditional African is the visible world. It is a tangible world peopled by beings and things, both animate and inanimate. Almost everywhere the typical traditional social unit is the village, made up of families and ruled by a *bale* ("head-man"). A number of villages are formed into a group ruled by a *mogaji* ("a chief"). In some of the early metropolitan centers, such as Oyo in southern Nigeria and Timbuktu in Mali, where communication is easy, nations have sprung into existence under kings.[4] In the historic past, extensive, if even ephemeral, empires have been formed by such conquering chiefs as Asipa, the Alaafin of Oyo (king or traditional ruler of Oyo); Oluyole, the founder and first chief of Ibadan; and Akenzua, the Oba of Benin (king of Benin).[5] The basic motivation for societal existence is the preservation of life. With adaptation to the environment, self-conscious pursuit of development, and expansion in the quality of life as the most urgent survival requirements, one finds human efforts invested in the direction of obtaining food, shelter, and clothing. In an illuminating approach, which is unfortunately marred by a less communicable choice of words, Eugene Ruyle, writing on an aspect of the social organization of the aboriginal Kwakuitl, sees this dimension of human existence in terms of energetics:

> There are two interrelated but analytically distinct thermodynamic systems associated with all animal populations. The first, in which food energy is invested by members of the population, may be termed the *food energy system*, relating the population to the food web of the ecosystem. The second, the patterned energy expenditure of the members of the population interacting with each other and with environmental objects in the satisfaction of their needs, may be termed the *ethnoenergy system*.[6]

The economic system in any societal existence correspondingly depends on the knowledge of the environment and how much humans can manipulate and overcome nature. The cultural ontology of the African puts him right at the center of the environmental stimuli. Mbiti has observed this fact in his extensive study of over two hundred and seventy tribes of Africa. He commented:

> Africans have their own ontology which is an extremely anthropocentric ontology in the sense that everything is seen in terms of its relation to man. . . . Man is the center of this ontology; the animals, plants, and natural phenomena and objects constitute the environment in which man lives, provide a means of existence and, if need be, man establishes a mystical relationship with them.[7]

The world as a natural order which inexorably goes on its ordained way according to a master plan or a natural law as found in a mechanistic worldview is foreign to the African mind. His world is a dynamic one. It is a moving equilibrium that is constantly threatened and sometimes actually disturbed by natural and social calamities. The events that upset it include natural disasters such as long, continual droughts, long periods of famine, epidemic diseases, as well as sorcery and other antisocial forces. Africans believe that these cosmic forces and social calamities that disturb their world are controllable and should be manipulated by them for their own purpose. The warding off of these cosmic and social evils, called *ibi* in Yoruba and *honhom fi* in the Ga language of Ghana, becomes the central focus of religious activities among the various African peoples. Writing on the subject of *honhom fi*, Max Assimeng, a senior lecturer in sociology at the University of

Ghana at Legon, observed: "Religion in traditional Ghanaian society may thus be said to concern essentially how man should keep a proper and undiluted ritual distance from this element of *honhom fi.*"[8] Saying the same thing differently in reference to the Igbo of Nigeria, Uchendu stated:

> The maintenance of social and cosmological balance in the world becomes, therefore, a dominant and pervasive theme in Igbo life. They achieve this balance, for instance, through divination, sacrifice, appeal to the counter-vailing powers of their ancestors (who are their invisible father-figures) against the powers of the malignant, and nonancestral spirits, and, socially, through constant realignment in their social groupings.[9]

For the traditional African, "religion begins not with a belief in God but with an emotional opposition to removable evils."[10] Let us pause in our examination of this struggle to maintain a cosmological balance in order to consider the world of the spirits.

The World of the Spirits

To the African mind, the visible world of nature is not alone; it is enveloped in the invisible spirit world. Constant natural disasters and social calamities such as sickness, plagues, famines, and large-scale mortality, especially of infants, impress upon him the existence of forces regarded fatalistically as beyond his control. From the shaky and tenuous existence within the context of nature emerges the overriding feelings of awe, respect, wonder, fear, and worship of such natural phenomena as rivers, trees, rocks, earthquakes, thunder, moon, sun, stars, hills, and certain species in the animal kingdom with which clans have ritualistic identification in the form of totemism. Edwin W. Smith reported that:

> Most of the Bantu tribes show some trace of totemism; that is to say, they are or were at one time divided into clans, each bearing the name of some animal, plant or object, such as the "Elephants," the "Grasshoppers" or the "Baobabs."[11]

Among the Yoruba of southwest Nigeria one commonly hears people addressed by their praise-name or appellation as *omo ekun* (literally "son of leopard"), *omo erin* ("son of elephant"), *omo oya* ("son of River Niger"), and the like. More often, the early foreign investigators fell into the snare of taking appearance for reality without adequate verification. For instance, the term "fetish" was used widely by some of the explorers to describe the religion of the whole of Africa, while Africa's god was called *Juju*, a French word meaning "toy."[12] On the contrary, African tribes commonly believe that people would hardly revere and worship entities which they regard as "ordinary" and which they can understand and manipulate. For them, behind the visible lies the invisible; behind the material lies the spiritual; behind the tangible lies the intangible; and behind the living lies the dead. Idowu epitomized this in what he labeled as the basic motif of Yoruba cultic art:

> O world invisible, we view thee
> O world intangible, we touch thee,
> O world unknowable, we know thee
> Inapprehensible, we clutch thee![13]

Thus, through the visible natural phenomena, appeals are made to the invisible powers or forces, which they conceive as having ultimate control over their interests and destinies. As Ernest Harms has noted, "Religion is concerned with the phenomena of human experience in the theistic sphere and the conditioning systems created by man for living with his gods."[14] One is not surprised to find that the hierarchical sociological pattern operative in the visible world is transferred into the spirit world. Nearest to people are the spirit-charged entities including the earth, rivers, mountains, trees, wind, and the luminaries, which naturally become to them symbols of worship and sometimes objects of direct worship. Next in the cosmic hierarchy are the dead ancestors, who, by virtue of their seniority, are believed to mediate between the gods and humanity. These are followed up the pyramid by the divinities, who are recognized for being the recipients of people's worship and sacrifices. At the top of the pantheon is the Supreme Deity, variously but prominently addressed as the Creator[15] of all things.

The spirit-charged entities

The earth with all of its hosts and the luminaries are believed to have been created and sustained by the Supreme Being: "They are God's children, as it were, albeit more elderly than man."[16] They are believed to possess the greatest of vital forces, the fertility and potency. Although all of these entities are important to humanity, the ones highly esteemed are the earth and the rivers or sea. The reason is obvious:

people live off them, being related to the perennial survival requirements of people already mentioned. In many of the traditional myths
and legends, the earth is venerated. It is believed to be indwelt by spirits. It is not uncommon for people to call on the spirits of the earth to
witness a pact because of the belief that the earth can punish anybody
who breaks the pact. Proverbially the Yoruba say:

> *Bi enia ba yo ile da* (*ile* is literally "the earth")
> *Ohun abenu a ma yo se.*

> If a person secretly breaks a covenant,
> Secretly (or quietly) he will suffer the consequence.

Ogboni is a strong and powerful secret cult of the earth among the
Yoruba. The members are believed to "worship and control the sanc-
tions of the earth as a spirit. Earth, to them, existed before the gods."[17]
The role and competence of the earth and the sea, for which several cultic observances are ritually enacted, can be likened to revitalization and
potency-renewal cultic activities in primal societies and elsewhere.[18]

The ancestors

Though nearest to humans in terms of visibility are the spirit-
charged phenomena just discussed, people's closest links with the spirit
world are ancestors, who Mbiti describes as "the living dead." African
tribes almost universally believe that death does not write *finis* to
human life.[19] Death is a transition; thus, such terms as "to depart," "to
follow those who have gone before," and "to answer the call" are used
to describe it. Believing that the departed continue to exist in another
realm, African peoples cultivate the custom of burying foodstuffs,
clothing, and other belongings with the dead. An ancient practice was
to bury some of the wives and servants with their dead chiefs and kings
so that the deceased rulers would not live alone in the next world. The
world of the dead is a world of activities: "There is a communion and
a communication going on all the time between those who have gone
into the life beyond and those that are here on earth."[20] Among the
Agikuyu people of Kenya, the departed spirits fall into three divisions:

1. *Ngoma cia aciari:* the spirits of the father or mother which communicate directly with the living children and which can advise
   or reproach them as they did in their lifetime.

2. *Ngoma cia moherega:* the clan spirits which are concerned with the welfare and prosperity of the clan, administering justice according to the behavior of the clan or any of its members.
3. *Ngoma cia riika:* the age-group spirits which are interested in the activities of their particular age groups. This group is sometimes called tribal spirits because it is the age group that unifies the whole tribe. The spirits of this group are the ones who enter into tribal affairs.[21]

Constant interaction is maintained between the dead and the living. The dead are believed to be reincarnated. Thus, a baby boy born after the death of his grandfather is given the name *Babatunde* in Yoruba, meaning "father has come again." Through sacrifices the living remember[22] the dead and seek their help. *Mutigairi* in Gikuyu means both "to be remembered" and "being immortal"; it is especially used of good persons. Life from day to day in a typical African village has no meaning at all apart from ancestral presence and power. The father of a family begins the day by praying to them, offering kolanuts and palm wine or water. This is his daily priestly function for himself and his family. Annually, a remembrance feast is held in honor of the ancestors. All members of the family participate in this, sometimes offering fowl or goats. Occasionally, other sacrifices may be offered upon the demand of the ancestors whenever a member of the family is sick or in case of calamity. This is usually prescribed by a diviner. To Africans, evidence seems to be everywhere that ancestors live on and are in close link with the living.

The divinities

Next in line in the spirit world hierarchy are the divinities or gods. They are called *Obosom* among the Twi people of Ghana and the Republic of Benin; *vodu* among the Ewe of Togo; *chi* among the Igbo; and *orisa* among the Yoruba, both of Nigeria. Scholars agree that they are uncountable in number even in cases where numerical limitation seems to be implied.[23] They are of three categories: deified ancestors or heroes, deified objects, and created agents both good and evil. Attempts to explain the etymology of the term *orisa* by the process of separating it into component parts, *ori* and *se,* or by inventing myths have been proved to be inadequate and incorrect.[24] As Oduyoye has demonstrated, not simply part of the word *orisa* means "head," but rather the whole word, built around the consonantal root -r-s-. This root spreads across Africa as far south as Malawi.[25] It is an Afro-Asiatic term having its cognate in Hebrew *rosh*, Arabic *ra's*, Aramaic *re'sh*, and Akkadian *rishu*—all meaning "head." Moving from the seen to the unseen, the Yoruba employ the physical head to designate the concept of headship by status as in *Oluwa* ("lord, master"), which is applied not only to an earthly master but also to the divinity. They assert, *"Eniyan ni d'orisa"* ("It is human beings who become orisa or god"). Fadipe stated: "We know that at death a man becomes an *orisa* to his children. The founder of each family is likewise an *orisa* to all the members of the extended family."[26]

History tells us of a man, Sango, the fourth Alaafin of Oyo, who lived about two centuries ago.[27] He was a powerful and wise monarch. He was also a great medicine man who claimed to be able to kill people by ejecting fire from his mouth. His reign was tyrannical and cruel. Following an unsuccessful plot to get rid of two of his ministers whom he dreaded, he fled, accompanied by his three wives—Oya, Osun, and Oba—and some of his loyal followers. He wandered in the bush, being gradually deserted by all, until only his favorite wife Oya remained. In despair, Sango hanged himself from an *ayan* tree. In revenge, his supporters secured medicinal means from Ibariba people, by which they were able to attract lightning. When the conflagrations became excessive and the townspeople were panic stricken, the friends of Sango then came forward saying: "You said *Oba so* ('the king has hanged himself'); *Oba ko so* ("the king has not hanged himself"), he is only angry with you." He was thus proclaimed a god and worshiped with oxen, sheep, fowl, palm oil, and wine offered in sacrifices to him for forgiveness. The article of faith rehearsed since then until today is *Oba ko so* ("The king did not hang himself"). Sango is the god of lightning and thunder.

As some of the ancestors and national heroes have been deified, so have some objects. Often the belief is that some unusual natural phenomena are spirit-charged, as already discussed. At times a few of them are personified as gods and goddesses. Among the Ibo the earth is regarded as the great Mother Goddess. The Ashanti of Ghana regard the earth spirit as the consort of Nyame, the Sky. No Ashanti farmer would till the ground without first asking permission by offering sacrifices.[28]

Beside deified ancestors and objects, there are other divinities believed to have been created by the Supreme Being to serve as agents. There are multitudes of them of different ranks charged with specific functions for humanity and society. Unlike the belief of the Near East religions that humans were created to serve the gods,[29] the African traditional religionists believe that the divinities exist for the benefit of humans. Sometimes they are identified as "the divinities of heaven," while many of them are regarded as household gods. In his book *Among the Ibos of Nigeria,* G. T. Basden described one of these divinities:

> The most universal of the household gods, and that which is given first rank, is the Ikenga. No house may be without one. It is the first god sought by a young man at the beginning of his career, and it is the one to which he looks for good luck in all his enterprises.[30]

While Idowu would state theoretically that the divinities are no more than ministers and functionaries in the theocratic government of the universe under the command of the Supreme Deity,[31] evidences abound that in the practical, day-by-day cultic life of the traditional religionists, these divinities are regarded as separate and independent. In his contribution to the symposium later published under the title *Biblical Revelation and African Beliefs,* Stephen Ezeanya testified to this fact:

> Those spirits [referring to divinities] are self-sufficient and do not therefore have to receive gifts from the Supreme God in order to distribute such to humans. They can bestow these gifts of themselves, thereby acting independently of the Supreme God.[32]

He later suggested that having been created by God and invested with powers and responsibilities, they became totally free and act without any prior consultation or seeking for his permission. "Like the Greek gods of old," he concluded, "they have some of the human limitations. They can be hungry, angry, jealous, and revengeful. Thus man must always seek to be on the best of terms with them."[33] All over Africa, places of worship in the form of shrines, groves, and temples are set aside for them and regular priesthood is kept. They are also directly worshiped.

The question of their origin remains in obscurity. Some believe that they are direct creatures of God, as are humans.[34] Others believe that they are conceptualizations of certain prominent attributes of deity, especially as discerned through natural phenomena. The present research reveals that while some of the divinities appear to be spirit realities, others are human conceptualizations. Another fact to be noted in passing is that while some of the divinities are regarded as good, others are regarded as evil.

The Supreme Deity

At the peak of the cosmic pantheon is the Supreme Deity. He is believed to be the owner of the world of humans as well as the spirit world. By names and attributes he is identified with the two worlds and yet is not part of either of them. As head of the divinities, he is addressed by the Yoruba as *Orisa nla* ("Great Orisa") or *Obatala* ("Exalted King"); and as head of the world of humans, they call him *Olori aiye* ("Chief of the World"). Many questions naturally arise: Who is this God? What was his origin, if any? What connections does he have both with humans and with the spirits? Does he really exist, and, if so, where? How do people know him? Is he interested in human affairs? Is he ever worshiped? How does he compare to the ideas of God in other religions? These and many more questions about God in traditional religion are the task of this present study. Suffice it to say for now that though there are many sides as to the tribal perception of God due to linguistic, geographic, and cultural variations, the belief in a supreme deity is a prominent theme among Africans. An Akan proverb says: "No one teaches the child about God."[35] The existence of God is self-revelatory. The question is: How do Africans perceive it?

How Africans Perceive God

Africans perceive God through rational intuition, natural phenomena, oral tradition and history, providence and preservation, experience, and cultural diffusion.

Perception through Rational Intuition

The advocates of rational intuition insist that human beings know immediately that certain propositions are true without resorting to inference. Avoiding the philosophical extravagance of men such as Descartes, who sought to derive all content of knowledge from the intuitive certainty of human self-existence, Augustine and Calvin claimed that on the basis of the divine *imago* in humanity, all people possess certain underived *a priori* truths without any process of inference whereby these truths are derived. *Imago Dei* presupposes personal communication between the Living Being who reveals himself and the living person to whom the revelation is made. Augustine held that:

> On the basis of creation [i.e., humans made in the image of God] the human mind possesses a number of necessary truths. Intellectual intuition conveys the laws of logic, the immediate consciousness of self-existence, the truths of mathematics, and the moral truth that one ought to seek wisdom. More-over, in knowing immutable and eternal truth we know God, for only God is immutable and eternal. As knowers all men stand in epistemic contact with God.[36]

The Akan proverb mentioned earlier implies that the existence of God is immanent and self-evident. This is perceived through the people's own existence. The Ghanaians say, "Where there is life, there is God." The life force, called *kra* ("soul"), is believed to be provided by God to make every individual a living person. Commenting on this, Peter Sarpong said:

> The soul is the spiritual bond between man and God, the humanizing force in man. As the soul is supposed to emanate from God and God is the source of everything that is, the final explanation of all phenomena, good-luck and ill-luck are associated with the soul.[37]

The Akan believe that at creation each individual receives vital force from the Creator, bids him good-bye, and embarks on a journey to the visible world. Whatever God tells him, then, is confidential. This divine provision and prescription, whatever it is, indicates the lifestyle (*kra-bea* or *nkra-bea*, "style or manner of farewell") of the individual.

In their anthropology the Yoruba discern that a human is composed of *ara* ("physical body"), *emi* ("breath" or "spirit"), and *ori* ("soul" or "life principle"). They seem to be predestinarian in their theology of *ori*. For instance, they say: *A kunle yan, ohun ladaiye ba* ("whatever destiny chosen kneeling down [i.e., when the individual takes leave of the Creator] is what one meets in this world"). An ill-fated person is called *olori buruku* ("a person with a bad head"). Luck is called *ori re* ("head of goodness"). From these ideas of good and bad "head" has come the belief that it is possible to cleanse one's luck and change one's ill fate by ritually washing one's head.[38] Metaphorically, they employ the physical head to refer to what they call *ori inu* ("inner head"). This is well illustrated by one of their songs:

Bi o ba maa l'owo,
Bere l'owo ori re;
Bi o ba maa s'owo
Bere l'owo ori re wo.
Bi o ba maa ko 'le,
Bere l'owo ori re
Bi o ba maa l'aya
Bere l'owo ori re wo . . . .

Whether you are going to be rich,
Find out from your *ori;*
When you want to go into business,
Consult your *ori;*
When you are about to build a house,
Consult your *ori;*
When you want to get a wife
Ask your *ori . . . .*

The theological implication of the association of *ori* with *orisa* cannot be overlooked. Intuitively the Yoruba say:

Ise ori ran mi, oun ni mo n je;
Ona ti orisa yan fun mi, oun ni mo n to.

It is the errand which *ori* sent me that I am running;
It is the path which *orisa* laid out for me that I am following.

Pregnant in their belief and religious awareness is the inner link of humanity with the supersensible world, especially the divinity. Harry Sawyerr endeavored to put this within a theological framework when he wrote:

Nearly all African groups believe that man is made up of a divine spark which vitalizes the blood of the mother and gives the fetus life. This divine element brings the newly born infant into a lineage with God.[39]

The core of African belief can be summed up as: "God is; hence man is." That Calvin would support such an assertion is evident by his statement in the *Institutes*:

The knowledge of the existence of God is innate, and a necessary attribute of man: this is a doctrine, not first to be learned in the schools, but which every man from his birth is self-taught. This, indeed, and the worship which accompanied it, is the only thing that makes men superior to the brutes.[40]

Further, the apostle Paul agrees that humans, by virtue of their being made in the image of God, possess the capacity to perceive the existence of their Creator. Paul categorically declared:

> When Gentiles, who do not possess the law, do instinctively what the law requires, these, though not having the law, are a law to themselves. They show that what the law requires is written on their hearts, to which their own conscience also bears witness; and their conflicting thoughts will accuse or perhaps excuse them. (Rom. 2:14–15)

Africans perceive the Supreme Deity through rational intuition, even as the Akan proverb says: "No one teaches the child about God."

Perception through Natural Phenomena

Coming from an organistic worldview, Cicero once said, "What the gods are like is a matter of dispute, but that there is a god is denied by no one." His world was a deified one. While Africans do not deify the world in the same sense as the Greeks, they regard the cosmos to be religious. The natural phenomena and objects are intimately associated with God as their Creator. They not only originate from God but also bear witness to God. In Eliade's words, "Every cosmic fragment is transparent; its mode of existence shows a particular structure of being; and hence of the sacred."[41] The traditional African natural theology was unsystematic. Nevertheless, Africans were able to perceive the Creator through the creation.[42]

The Akamba of Kenya in East Africa consider the heaven and the earth to be the "Father's equal-sized bowls: they are His property both by creation and the rights of worship, and they contain His belongings."[43] The sun, moon, and stars are featured in myths of many peoples, and though sometimes deified they are believed to be aspects of God such as his omniscience, power, and even nature. Thunder is taken, by many, such as the Bambuti of Zaire, Bavenda of South Africa, and the Ewe of Ghana and Togo, to be the voice of God. The Kikuyu of Kenya interpret it to be the movement of God, while the Yoruba and Tiv of Nigeria regard it as an indication of God's anger. The Shona of Zimbabwe think earthquakes are caused by God walking in them. Outstanding trees, mountains, and hills are generally regarded as sacred. Unlike Kant's unknowable "noumenal world" and Hegel's Absolute Idea, from these and many more natural pictures, the world is clearly to the African a religious home which awakens him to conscious response. However imperfect the world may be, the traditional African peoples are able to perceive through the natural phenomena the eternal power, the personality, and the wisdom of God. That this is not an empty assertion could be supported by such passages as Psalm 19:1–6; Acts 14:15–17; 17:27; and Romans 1:19–23. Chafer claims that:

> The heathen are universally convinced of the fact of a Supreme Being and, because of that conviction, are looking for evidence which, in their estimation, expresses His favor or His displeasure.
>
> In general, a divine revelation is accomplished whenever any manifestation of God is discerned or any evidence of His presence, purpose or power is communicated. Such manifestations are discoverable all the way from the grand spectacle of creation down to the least experience of the lowest human creature.[44]

Revelation is God's initiative; perception is a human task. Nature can and does teach us much about a God who exists; it cannot by itself prove that he exists. Thus, revelation through nature needs augmentation.

Perception through Oral Tradition and History

Speaking on the validity of general revelation, Lewis S. Chafer remarked: "No man on earth could be entirely void of divine revelation."[45] Chafer is by no means alone in this affirmation. Here is what George Peters said:

> I accept the Genesis record as historical and firmly hold to the fact that the revelation of Genesis 1–11 came to the entire human race, even though its writing was accomplished much later by Moses. From Genesis 12 and the rest of the Old Testament, God reveals Himself uniquely to and through Israel, although the design of this revelation was for the world.[46]

Three significant revelatory events recorded in Genesis 1–11 are noteworthy: the creation, the entrance of sin into the world, and the universal judgment of the world by the flood. These events reveal certain attributes of God such as his personality, purity, and eternal power. Not merely by coincidence are these events told in one form or another in the various mythologies of primitive religions.[47]

According to the traditions of the Yoruba, the earth was created in four days. The fifth day was designated for rest and worship. Ile-Ife, an important cultural city in Oyo State, Nigeria, is believed to be the sacred spot where creation all began, thus becoming the origin and center not only of the Yoruba but also of the whole world of nations and peoples. *Ife*, from the verb *fe* ("to be wide"), means "that which is wide." Tradition also holds that originally heaven was very near to the earth, so near that one could stretch up one's hand and touch it. It was a time when no limitations of communication existed between heaven and earth. But humanity violated the divine command and a frustrating, extensive chasm came into existence between heaven and earth. Stories of the nature of the offense are fantastically told. Nevertheless, this myth of a lost paradise explains the origin of suffering, illness, death, and the separation from God in terms of a heaven–earth polarity.[48] The difficult task of religion is to overcome this polarity through ritual action.

In a personal interview with John Mpaayei, I was informed of the reason the Masai of Kenya feel free to take their neighbor's cattle with impunity. According to their oral traditions, they were made to believe that God gave the first cattle to the first Masai in the beginning. This perspective has been perpetuated so that even today Masai feel all the cattle in the world belong to them and they can take any freely.[49] Current papers in East Africa carry news of occasional raids which sometimes result in the loss of human lives. Erich Sauer's comment is very appropriate here:

> At the commencement of human history there is present faith in the one God, who revealed Himself in a three-fold manner: in nature (Rom. 1:19,20), in conscience (Rom. 2:2–15), and in history (Gen. 1–11). The later heathendom is, therefore, a perversion of this threefold original: distortion of the remembrance of the original revelation, misinterpretation of the revelation in nature (Rom. 1:23), and a confused conflict of soul with the revelation in conscience, these are the three fundamental elements in all heathen religion.[50]

Regardless of the perversion, the divine influence upon humanity through the universal revelation persists. Its vehicles are more than the three suggested by Sauer. At least three others should be briefly considered.

Perception through Providence and Preservation

The Westminster Shorter Catechism teaches: "God's works of providence are his most holy, wise, and powerful, preserving and governing all his creatures and all their actions."[51] Nehemiah magnificently stated:

> "You are the LORD, you alone; you have made heaven, the heaven of heavens, with all their host, the earth and all that is on it, the seas and all that is in them. To all of them, you give life and the host of heaven worships you. (Neh. 9:6)

Charles Hodge ably brought out the fact of what he calls a "concursus" of divine causality with the causality of created things. He argued that we must:

> rest satisfied with the simple statement that preservation is that omnipotent energy of God by which all created things, animate and inanimate, are upheld in existence, with all the properties and powers with which he has endowed them.[52]

God, in the traditional African mentality, is not a mere spectator of natural processes as in deism. Though they may not worship him directly, Africans universally acknowledge God's goodness to them. The Yoruba call him *Olupese,* a name synonymous with *Suku* of the Ovimbundu of Angola. Both literally mean "He who supplies the needs of his creatures."[53] The African farmers offer prayers to God for rain, fertility, and good yield. An example of these is prayer number fifty-five in Mbiti's book:

> Title: For Increase of Cattle
> God, we are hungry,
> Give us cattle, give us sheep!

At their sacrifices, the officiating elder prays:

> God, increase cattle,
> Increase sheep, increase man![54]

Different peoples of Africa acknowledge the sustaining and preserving work of God in various ways. The Bambuti of Zaire say, "If God should die, the whole world would also collapse."[55] A fair apprehension of God's providence by Africans has been described by Lystad, speaking of the Ashanti of Ghana:

Even though God may seem withdrawn from man, he has not forsaken them, and has created the divinities who provide the day-to-day assurances that men are not alone in the world, and who sustain and protect them.[56]

Though their perception is not without error, the fact remains that through God's faithfulness to his covenant with Noah and all the nations of the earth, God unveils himself (cf. Matt. 5:45; Acts 17:25–29; Col. 1:16–17; Heb. 1:10).

Perception through Experience

Taking the scientific method of the British physicist Sir Isaac Newton as his model, Hume attempted to describe how the mind works in acquiring what is called knowledge. He concluded that no theory of reality is possible: there can be no knowledge of anything beyond experience. Without endorsing the theological ramifications of knowledge based purely on experience, experience could be used as a medium through which God's self-disclosure can be perceived.

The city of Abeokuta, capital of Ogun State, is an important traditional town in southwestern Nigeria. The original settlers of this town, Egba Alake, Egba Oke-Ona, and Egba Agura, migrated in 1830 from their destroyed forest homesteads between Ibadan and Oyo to occupy the present-day location. They were traditional religionists, worshipers of many gods, though believing in a supreme being. Of them, S. Abiodun Adewale notes, "The oracles were consulted frequently to ascertain the future and no time was wasted to perform the prescriptions of the oracles."[57] Tradition teaches that *Ifa* oracle ("Geomantic form of divination"),[58] which led these people to their new location, also predicted the coming of the white people whose teaching was to be permitted. Townsend, one of the pioneer missionaries to Abeokuta, reported:

> The great oracle, that is to them as a Bible, has been consulted again and again about us, and has, I am told, never been induced to utter a word against us. On the contrary, it has said that the white people must be permitted to teach.[59]

The experience of the Egba in their settlement and subsequent victory over their enemies was of religious significance to them. It was attributed to God's help. It also paved the way for later massive conversion among them.

Perception through Cultural Diffusion

Culture is a dynamic element. Consciously or unconsciously, as people migrate from one part of the globe to another, they share their cultural and religious ideas both in forms and structures with others. Several examples could be cited from the Bible of individuals who enjoyed the benefits of God's special revelation though they did not belong to the nation Israel. How else can one explain such cases as Melchizedek, Hagar, Rahab, Pharaoh, Balaam, Nebuchadnezzar, Belshazzar, and Cyrus? In each of these cases the person, though a Gentile, had a knowledge of God. Also evident in these cases is the fact that there was always a messenger of God on the scene to interpret the revelation. The principle of cultural diffusion explains in part the elements of truth observable in non-Christian religions.

In the very first century of the Christian era, some Africans were exposed to the gospel. Acts 8:27–38 records a remarkable conversion of a man of Ethiopia. Two of the prophets and teachers who were present at the church in Antioch (Acts 13:1) were from Africa: Simeon who was called "Niger," the Greek term which means "black"; and Lucius of Cyrene, a town in what is now Libya in North Africa. Another African, Simon of Cyrene, was present in Jerusalem during the trials of Jesus Christ and even had the unique privilege of carrying the cross on which Christ was crucified to Golgotha (Luke 23:26). From these instances the point becomes clear that Africans have always been in contact with the Judeo-Christian world and that through cultural diffusion their perception of God may have been sharpened.

Conclusion

On the basis of the African worldview and the perception of the Supreme Deity, we can conclude of Africans that, knowing God, they know in part; and seeing him, they see through the mirror of creation dimly. Even though in times past God has "allowed all the nations to follow their own ways" (Acts 14:16), God has never left himself "without a witness." Therefore, Africans are without excuse. Their predicament is in the limitation of natural revelation, which cannot tell them that the once unapproachable God can be approached through faith in Jesus Christ, whom the Supreme God sent to bridge the chasm they too perceive between heaven and earth. In other words, the traditional African knows "the Lord who made the earth," who fills heaven and earth (Jer. 23:24; 32:17–23; 33:2) but not the Lord who is unique, whose "name is Jealous" (Exod. 34:14).

We have seen how the transcendent quality of the Supreme God permeates all African (and in the previous chapter Afro-Caribbean) traditional religion. The next chapter will explore further how the Supreme God, though revealed by general revelation, yet stands above all traditional and indigenous religions, revealing to all traditions a single, great, unifying hope.

Seven

The God above Tradition
Who Speaks to All Traditions:
An African (Ghanaian) Perspective

Edward John Osei-Bonsu

Edward J. Osei-Bonsu, born in Aduamoa-Kwahu of Ghana, has a D.Min., M.R.E., and MATS from Gordon-Conwell Theological Seminary and a B.A. from Pan Africa Christian College, Nairobi, Kenya. He is Associate Minister of Family Life and Christian Education of Calvary Baptist Church, Accra, Ghana, and Adjunct Lecturer at Maranatha Bible College and Calvary Leadership Institute. He has ministered among the Akan traditional people in Kwahu for over 20 years.

Adelaide became a Christian some twelve years ago when she was in the University. But after graduation she has had lots of challenging life experiences. These have led her to visit over six different indigenous church houses and over five fetish shrines. Adelaide entered into deep spiritual bondage. When she ended up in my church, she acted and behaved abnormally, like someone who is mad. But, today Adelaide has received her deliverance by the exorcism ministry in our church where we directly entreat God for healing and freedom. Adelaide's case is typical of the ministry challenges Christians face when ministering within the traditional African context.

The New Testament distinguishes between two kinds of traditions: a divinely instituted tradition where God's special revelation is handed down from generation to generation (2 Thess. 2:15; 3:6) and human traditions where errors about God are transmitted (Mark 7:8–13). God is a God of tradition in that God has revealed truth in nature and through God's words, preserved in the Bible and exemplified by God's great, specific Word: Jesus Christ. But God is also a God above tradition and while many human traditions contain truth about God, God transcends their errors. The task of the church is to perceive and preserve the truth about God. The church must be careful not to pollute with error the truth Christ has revealed. It must also be ready to recognize truth in other traditions while carefully and lovingly separating it from any error in which it may be encased. These truths are particularly relevant when tradition and religion are culturally intertwined.

Ghanaians, as all African peoples, have tradition. Attached to this tradition is their system of belief where they express their love and trust to a *God*. This belief is recognized through their worship, conduct, devotion, and ceremonial observances. Their traditional religion brings out the belief in a God who is a Supreme Being, but is seen to come to his people through other supernatural deities called gods, who derive their powers through the Supreme Being. Besides the Supreme Being and his lesser "messengers" are the ancestors or ancestral spirits who play prominent roles in the lives of their living relations. Added to these lesser gods and ancestors are natural objects called talismans, charms, amulets, and mascots, which provide "protection" for the people.

Unlike traditional religion, "indigenous religion" accepts the Bible as the Word of God and accepts Jesus Christ, acknowledging him as the Son of God and Savior of the world. But, like the traditional religion, it attaches great importance to the material needs of its followers. Its basic features address all areas of human life. People go to its practitioners not because they want to worship God, but want to have their needs met. The indigenous religion, called the "spiritual church" in Ghana, is reminiscent of the traditional religion. The "spirit" of healing and caretaking by both religions has deeply eaten into the hearts of the Ghanaian people. One is hard pressed to separate tradition from religion and the worship of idols, ancestors, and human beings from the worship of God.

The problem calls for a careful assessment in order to forge a suggested guideline for ministry. In this chapter, therefore, I will examine

African traditional and indigenous religion as a whole from the particular standpoint of my own experience in the context of Ghana, testing its doctrines from its general revelation about God against the specific revelation recorded in the Bible.[1]

What Are "Traditional" and "Indigenous" Religions?

According to *Webster's Dictionary,* "tradition" is defined as "the delivery of opinions, doctrines, practices, rites and customs from generation to generation by oral communication."[2] *Vine's Expository Dictionary of Bible Words* also defines "tradition" as "paradosis"—"a handing down or to hand over, deliver ordinances, law or precepts" (see Matt. 15:2; Mark 7:3; 1 Peter 1:18).[3]

To put these understandings together, "tradition" could be defined as the "handing over, transmission or delivery of opinions, ordinances, practices, rites and customs of *a people* from generation to generation by oral communication," for example, as African tradition, American tradition, Ghanaian tradition, Jewish tradition, and so on.

Webster's Dictionary defines "indigenous" as "native"; "born, growing or produced naturally in a country or region." Webster's defines "religion" as (1) "a specific system of belief, worship, conduct, etc. often involving a code of ethics and a philosophy"; (2) "a state of mind or way of life expressing love for and trust in God, and one's will and effort to act according to the will of God. . . ."[4] *Chambers' English Dictionary* also defines "religion" as "belief in, recognition of, or an awakened sense of a higher unseen controlling power or powers with the emotion and morality connected therewith; rites of worship; any system of such belief or worship; devoted fidelity."[5] According to *Strong's Exhaustive Concordance,* "religion" is a "ceremonial observance." Paul said in Acts 26:5: "According to the strictest sect of our religion, I lived a Pharisee" (NIV).[6]

If all is put together, "religion" could be defined as "a specific system of belief where people express their love and trust to *a God* or recognize him through worship, conduct, devotion, and ceremonial observances." Looking at the above definitions, Ghanaian and indeed African traditional religion could be literally described as a handing over of or transmission of a system of belief where people express their love and trust to a god (or gods), recognizing him (or them) through worship, conduct, devotion, and ceremonial observances according to their ordinances, practices, rites, and customs.

Ghanaian Traditional Religion

Ghanaian traditional religion could be described in terms of being an African traditional religion. Even though one runs the risk of generalizing when he or she speaks of traditional religions in Africa, yet a common factor underlies the religious beliefs and practices found in various societies and ethnic groups in Africa as a whole. For example, Kwabena Amponsah writes:

> There appears to be a common basic belief in West Africa that is the belief in the existence of Supreme Being. The concept of God is common in all West African societies, the differences occur because of local colouring. . . . the name of God appears in various forms in West Africa according to the language spoken in each locality. It is the variety of cultures which make the concept appear different.[7]

Kofi Asare Opoku also confirms:

> Africa is so vast and has such a large number of societies which differ from each other considerably that one runs the risk of generalization when one speaks of traditional African religion. And yet there is a common thread in indigenous values, views and experiences which shows a large measure of uniformity.[8]

Generally, traditional religion in Africa has been given different names and terminologies:
African traditional religion has been described as *animistic:*

> This is probably the most commonly used term in reference to African traditional religions. . . . Animism is derived from "anima," breath, which in Latin came to have the secondary sense of soul, very much as did the equivalent word "spiritus," whence our spirit. Hence animism might stand for any doctrine having to do with soul or spirit and later, with souls of spirits.[9]

Opoku also argues: "Traditional African religion has often been described as *animism,* a word first used by the British anthropologist E. B. Tylor. . . . According to Tylor, the people he described as primitive believed that the soul of a human being could leave his body and enter other men, animals or things and continue to exist after death."[10] Opoku contends that the use of the term "animism" for traditional African religion is a "misnomer": "Africans do not believe that every object, without exception, has a soul. Rather, they believe that spirits can have certain objects as their habitat or abode, and that they can be embodied in or attached to material objects, and through these objects exert their influence."[11]

He, therefore, concludes that animism should not be used to describe traditional African religion. Byang Kato also believes that using the term "animism" to describe traditional African religion is inadequate. He points out that it limits African traditional religions to the belief in spiritual beings. However, they contain more than just a belief in spiritual beings. Kato writes: "African traditional religions do have a belief in spiritual beings, but their religious system covers more. Complex practices cannot be said to be only a belief in spiritual beings. Animism may not be a bad word, but it is certainly inadequate as a description of African traditional religions."[12]

Limiting traditional African religion only to a belief in spiritual beings or the existence of spirits cuts out important aspects of the religion. Animism is not a suitable word or term to be used to describe traditional African religions.

Paganism is another word often used. *Webster's Dictionary* describes a "pagan" as a person without religion. In that sense, "paganism" could be used to describe Europeans, Americans, Australians, Indians, and others as well. Byang Kato adds:

> The Scriptures know of only two groups of people, the people of God and the people of the world. . . . The terms "pagan" or "heathen," if used at all in the Scriptural sense, would refer to all unbelievers whether they are found in New York City, New Delhi or Nairobi. The distinction is not cultural, but a covenant relationship with God. African traditional religions cannot be distinctively defined as "paganism." These terms are too broad to describe the religion of a particular people.[13]

Opoku also writes: "Originally, a pagan was a person who was not a Jew, Christian or Muslim, but in the course of time, the word acquired a derogatory connotation, especially in its application to Africa, and was used to refer to people who had no religion as well. Africa, of course, has a religion."[14]

Again, paganism is not a suitable term to be used to describe African traditional religions. Africans generally believe in God and believe that they can reach God through their belief systems—their own cultural religious practices.

Fetishism is the third word. Fetishism is derived from the Portuguese word *fetico*, which means any object, animate or inanimate, natural or artificial, regarded with a feeling of awe, as having mysterious powers residing in it or as being the representative or habitation of a deity. Things like talismans, amulets, and mascots are used as fetishes. Even though in African traditional religions such objects are used by some worshipers and devotees, "fetishism" could not be used as synonymous with African traditional religions, because, according to Opoku: "The word could also be used for similar objects of other peoples outside Africa, but in those non-African instances, the objects in question were never referred to as fetish, but by their actual names—talismans, amulets, and mascots. Moreover, the clear distinction made in the African language between human-made religious objects and spiritual beings or deities has not been considered. In the Akan language (in Ghana), for example, a *suman* human-made religious object or charm is not the same thing as *obosom* which is more appropriately translated as 'deity.'"[15]

Therefore, traditional religion means more than only using an object for charms. Kato rightly sums it up: "The term fetish appropriately describes certain outward practices of African traditional religions, but once again the description does not cover the whole system. It is only one aspect of it."[16]

Idolatry simply means the worship of idols or images. Though idolatry is evident in African traditional religions, the term is inadequate to describe the whole system. In fact, undeniably idol worship is a part of African traditional religions, but the whole religious system is more than just idol worship. Kato supports this contention:

> Webster defines idolatry as a "representation or symbol of deity used as an object of worship." These representations abound in African traditional religions, though they are not the whole religious system. Other facets of religious practices form a part of African traditional religions. While idolatry forms a major part of these religions, it is inadequate to call African traditional religions only as idolatry.[17]

What, then, is an adequate description of African traditional religion? Opoku says that in order to be faithful to the nature of religion in Africa, we need to call it by its name: African traditional religion. If we want to be more specific, we should simply qualify it with the name of the particular society in question, instead of using the terms "animism," "paganism," "fetishism," etc."[18] Kato also says:

> The religions are distinctively African, though similarities are traceable in the Caribbean Islands and other Latin American countries. The religions are traditional as opposed to the new religions in the continent such as Islam and Christianity. Tradition is the "handing down of information, beliefs and customs by word of mouth or by example from one generation to another, without written instruction." The definition fits the pattern of African religions. . . . But African traditional religions must be spoken of in plural because of the numerous types of religious practices among different tribes. We speak of African traditional religions in the plural because there are about one thousand African peoples (tribes) and each has its own religious system. Other terms such as animism and idolatry may be used provided the limitation of these terms is recognized.[19]

In trying to describe African traditional religion, the author would like to agree that it should be called by its name; then it should be localized depending on a particular society in question. For example, in Ghana it should be called Ghanaian traditional religion. Even under Ghanaian traditional religion, it could still be localized depending on a particular tribe, for example, Akan traditional religion. In Nigeria, it should be called Nigerian traditional religion, and then Yoruba traditional religion for the Yoruba people. Still, we could say that, in their practices, the devotees of African traditional religions are:

1. Animistic—because they believe in spiritual beings (not in the sense that every object, without exception, has a soul), if Webster's fourth definition of the word is taken (that is, a belief in the existence of spirits, demons, and the like).
2. Idolatrous—because they worship idols—other deities apart from God. Or we could call their practice polytheistic, understanding that these "other" gods emanate from and depend upon the Supreme Being.
3. Fetishistic—because some use protective charms, like amulets, talismans, and mascots.

All these practices may be colored by cultural, tribal, linguistic, and other settings. Practices also may differ depending on the geographical location of a particular ethnic group. Therefore, differentiating a people with their particular religion, as in the use of the title "Ghanaian traditional religion," would be appropriate.

General Features of Traditional Religion

Traditional religion in Ghana, like other religions, is made up of a set of beliefs and practices. Opoku has presented a set of beliefs[20] which I believe *corresponds* with the main features of Ghanaian traditional religions.

1. He notes a widespread belief in God, who is known by various local names.
2. Next to God are the ancestral spirits who play a very prominent role. The ancestors, like God, are always treated with reverence.
3. Further are the supernatural deities or lesser deities who derive their powers essentially from God.
4. Besides the natural objects which are believed to be the habitats of the lesser deities, animals and plants are regarded as emblems of hereditary relationship. This is what is implied by the term "totemism."
5. In addition to the divinities or supernatural entities, other spirits or mystical powers are posited which are recognized and reckoned with for their ability to aid or harm humans. Among them are agents of witchcraft, magic, and sorcery.
6. Charms, amulets, and talismans are also regarded. These are used for protective as well as for offensive purposes.

Minor Deities or Lesser Gods

The Ghanaian traditional religion believes in minor deities or lesser gods called *abosom* for the Akans, *won* for the Gas, *Nnadu* for the Krobos, and *Mawu* for the Ewes. To the Akans, the term suggests that the gods worshiped by the Akans were formerly only stone (*obo*, "stone," and *som*, "worship.") Others believe that the term is derived from two words (*oboa*, "help"; *som*, "serve or worship"), that is, the general consensus is that the lesser gods help the devotee to worship or serve the Supreme Being.

They range from big tribal gods, intermediate family gods, to little private or individual gods. According to the Ghanaian traditional religion, the lesser gods derive their power from the Supreme Being, *Onyame, Nyonmo, Mao, or Mawuga*. A god also requires a temporary abode and a priest or priestess. The spirit of the god may enter the priest or priestess and speak through him or her. These lesser or minor deities then become the mediators between God and humanity.

Some principal deities of the Akans are:

1. The Spirit of the Earth: In Akan society, she ranks after God and the second deity to be offered a drink at libations. She is known as *Asase Yaa* in Asante and other Akan areas, and *Asase Efua* among the Fante. She is also sometimes referred to as *Aberewa* ("old woman/mother").
2. Spirits of Water: They believe that these are deities inhabiting the waters, great and small. Some worship these water divinities at their shrine with the appointment of a special priest or priestess in attendance.

All these divinities, according to the Ghanaian traditional religion, do not exist independently but through them people relate to the Supreme Being—God. They are intermediaries and immediate objects of worship. They derive their power from the Supreme Being, and they would be powerless without reference to the Supreme God, the source of all power.

Ancestral Spirits

Paramount in the Ghanaian traditional religion is belief in the spirits of the dead and their influence over the living. These ancestral spirits are believed to have authority. The Akans call them *nananom nsamanfo* or *niime* and *jemawodjii* for the Gas. The dead are believed to be everywhere at anytime. They are always revered and held in high esteem:

> The ancestors are our elders and the reverence given to them is reminiscent of reverence and homage paid to saints and angels in the Catholic Church. . . . The relationship between the living and the ancestors is symbiotic, the living have their part to play in providing for the ancestors and the ancestors have their part to play in protecting and pleading for their relatives at the court of the Supreme Being. They act as friends at court to intervene between man and the Supreme Being and to get prayers and petitions

answered more quietly and effectively. The ancestors are constantly kept in mind and informed of whatever is happening as "living" members of the family. They are informed of what is going on in the family and requests and petitions are addressed to them.[21]

In fact, the ancestral spirits are not the source of blessings to the people but are intermediaries between the Supreme Being and the living. The ancestors show keen interest in what is happening among the relatives or family members who are living and serve as their guardians in their activities and ethics.

Charms and Fetishes

Charms and fetishes are articles which are worn or hung in a house for protective purposes. The Akans call these protective charms *asuman;* the Krobos call them *kotoklo.* The use of charms *(asuman)* is widespread. These are repositories of "power" *(tumi)* and consist of a variety of substances.

Constructing a chart of the distinctives of different tribal beliefs underscores their parallels and similarities (see next page).

Romans 1:19–20 tells us God reveals much through general revelation. In Ghanaian traditional religion, as we can see from the chart, God is perceived as a Supreme Deity who is chief and head and creator of all other spirits. The Supreme Deity demands sacrifice and judges and punishes wrong after death. God is the source of all good. Sometimes, as the Sisaala perceive Wia, God does influence everyday activity and, in the case of Uwumber of the Kokomba, even has a way of entering into people. As the Kasena recognize, God controls people's lives. But more often God is far removed from people and they are not able directly to communicate their concerns to God. So, fetishes and charms intervene, as do lesser deities and ancestors who demand to be objects of worship.

Further, as this chart's summary of religious practices clearly shows, all the ethnic groups in the country have a common traditional religious belief and practice. Therefore, the term "Ghanaian traditional religion," when used, describes all the various religious beliefs of the Ghanaian people—whether the person is from the Gur language family or the Akan language family.

In addition, more detailed examination will reveal that no apparent distinction exists (though in practice one does) between Ghanaian tra-

Table A—People of the Gur Language Family Groups of North Ghana

People	Location	Percentage of Adherents to Traditional religion	Deities	Ancestor Worship?	Distinctive Features
Dagaaba	Northwest corner of Ghana, covering 4000 sq. km.	60%+	Tengbam is chief deity supported by weni or njimin	Yes	Naanjim or Naamnin is God, but humans cannot communicate with him
Wala	Live in Wa areas covering 2000 sq. km.	40%+	Same as above	Yes	Same as above
Birifor	Strip along border of Ivory Coast, covering 2000 sq. km.	90%+	Naagmin is the Supreme God, but is far removed from the people	Yes	Tingaan and other smaller deities worshiped; animal sacrifices performed yearly
Safalba	West of Bole about 60 sq. km.	95%	Same as above	Yes	Same as above
Frafra	Covers most of Navrongo, Bongo-Nabdam, and Bolga. 1900 sq. km.	80%+	Naayinne is the chief God worshiped through various shrines	Yes	Yinne, Bakologo, Madonna, and Sodoma are shrines, which differ according to location. Naja'ana is their household totem
Nabdem	Southeast corner of Bongo Nabdem covers 250 sq. km.	80%+	Similar to the Frafras	Yes	Similar to the Frafras
Kusasi	Covers 2200 sq. km. from Kusanaba Zebilla, Bawku etc. in the far northeast of Ghana	88%+	Na'awim is the Supreme God. They sacrifice to host of gods; among them is "buza"	Yes	"Tubig" cares for infants; "No tood" protects against curse; "Suenling" helps win court case
Talensi	Tongo district, covers 370 sq. km.	80%+	Similar to the Frafras	Yes	Similar to the Frafras
Mamprusi	Covers Walewale and Nalerigu district, 4700 sq. km.	82%+	Naawuni is the Supreme God	Yes	Bubuja enforces oaths and Gambaga specializes in snakes and witchcraft

Group	Location	%	Supreme God	Belief	Notes
Dagomba	Covers Tolon, Savelugu, Tamale, and Yendi, 11,900 sq. km.	42%+	Naawuni is the Supreme God; Pabo and Yanderi are two most powerful gods	Yes	Sapani and Tagragenti harrass people at night; Tiyawonya is used to harm one's enemies; animal sacrifices are made to gods
Nanumba	Northern half of Bimbilla, 1750 sq. km.	85%+	Similar to the Dagombas	Yes	Share same practices with the Dagombas
Hanga	20–50 km. northeast of Damongo, covers 500 sq. km.	93%+	Bore is the Supreme God	Yes	Worship Bore through ancestors, gods, and fetishes
Bulsa	Close to Sandema, covers about 2000 sq. km.	85%+	Nawen is the Supreme God, Chief of the sky and Creator of all gods and spirits	Yes	No sacrifices made directly to Nawen
Bimoba	Eastern part of Tompare Garu and Nalerigu covers 800 sq. km.	90%+	Yennu is the Supreme God; next is worship of smaller deities and ancestral spirits	Yes	No sacrifices made to Yennu, but he judges and punishes wrong after death
Kokomba	Northeast border of Ghana, 50 km. wide and 175 km. from north to south	92%+	Uwumber is the Supreme God and Creator, source of all good	Yes	Uwumber enters into people through Ungwin; he creates lesser gods and is worshipped through shrines of the earth
Sisaala	Covers Tumu to Burkina Faso border, 5000 sq. km.	73%+	Wia is the Supreme God, influencing everyday activity	Yes	Fetishes linked to a secret society with a form of initiation called *juansing*
Dega	Covers border between Brong Ahafo and northern region, 1700 sq. km.	82%+	Korowii is the Supreme God, head of all; Longore Teo is the god of all Dega	Yes	Special clans have other gods. Fetishes are owned by clans, households, and individuals
Kasena	Extends from Paga to the northeast corner of Tumu, covers 2200 sq. km.	80%+	We is the Supreme God and Creator; have lesser gods	Yes	Supreme God controls people's lives; have shrines to the chief god or fetish

Table B—People of the Akan, Ga Adangbe, and Ewe Family Groups of Southern Ghana

People	Location	Supreme Deity	Lesser Deities	Worship of Each	Ancestral Worship?	Fetish
Akans	Covers about 7/8 of the southern part of Ghana; made up of tribes: Akuapem, Akyem, Kwahu, Asante, Ahafo, Brong, Sefwi, Aowin, Nzima, Ahanta, Fante, Denkyira Assin and Asante-Akyem	Onyame, Amowia, Amosu, Amoamee, Oboadee, and others	Abosom: they help devotee to worship Supreme Being. Asase Yaa, Asase Efua, Aberewa are the spirits of the earth and water	The Supreme God is worshiped through the medium of lesser gods	Believe in the spirits of the dead and their influence on the living; they believe in the authority of Nananom nsamanfo	Believe in wearing protective charms and fetish-like talismans and amulets which are called *asuman* (repositories of the *tumi* [power])
Ga Adangbe	Covers far south part of Ghana on the Atlantic Ocean. Adangbe family group is made up of Gas, Krobos, and Adas	Ataa Naa, Nyonmo, Mao, and Tsatse Mao are the names of the Supreme God	Lesser deity for the Gas is *won*; the Krobos are *Nnadu* and *Kotoklo*; the Adas have *dzemawoi* and *amega*	The Supreme God is worshiped through the lesser deities	Believe in worship of ancestors; libation is poured for *Niime* or *Jemawojii*	Use charms, amulets and talismans or totems for protection
Ewe	Eastern part of Ghana stretching from the Atlantic coast along the border of Togo to the north of Ghana	Mawu or Mawuga; he is the one among many gods; he has various praise names— Ganhunukpo; he is almighty *Semedoto*, the creating spirit	Vudu or Vodu	Yes	Yes	Yes

ditional religion and Ghanaian indigenous religion, which mixes Christianity in with traditional beliefs.

In what way can I conclude that despite the influx of one more deity (called Jesus), no apparent distinction occurs? In their shared theology, the Ghanaian indigenous and traditional religions believe that God, who is the Supreme Being, is far removed from the people and rarely worshiped directly. Only in isolated instances can the Supreme Being be said to be worshiped. The Supreme Being is worshiped through the lesser gods. In indigenous religion, Jesus becomes just another lesser god.

Ghanaian Indigenous Religion

Ghanaians as a people honor tradition. That is, they have doctrines, practices, rites, and customs "handed over" or "transmitted" to them by their ancestors. Attached to this tradition is their system of belief wherein they express their love and trust to and dependence on *a God*. This belief is recognized through their worship, conduct, devotion, and ceremonial observances. In the preceding pages, the amalgamation of the doctrines, practices, rites, customs with the beliefs, worship, conduct, devotion, and ceremonial observances have been discussed under (1) traditional religion, and (2) indigenous religion.

Traditional religion brings out the belief in a God who is a Supreme Being, but comes to his people through other supernatural lesser deities called gods, who derive their powers through the Supreme Being. Besides the Supreme Being and his lesser "messengers" are the ancestors or ancestral spirits who play prominent roles in the lives of their living relatives. Added to these are natural objects called talismans, charms, amulets, and mascots, which provide protection for the people.

The people, on the other hand, offer their devotion to this God through the mediation of traditional priests or priestesses and/or a family head. The ministry of these "mediators" is considered to provide "care" for the people. This "care" is administered through traditional practices, rites, customs, and ceremonial observances. In traditional Ghana, one cannot live without these practices and beliefs, because tradition and religion are seen as inseparable. To the Ghanaian people, salvation is considered to be deliverance from material ills such as fear, hunger, and sickness, and the substitution of abundant material prosperity in place of these ills. For adherents, the irreligious person is the one who suffers. Therefore, the people who go to the shrines of these mediators are offered care as they perform their part of the rituals, customs, and ceremonial observances.

The indigenous religion amalgamates Christianity with the "native" religion of the people of Ghana. Even though the religion attempts to be faithful to Christianity, it is born out of Ghana with its practices traditionally inclined. In fact, B. Kese-Amankwaa judges the indigenous church as a "positive repudiation of Christianity." Though proponents use the scaffolding of the Christian church, he contends that they "erect new structures for the self-expression of the traditional religion."[23] However, unlike the traditional religion, the indigenous religion:

1. accepts the Bible as the Word of God.
2. accepts Jesus Christ and acknowledges him as the Son of God and the Savior of the world. But like the traditional religion, ministers attach great importance to the material needs of their followers.

Indigenous religion's basic features address all areas of human life with practices similar to traditional religions. It has healing, divination, respect for the departed, use of prophecy and dreams, and visions and revelations as mediums by which it offers pastoral care to its devotees. A communal spirit, which is also a "landmark" of Ghanaian tradition, pulls people from all walks of life to its fold. It offers "care" to them through the mediation of prophets, prophetesses, and other leaders considered as "seers," who offer hope and assurance to their followers. All these are done in the spirit of care which is affirmed by Paul Makhubu when he observes:

> This "caring spirit" concept stems from African culture and custom. Among the blacks there were no orphans or conspicuous widows. The poor were helped to make a living. A young man who had no money or cattle for *lobola* (marriage rites) would be given a wife. . . . A man with no cattle would be loaned cattle for milk and to plough. . . . African independent churches do not separate the needs of the body from that of the soul. They minister to the whole person in this system of caring.[24]

This "spirit" of care by both religions has deeply penetrated the hearts of the Ghanaian people. In fact, one cannot separate tradition from religion.

Biblical Christianity Confronts Traditional and Indigenous Religion

Biblical Christianity does not favor the practices of Ghanaian traditional religion. Yes, God is the Supreme Being and God expects his people to communicate to him directly. God says repeatedly in his Word that communicating to him through minor deities called lesser gods is idolatry, which he detests as abomination. The Bible says:

> You shall not make for yourself an idol, whether in the form of anything that is in heaven above, or that is on the earth beneath, or that is in the water under the earth. (Exod. 20:4)

> Do not make idols or set up an image or a sacred stone for yourselves, and do not place a carved stone in your land to bow down before it. I am the LORD your God. (Lev. 26:1 NIV)

> Be careful, or you will be enticed to turn away and worship other gods and bow down to them. (Deut. 11:16 NIV; cf. 7:25)

> I am the LORD; that is my name! I will not give my glory to another or my praise to idols. (Isa 42:8 NIV)

> Little children, keep yourselves from idols. (1 John 5:21)

The Scripture refutes the traditional belief that "no ordinary human could talk to God directly"; therefore, a need exists for lesser gods or a go-between. Also the concept that the gods and ancestors are mediators between God and the living, and the Ghanaian or African custom of not approaching the king or senior person directly create the mental attitude that since no ordinary person could talk to the king or chief face-to-face, for humans to go to God is, therefore, extremely disrespectful. All of these beliefs and concepts, therefore, account for idolatry in Ghanaian traditional religion. Since God, who, as the Supreme Being, cannot be approached directly, a go-between—minor deities or lesser gods and ancestors—must be enlisted to represent a suppliant.

Rather than religious "care," I believe that such a system creates *bondage*. A devotee to traditional religion who receives *care* from the traditional sources is placed under an oppressive load of numerous taboos. Failure to observe all forbidden practices results in punishment from the ancestors or the gods or even an immediate death. For example, one who receives protection against snakebites will be bitten by a snake if he or she fails to observe taboos assigned to that protective charm.

The indigenous religious care is also fraught with problems. Essentially, this syncretistic religion is a pseudo-Christian cult. Humanistic in nature and in its approach to care, it does not encourage adherents to seek God for God's own sake, but rather to venerate the ancestors and appease the spirits in order to receive favor in return.[25] Devotees to this religion only go there when they have needs. As a result, leaders of this religion are tempted to have a vested interest not in the people they help, but in themselves. They seek fame; they become "lords" and "messiahs" as they mediate between God and the suffering of needy people. The people look to them for healing, deliverance, and prosperity and not to God. Their interest in God is utilitarian. Still, their appeal and, thus, their religion's growth is phenomenal. In fact, many people from mainline evangelical churches go to them when they are faced with existential problems. We recall B. Kese-Amankwaa's observation:

> Traditionally, the African looks to his religion for everything. A religion which will not help one out of an existential difficulty is of no use to the traditional African. To him suffering is incompatible with the believer's closer walk with God. The average African traditional believer cannot imagine why anyone who discharges his religious duties sincerely should not prosper. And since the local prophets claim to be able to heal the sick, restore sight, and pray for money, one does not need to ask why their temples are always full.[26]

Even though the above concept is a wrong attitude for one's walk with God, since it is considered as primarily utilitarian, I believe that we can envision ways to change this erroneous concept. These ways would help Ghanaians, in particular, to know God in a personal and intimate way, while God would still meet their personal needs in times of existential difficulty or crisis.

Ghanaians would not have to choose between worship and benefit. One way is an *active care* where the Christian churches would "engage in practical existence expressed in terms of fellowship, providing identity for their members, and responding to immediate physical and pastoral needs."[27] Another way would be affirming where the communal and caring spirit in the Ghanaian tradition would be upheld and nurtured in the Christian church. Further, in the practice of pastoral care in Ghana, the Christian church must take into consideration that Ghanaians as a people have tradition. Therefore, some traditional, not religious, practices must be considered and contextualized as we offer care. Good traditions on which Ghanaians can truly depend are the:

- traditional communal spirit of care and concern for one another;
- traditional hospitality;
- traditional extended family system which brings commonality in sharing;
- traditional way of worship with drumming, dancing, clapping, singing in their own ethnic language, expressing their respect, honor, adoration, and devotion by their total commitment to, obedience to, and fear of the Supreme God, which will help them have a closer relationship with God, so that they can go to him directly without going through inferior gods who have nothing to offer;
- traditional respect to the elderly.

The understanding of a Supreme God points to the Bible's revelation that God is indeed holy and worthy of awe and respect. The God of the Bible is a God of generation after generation. Highlighting a culture's positive traditions brings identification and belonging. For example, language brings commonality. Hearing ministers of God declare the wonders of God in one's own native language or tongue could be quite comforting and edifying. The Ghanaian Christian who gives care to his or her parishioners, while being sensitive to such issues, will provide lasting benefits for the Ghanaian people. Carefully sorting helpful tradition from unhelpful religion, Christians have to lead people to God so that they can trust God with their whole hearts, without going through the medium of idol worship, ancestral veneration, fetishism, and other practices which are abominations to God.

All of these truths have become apparent to me in my own religious journey from traditional to indigenous to Christian belief.

From Bondage to Freedom

I was born into an idol-worshiping home. My father and mother were devotees of the "Ayago" shrine in a village in the Kwahu traditional area. As early as the age of six, I was sent to the shrine of "Nana Ayago" for protection. I used to go with my father every month to make sacrifices to the gods. When we went, some ceremonies and rites would be performed on my behalf. I was given a protective ring to wear. I was not allowed to visit the farm or the bush on Fridays, or I would be bitten by a snake. I was also forbidden to eat certain foods.

For several years, my family was in bondage to this fetish shrine. Even though my parents were poor, when it came to sacrifices my father had to find means to get sacrificial items like goat, fowl, calico, cowries, and cash to take to the shrine. I was faithfully attending the Roman Catholic Church in my village during these years. I was even an altar boy.

After I had completed primary school and began attending high school in the city of Koforidua in the eastern region of Ghana, I had to visit the shrine to renew my protection whenever I was on a holiday. This continued throughout my college years. After graduation I moved to the capital city, Accra, in the Ga traditional area.

In Accra, I was faithfully attending the Roman Catholic Church but was still searching for absolute protection because city life had very different and frightening challenges. In my search, I finally ended up in a "spiritual" (or indigenous) church. Tuesday nights were all-night prayer meetings, but almost every day I visited the prophetess. I had to walk a distance of about five miles to the seashore (on the Atlantic Ocean) to fetch seawater for the prophetess. She would then pray over it and I would take it home. Every morning when I woke up, I had to wash my face with this "holy water." This was to protect me against witchcraft or any misfortune.

Lives in spiritual bondage comprise the problem confronting the Christian church in Ghana today, ministering in the face of such traditional and indigenous religious beliefs. Today, liberated by Jesus from performing such rituals, I hold the view that no compromise is needed, but through active pastoral care the Christian church needs to communicate to Ghanaians that they can go to God directly. The way is wide open—salvation through God's Son Jesus Christ! Through the incarnation, death, and resurrection of Jesus Christ, God's only begotten Son, Ghanaians have access to God simply by believing him. Jesus says: "I am the *way*, and the *truth*, and the *life*. *No one* comes to the Father except through me" (John 14:6 italics mine). Again "There is salvation in no one else, for there is *no other name* under heaven given among mortals by which we must be saved" (Acts 4:12 italics mine). Christianity is an exclusive religion.

Acceptance into the community of the living and the living dead, deliverance from the power of the evil spirits, possession of life force, absence of material ills such as fear, hunger, and sickness, and abundant material prosperity alone do not make a person fulfilled in life. But real fulfillment is found in salvation through Jesus Christ. This is where real life and care begin. Jesus says, "Strive first for the kingdom of God and his righteousness, and all these things will be given to you as well" (Matt. 6:33). True Christianity works inversely to traditional and indigenous religion. God is worshiped; then needs are met. The meeting of needs, the impetus of participation in both traditional and indigenous religion, does not precede worship or impel it. Further, God is not far removed from us. He is not an absentee God who needs smaller deities to deputize for him. He is and will be with us. If we did not know, now we know. Tokunboh Adeyemo puts it well: "Africa's broken rope between heaven and earth has been once and for all re-established in Christ. Africa's God, who, as they say, withdrew from men to the heavens, has now come down to man so as to bring man back to God. Evil forces and death which linger on the doors have been overcome by Christ. Beyond death lies not the dusty ruins of the conflict, but the shining light of the resurrection and conformity to Jesus Christ for everyone who believes."[28]

Christian ministry and pastoral care in Ghana must begin from this true biblical premise. Pastoral care in Ghana must sound the message loudly and clearly. It must strive to liberate men and women from bondage to traditional and indigenous religions. It must not be cowed into submission by the threats of traditional beliefs or syncretized with them in indigenous systems. Christianity transcends traditions. While it can incorporate good traditions, it is the revelation of God who is above all tradition.

Like African tradition, Asian religious tradition also has a distinct theology of the doctrine of God that orients the emphasis many Asians put on God when coming into Christianity.

Eight

Viewing God through the Twin Lenses of Holiness and Mercy: A Chinese American Perspective

Grace Y. May

Seeking to integrate culture and theology, **Grace Ying May** is presently pursuing a Th.D. at Boston University School of Theology. She is a Chinese American serving as Director of Christian Education at the Roxbury Presbyterian Church in Boston, Massachusetts, a predominantly African American church. She has an M.Div. magna cum laude, from Gordon-Conwell Theological Seminary and a B.A., cum laude, from Yale University. She has published several articles with *Priscilla Papers*. As well as in the church, she has served in leadership roles in academia, missions, and conferences.

I used to dread communion services. The mood was somber, and my foreboding increased before the distribution of the elements, when the pastor warned us, "For he that eateth and drinketh unworthily, eateth and drinketh damnation to himself" (1 Cor. 11:29 KJV). After the pronouncement, a sense of judgment hung heavy in the air. I bowed my head and closed my eyes. While the tiny glass cups and bits of bread were being passed from row to row, I anxiously confessed my sins and earnestly sought the Lord's forgiveness. As loath as I was to undergo the period of soul searching, in almost every instance I benefited from the exercise. The Lord's pardon released me from my sense of guilt and shame. No longer afraid of God, I found God's presence reassuring. As a youth, I was developing an understanding of God's holiness and mercy. I equated a need for personal holiness with the proper observance of the Lord's Supper.

In my years in the Chinese American church I have observed that the emphasis on moral rectitude and purity permeates not only our communion service, but our whole approach to spirituality. We have a keen sense of God's holiness and accept the corollary truth that those who worship God must be holy. What our church lacks is an equally strong emphasis on God's mercy.

In this chapter I will explore the biblical concepts of holiness and mercy against the backdrop of the Chinese American church's theology and experience. Although I realize that as a second-generation Chinese American, Confucianism has exerted less influence on my generation than on my parents', I would be remiss if I did not start by considering some of the cultural roots of our pietism. After tracing some of these influences, I will briefly mention some of the internal conflicts that second- and third-generation Chinese Americans face.[1]

Our main focus, however, will be on the interplay between the Scriptures and the contemporary Chinese American church. Thus, I will examine the biblical support for the Chinese American church's concern for holiness. Following the discussion on holiness, I will take a look at how the Scriptures describe the same God as full of mercy. Through specific contemporary applications, I will consider how a proper emphasis on God's mercy can balance and enhance our appreciation of God's holiness. Finally, I will reflect on the culmination of God's holiness and mercy intersecting our lives.

No culture is static, and the culture of the Chinese American church is no exception. By "Chinese American," I am referring to those who are Chinese by descent yet more comfortable with American thought, culture, and speech. Like any other church, the Chinese American church exists in a continuum, consisting of individuals who have assimilated at different rates and in varying degrees. In a church with a large immigrant population, old world and new world traditions compete for the right to define the reigning cultural norms. In a bicultural church, distinguishing between our parents' voices and our own proves especially difficult.

The matter is complicated by the fact that most Chinese American congregations originated as youth ministries. Catering to expanding family needs, Chinese-speaking parents insisted on developing an English ministry, instead of attending a European American church with a vibrant youth ministry. Recognizing parents' desires to remain in a Chinese-speaking church with their children, Chinese-speaking church leaders attempted to provide for the younger English speakers. Consequently, the English-speaking congregation functioned more as an appendage to the Chinese service than as a separate, autonomous ministry of the church. Presently, though, Chinese American churches attract a far broader spectrum of people, including families, young professionals, and students of all ages.

Based on my own and others' experiences of worshiping and serving in the Chinese American church, I hope to paint a collective reflection of what God's holiness and mercy look like in the Chinese American church.

Our Ancient Roots: Confucianism

Before we can adequately evaluate the present state of the Chinese American church, we would benefit from considering the roots of some of our values. Long before any Christian missionaries made their first journey to China, Confucianism flourished, arguably exerting more influence on Chinese civilization than any other worldview. Although its founder, Confucius (551–479 B.C.), lived over two thousand years ago, neo-Confucians revived his thoughts and his writings centuries later, thus preserving a tradition that has survived to the present time. Confucius extolled filial piety (hsiao)[2] and propriety (li). A strong advocate of social order, Confucius upheld hierarchy and submission as the modus operandi of the Confucian state and family.[3] To know one's place was essential to leading a virtuous life. Just as a subject owed absolute loyalty to the emperor, similarly, children were duty bound to honor and obey their parents in everything. In response to a young noble's question about filial piety, Confucius said:

> Never disobey. . . . When parents are alive, serve them according to the rules of propriety. When they die, bury them according to the rules of propriety and sacrifice to them according to the rules of propriety. (*Analects* 2:5)

Not only did Confucius assume that children would support their parents in old age, but he believed children should fulfill their family obligation with a sense of reverence (*Analects* 2:7).[4]

Confucius believed that people could realize virtue *(jen)* or perfection in their lifetime. Given the belief in the perfectibility of humanity, later Confucians taught the inherent goodness of humankind. The process of self-cultivation entailed prodigious amounts of self-discipline and hard work.[5] Education was indispensable in attaining virtue. Based on a systematic diet of Confucian teachings, the civil service examinations (begun in their earliest form in the Han dynasty in the third century and enduring into the twentieth century) formalized the Chinese pursuit of excellence.[6] In China's meritocracy, the goal was sagehood and a respectable position in the government.

To be a sage was the moral equivalent of being holy. *The Doctrine of the Mean,* one of the early Confucian classics, extols the sage or saint as follows:

> It is only he, possessed of all sagely qualities that can exist under heaven, who shows himself quick in apprehension, clear in discernment, of far-reaching intelligence, and all-embracing knowledge, fitted to exercise rule: magnanimous, generous, benign, and mild, fitted to exercise forbearance . . . fitted to maintain a firm hold; self-adjusted, grave, never swerving from the Mean, and correct, fitted to command reverence . . . . He is the equal of Heaven.[7]

In Chinese, the same word that describes the "sage," *sheng,* is part of the compound term for the Bible, *sheng jing* (literally, "sacred Scripture"). Borrowing the word to denote Christian "holiness," Christians have likewise inherited a scholarly tradition that emphasizes the *rational side of spirituality and morality.* The inextricable relationship between moral cultivation and rigorous study gave rise to a form of scholasticism that still shapes modern Chinese American values both in and out of the Christian community.

Chinese American Crosscurrents: Reevaluating the Myth of the Model Minority

While the values commended by Confucius kept the family intact, the same code of ethics added special strains to the immigrant struggling to adjust to a new and different world. The second generation often bore the brunt of upholding Chinese customs while attempting to assimilate into the surrounding culture. Through the lens of Confucianism, education appears to confer godliness. But what is the cost of achieving good grades, especially in a dominant culture that also prizes creativity, social skills, and leisure? Today's Chinese Americans face a barrage of pressures: the high expectations of parents, steeped in Confucian values; the burden of living up to the mythical status of a model minority, based on the racist need to pit one minority group against another; and the aspiration to be recognized and not remain invisible, the product of a highly competitive society with no room for modesty. Together, these forces compound the difficulty of coping with failure and, contrary to the media coverage, many Chinese Americans do miss the mark.

Rev. Kenneth Uyeda Fong observes that Asian Americans struggle profoundly with a sense of shame. According to Fong, healthy shame makes people aware of their fallenness and their ongoing need for redemption and directs them to the cross; whereas "toxic shame is the dark feeling that [they] are flawed as a human being," without any hope.[8] People suffering from toxic shame try to hide behind pretense or legalism to cover the gaping hole in their soul.[9] Others, fearing rejection, overcompensate. One young Asian American confesses:

> I tried very hard to do good and to be good in order to earn my parents' affection and approval. I tried to make good grades in school. As I did this, I grew to accept only the good side of myself; I dared not face my shortcomings.[10]

For Asian Americans, a lack of acceptance by European Americans can intensify the sense of alienation and shame. Thus, the Asian American desire to succeed may derive partly from a positive work ethic (Confucian and possibly Protestant in origin) and partly from a debilitating need for others' approval (fed by Confucianism and an immigrant mentality).

When genuine triumphs do occur, Chinese and Chinese Americans celebrate their successes differently. In *The Joy Luck Club,* novelist Amy Tan powerfully choreographs the dance of approval between a mother and daughter. *Time* magazine hails Waverly Jong as a child chess prodigy, but her mother never congratulates her and only admonishes her to keep improving. In marked contrast, on the weekends Mrs. Jong parades Waverly through the streets of Chinatown, practically campaigning for the young champion. Miffed and embarrassed by her mother's doting in public and her nagging in private, Waverly gives up chess altogether.[11]

For the Chinese American, issues of acceptance and achievement often lead to frustration because of the sense of futility that accompanies one's efforts: "I can never do enough"; "I will never please my parents." To the extent that our parents and family give us our first exposure to God, Chinese Americans, in particular, must be careful to avoid seeing God as a reticent or overbearing parent and learn to see God as the one who offers unconditional love while upholding perfect standards.

Our God Is Holy

Confucian sagehood and the Chinese American pursuit of perfection, however, do not fully do justice to the divine self-portrait of holiness. In the Scriptures, "holiness" speaks to the "otherness" of God, the sum total of what makes God *unique and distinct.* By calling God holy, we are registering an "awareness of the division between the human and the divine."[12] We are acknowledging the difference between what is pure and what is not.

Moses, in Exodus 15:11, asks, "Who is like you, O Lord? . . . Who is like you, majestic in holiness?"[13] Hannah, in 1 Samuel 2:2, replies, "There is no Holy One like the Lord, no one besides you; there is no Rock like our God." Isaiah records the Lord's query, "To whom then will you compare me, or who is my equal?" (Isa. 40:25), while John unfurls the victorious song in the last day, "Lord, who will not fear and glorify your name? For you alone are holy" (Rev. 15:4). The Scriptures replay the question and answer over and over again in an attempt to underscore the fact that no one is like God. God is God, and no one can compare with God.

But, then, how does one conceive of a God beyond comparison? Biblical imagery locates God in the "holy city,"[14] in the "holy temple,"[15] and on the "holy mountain"[16]—places removed from the beaten track and reserved exclusively for God and God's holy ones. Yet, instead of remaining aloof from creation and enjoying purely celestial company, God spans the chasm between heaven and earth. "For thus says the high and lofty one who inhabits eternity, whose name is Holy: I dwell in the high and holy place, and also with those who are contrite and humble in spirit" (Isa. 57:15). God desires to dwell with the humble.

The Scriptures depict God eagerly attending to creation, granting petitions, entering into covenants, and revealing divine intentions and plans. The Holy One promises to deliver Israel from her enemies (Isa. 43:16; Jer. 50:29) and to teach and lead her in the way she should go (Isa. 48:17). Surrounded by a heavenly entourage, which chants "Holy, holy, holy, the Lord God the Almighty" (Rev. 4:8), God still desires to be enthroned by the praises of human voices. A marked humility exists in God's holiness, so much so that God dons flesh and bone to dwell among us as one of us. Borrowing from the rich temple imagery of the Old Testament, Paul relocates the holy temple. No longer an external building, God's dwelling place is with the people of God (1 Cor. 3:17; Eph. 2:21–22). The church becomes God's holy habitation.

For most Chinese Americans, believing in a holy God who is above us and distant from us is not nearly as difficult as believing in a merciful God who is near us and within us. If we were raised in a traditional household, we were taught to revere our elders. We showed our respect by remaining silent unless spoken to, keeping a certain physical distance, and not looking directly into someone's eyes. For many, even as adults, the idea of treating our parents as equals is at best remote.

What happens when we transfer the principles of filial piety to our worship of God? Addressing God as Father reinforces the image of a parental figure to whom we owe unquestioned allegiance and obedience, because in the Confucian family the father rules. Unfortunately, too many of us project a picture of our parents on God. We assume that because our earthly parents did not hug us or verbalize their love for us that our heavenly Parent is indifferent to our need for affection and affirmation. Consequently, we relate to God as a towering figure or a strict disciplinarian. We worship God, but we cannot imagine intimacy with God. We struggle with understanding God's love for us on an emotional and gut level.

Some criticize the present generation of Chinese Americans for having lost their awe of the transcendent. But, in my estimation, a Confucian sense of respect continues to permeate our worship services. Ministers will often exhort their congregations not to trivialize God by treating God merely as a friend. A period of silence for prayer and meditation follows the worship service, silence being a most appropriate response to a superior in a Confucian-based culture. Communion remains a serious time of introspection and confession, with the accent being on God's holiness and our unworthiness. The generalization about communion seems to hold true particularly when an overseas-born Chinese pastor leads the service, which is still frequent, given that only 21 percent of Chinese pastors are American born.[17]

Whatever Is Devoted to the Lord Is Holy

In addition to uniqueness and distinction, holiness in the Bible marks people and objects as being *devoted to God.* Under the old covenant, whatever God deemed holy was reserved for God's use and disposal. God's name was sacred, and therefore people were afraid even to pronounce it. To show respect for sacred space, God insisted that Moses remove his sandals when he stood on holy ground (Exod. 3:5). God permitted no one to enter the Holy of Holies except the high priest, and then only once a year as the Law stipulated (Lev. 16:2–34).

To insure that certain times were set aside explicitly to honor God, work was prohibited on the Sabbath and during other holy convocations.[18] To make an object holy, that is, to consecrate it, entailed ceremonial cleansing and adhering to certain other rules concerning its use.[19] The rosette on the high priest's diadem bore the inscription "Holy to the LORD" (Exod. 28:36) and indicated that not only the crown but also the sacrificial system and all that it symbolized belonged to the Lord. God required the priests to eat sacrificed food at a designated area in the temple (Lev. 10:12–14), to wear holy vestments (Exod. 35:19), to mix holy incense (Exod. 30:37; 37:29), to anoint with holy oil (Exod. 37:29), and to employ holy utensils in the service of the temple.[20] When the priests offered sacrifices on behalf of the people, the gifts had to conform to God's specifications. The Holy One, who always gave the best, accepted only the best: unblemished grain and animal offerings, the first fruits of the land, and the consecration of Israel's firstborn.

The Old Testament pattern of setting aside time, space, and objects to God finds parallels in Chinese American churches. In keeping with a revivalistic tradition, probably inherited from missionaries, Chinese American congregations regularly look forward to retreats. The main branch of the Overseas Chinese Mission in New York City (a church that offers services in Chinese and in English) holds two churchwide conferences annually and many other retreats throughout the year. Smaller congregations often join conferences sponsored by organizations, such as Ambassadors for Christ (a Chinese American parachurch ministry similar to InterVarsity). While holiness may not feature as the explicit theme of the conference, a retreat provides people with opportunities to be apart with the Lord, to set aside their daily routines, and to receive spiritual replenishment. To prevent the encroachment of sacred time and space, those organizing a retreat will forbid the use of radios and Walkmans and hold the retreat at a campsite.

While retreats reflect some degree of success on the part of independent Chinese American churches to foster a sense of holiness, the struggle to keep the holy and the profane distinct persists. A suburban Chinese American church wants to sell its old property to another church instead of a business, so as to keep the building serving sacred ends, but in the end financial pressures win out. An older Chinese American pastor enforces a dress code in church, believing that Christians should wear their best clothes to worship God. On one sultry evening when a young woman was unexpectedly asked to come up to the pulpit to make an announcement, the pastor publicly rebuked her for wearing shorts, because in his opinion she had desecrated the pulpit. Similarly, Chinese parents will tell their American-born children not to lay any objects on top of the Bible or to hold the sacred volume between their legs, so as not to show disrespect for God's *Holy* Word.

God Demands a Holy Life

The ritual and ceremonial laws contained in the Old Testament bring into sharp focus the *high moral standards* expected of God's people. The familiar words of Leviticus 20:26, "You shall be holy to me; for I the LORD am holy," calls God's people to pattern their lives not after their neighbors, but after a holy God. The essence of holiness is absolute purity from defilement, which demands separation from all that is impure and tainted by evil.[21] God called Israel to holiness, so that she would live. God gave the Ten Commandments and over six hundred other laws (Hebrew *mitvah*) not to burden, but to bless the people. If they followed the laws, God promised to protect them and insured that they would live bountifully in the land (Deut. 28:1–12). Moreover, by living distinct and pleasing lives before the Lord, the Israelites would serve as a sign to the nations. They would bear witness to the benefits and rewards of living in right relationship with the Creator. God had called Israel (Deut. 7:6) to be a holy people to bless all the nations of the earth (Gen. 12:3). Similarly, Jesus chose the church to extend God's reign in the world (Matt. 28:19).

Ethically, holiness is depicted as the opposite of uncleanness (Lev. 10:10). To be holy is to be blameless (Col. 1:22; 1 Thess. 3:13), which involves confessing one's sins and receiving God's pardon. Peter enjoins the church to exhibit godly behavior consistent with Christ's return (2 Peter 3:11). Paul's correspondence makes plain the moral connotations. Holiness requires abstaining from fornication and lust (1 Thess. 4:3–4) and living a life free from immorality, idolatry, adultery, homosexuality, greed, drunkenness, slander, and stealing (1 Cor. 6:9–11).

Purity in spirit has consequences in our physical conduct and comportment, and vice-versa. Therefore, leaders in the church have an obligation before God to be diligent in upholding such standards in their own lives (1 Thess. 2:10; Titus 1:8). At the same time, we as Christians need to be the first to remember that offering ourselves as a "living sacrifice, holy and acceptable to God" (Rom. 12:1) is a feat that we can only accomplish by God's grace (Eph. 2:8–9).

Sanctification, that process by which God makes us holy, not against our wills but with our cooperation, consumes the attention of the biblical authors. The writer of Hebrews explains why the theme of sanctification is uppermost in his or her mind: "The one sanctifying and the one being sanctified are all of one" (Heb. 2:11 my own translation), that is, stemming from one source, God. The same *holiness unites us to Christ*, who is "holy, blameless, pure" (Heb. 7:26 NIV). The purpose of leading holy lives is nothing short of bringing us into *union* with the Holy One. So paramount is the thought that believers are those who live and act differently from people who have not yet believed that the New Testament throughout refers to Christians as "saints" (Greek, *hagios*),[22] literally, "the consecrated ones" or "the holy ones," those set apart for God. The Chinese Bible translates "saints" as "those who follow holiness" (see, e.g., 1 Cor. 1:2). We become followers of God's holiness as we model our lives after Christ's.

Holiness Requires Sacrifice

As mentioned earlier, the Scriptures not only stress God's holiness but our need to be holy. But how can a holy God transmit holiness to an unholy people? The Mosaic law unveils not only a strict moral code of behavior but God's provision for ritual cleansing and the forgiveness of sins. The sacrificial system is God's way under the old covenant of maintaining fellowship with people without compromising the divine character. In the New Testament, God made the ultimate sacrifice: God's own Son was slain for our sins.

The Chinese American church preaches and teaches without apology or diffidence the substitutionary atonement of Christ. Songs and hymns lift up Christ's saving work on the cross. The message punctuates Sunday sermons and forms the core of evangelistic services.

Distinguishing between Ritual and Moral Purity

Exposure to the holy can have beneficial and harmful effects. In Exodus 29:37, the Lord notes that "whatever touches the altar shall become holy." Likewise, in Leviticus 6:27, the Lord states that "whatever touches the flesh [of the sin offering] shall become holy." In 1 Corinthians 7:14, Paul even applies the principle of communicability to married partners, when he asserts that the believing spouse will make the unbelieving holy. The three references indicate that the nature of the holiness is *not salvific.* In the Old Testament cases cited, the authors are referring to *ritual holiness.* In the New Testament case, holiness keeps the believing spouse from being profaned by sexual union with the unbelieving partner (cf. the warning against fornication in 1 Cor. 6:15–17).

Other Old Testament examples demonstrate that exposing the profane to the holy can be dangerous. God demanded the smashing of any clay vessel that came into contact with the sin offering. God took the life of a man who touched the ark of the covenant, which only the priests could carry (2 Sam. 6:6–7). In Ezekiel 46:20, God prohibited the carrying of the guilt and sin offerings into the outer court, where the offerings might transmit not only holiness, but death. In short, encountering God's holiness unawares can have severe consequences.

Moral sanctification, in contrast, never occurs by proximity. According to Haggai 2:12, simply coming into contact with consecrated meat does not make one holy. *Only God can impute holiness.* And God prescribes sacrifice as a means to that end.

The communicability of ritual holinesss, however, does have a counterpart in moral holiness. In God's mercy, the redeemed people of God have a share in God's holiness which can be contagious as we fellowship with one another (1 John 1:7; 3:2–3). Meeting together continually reminds us of our new status in Christ and the blood of Christ that cleanses us and gives us confidence to enter the Holy of Holies (Heb. 10:19–25).

In the Chinese American churches of which I have been a part, fellowship has been a mainstay both of our life together and of our outreach. Through structured and informal times of sharing, singing, praying, teaching, eating, and recreation, we have challenged one another to live like the body of Christ by *being* the body of Christ. In those moments when we relate struggles and triumphs or when we seek forgiveness for sins, we acknowledge our need for holiness.

The preaching in a Chinese American church reinforces the call for moral excellence. Sermons accent the need for cultivating spiritual disciplines, such as prayer and Bible study. In many respects, the attention to self-cultivation resonates with both our Christian and our Confucian heritage.

Potential Dangers in Our Emphasis on Holiness

With all the emphasis on moral rectitude and injunctions to live a life worthy of God's calling, we need to remember that no matter how hard we strive to be holy, in this life we will never attain perfection. This truth should not discourage us from trying, but should keep us humbly and actively depending on the Lord.

Self-Righteousness

One of our problems in the Chinese American church is that we have a proclivity to mistake the appearance of success for genuine well-being. We are prone to self-righteousness in an environment where we often determine spiritual maturity by the length of a person's quiet time or the number of times a person has read the Bible in its entirety. While such indicators may tell us the nature of a person's spiritual disciplines, they do not necessarily measure the level of obedience or intimacy in a person's relationship with the Lord. Intended to draw us closer to God, spiritual disciplines are not meant to be a rigid standard by which we judge others.

Self-righteousness, complacency, and spiritual smugness flourish among people who pride themselves on their own accomplishments. The 1990 United States census reported that 49 percent of Asian Americans polled had earned college degrees.[23] The same census indicated that Asian Americans boasted a family median income of $36,100 as compared with the national median of $28,910.[24] Many of us, thanks to the sweat and sacrifices of our immigrant parents and forebears, have achieved our version of the American dream. Yet, tragically, our material success has too often blinded us to our spiritual poverty.

Accustomed to corporate America's and Ivy League standards of success, many of us substitute these standards for God's. With trophies, scholarships, and degrees in hand, we insulate ourselves against God's evaluation of our "good works." Why is it, for example, that so few Chinese Americans enter the ministry? On the one hand, we still feel the tug between following God's call and listening to our parents, who, Christian or not, rarely hold ministerial vocations in high esteem. On the other hand, we should also confess that we are generally more attracted to the status and wealth associated with careers in medicine, engineering, and business. Preferring the world's accolades to God's, we lose our reference point. Co-opted by the enemy's value system, we lose the critical distance that God's holiness affords. Instead of asking what will bring us closer to God, we care more about enhancing our own image, and in the process become our own gods.

Although easier to measure than internals, externals are not all that concern God, who looks at the heart. If we in the Chinese American church define ourselves by our achievements, then we have forgotten our primary identity as recipients of grace. God came to save those who are aware of their need, not their accomplishments (Luke 5:31).

If we, Chinese American Christians, are satisfied with merely the appearance of holiness, God has strong words of rebuke for us. God calls "unholy" those who "holding to the outward form of godliness" nevertheless deny its "power" (2 Tim. 3:2, 5). Spiritual disciplines may well lead to ethical conduct and morality, but these are only penultimates. Our ultimate objective—the reason God calls us to be holy—is *to be like God* and to be *partakers of God's holiness* (Heb. 12:10). Like the law, which Paul describes as a tutor in Galatians 3:24–25, holiness brings us to Christ. We are to "pursue peace" and "holiness," because apart from them "no one will see the Lord" (Heb. 12:14). God commends holiness as a way of life, but not as an end in itself, for the Scriptures enjoin us to set our sights on *nothing less than God*.

Lack of Political Self-Awareness

While affirming personal holiness, God also demands corporate holiness, a quality that is conspicuously absent in the Chinese American church. Unlike the individualistic American self, "the self in Confucian cultures is a relational self."[25] The Confucian self locates itself in the complex web of relationships within the family, which in turn buttresses the authority of the state. Politically, Confucian cultures seek to preserve the status quo. The irony is that a large segment of the Chinese American Christian community has inherited the conservative leanings of both Confucianism and American society while claiming to be apolitical.

Various other factors contribute to the apolitic stance of the Chinese American churches: biblical teaching that overlooks the social import of the gospel, wariness and indifference to political involvement, and the comfortable middle-class status of many Chinese Americans. Whatever the reasons, the Chinese American church needs to develop a biblically informed social conscience. For God's holiness, as in the days of Amos and Micah, demands that we address the needs of the poor, the alien, and the disenfranchised. Otherwise, we will call down God's judgment on ourselves.

Lack of Joy

While reflecting on our need for corporate holiness can be sobering, all of our thoughts surrounding God's holiness need not be. Many Chinese Americans possess a rich sensitivity to the arts, but our affective side remains largely untapped by the church. Our compelling desire for propriety, what I referred to in the introduction as *li*, a legacy from our Confucian heritage, when taken to an extreme often stymies the desire to be more expressive. If we confine our worship only to the cognitive realm, we will have an impoverished understanding of God. If we avoid expressing our feelings to God, we will seek emotional stimulation outside the church. What a dismal conclusion to draw, that the Creator of our lives cannot handle our emotions. God seeks those who will worship God with all their hearts, minds, strength, and soul. Do we dare give God any less? In short, even the seriousness with which we approach God, a characteristic of our services that I admire, can turn dour if overemphasized.

As Chinese Americans, many of us struggle with the appropriateness of expressing our emotions in public, especially in a formal worship setting. Since childhood, our parents have taught us to show respect by remaining silent and acquiescing to authority. Certainly the Scriptures validate silence as a proper response to God. Habakkuk describes how a hush fell over the earth at the appearance of God's holiness (Hab. 2:20).

Nevertheless, the story of Nehemiah reveals another equally satisfying response to God's holiness that can balance and enrich the Chinese American worship experience. Nehemiah unabashedly calls the reply *joy*. On the day that the Law was read out loud, the prophet declared, "This day is holy to the LORD your God; do not mourn or weep . . . do not be grieved, for the joy of the LORD is your strength" (Neh. 8:9–10). Nehemiah effectively cuts short the weeping of the people, who had been cut to the core by the Lord's words, and leads the people in revelry and celebration over the completion of the city's walls. The psalmist writes, "Our heart is glad in [the Lord], because we trust in his holy name" (Ps. 33:21). God's holiness is cause for celebration. Paul speaks of joy in the Holy Spirit (Rom. 14:17) and credits the Spirit with being the source of joy for the redeemed community (1 Thess. 1:6). Far from being awkward or ill at ease with our excitement or happiness, God demonstrates that joy is the province of the Spirit.

My experiences in the African American church have opened my eyes to the joy that can surround communion. Instead of communicating that the Lord's Table is reserved for those who are "worthy," the pastor of the church I serve emphasizes that none of us is worthy, and the recognition of our "unworthiness" is precisely what makes us eligible to receive God's mercy, and therefore Christ's body and blood. After the invitation to partake of the Table, the choir and congregation sing rounds of "Let Us Break Bread Together." The music and the singing start softly and rise in a gradual crescendo, as we pass the bread and wine and celebrate God's outpouring of mercy and forgiveness.

When we as Chinese Americans, no matter how rich or poor, can see ourselves as desperate and needy recipients of God's welfare, then we, too, can revel in the unconditional love that encounters us at the cross. Instead of feeling obligated to ask for cleansing, we can freely give God thanks for forgiving us. Then joy over God's company will overwhlem us as we accept the invitation to dine in the presence of a holy and merciful God.

The Lord's Supper provides a foretaste of the final banquet, where in a matchless display of grace and generosity, God will bring people from every tribe and nation to the Table. Even now, as Chinese Americans let go of our ethnic pride and venture beyond our own tradition, we will taste and see a God who is far larger than we anticipated. Exploring God from the vantage point of different denominations, different ethnic backgrounds, and different parts of the world, we will see that

God's self-offering is not to one people but to all the peoples of the world. Thus, in the fullness of Christ's body, we will gain the boldest, sharpest, and most nuanced picture of God. Around the Table, we will experience the culmination of God's saving work—a holy God extending mercy to *all* who believe.

Our God Is Also Merciful

In Hebrew and Greek several different words communicate the single word translated "mercy" in English. In the Hebrew Bible, *hesed*[26] denotes covenantal love; *rāham,*[27] the compassion of a father or mother; and *hānan,*[28] the unearned favor of a superior. The Greek New Testament employs words, such as *eleos,*[29] compassion and relief shown to the sick or desperate; *oiktirmos,*[30] pity we receive and extend; and *splagchnon,*[31] earnest heartfelt love. This family of words describes what we in English commonly construe as "mercy," "compassion to one in need or helpless distress, or in debt and without claim to favorable treatment."[32] To depict God's mercy in action, I will trace the saga of the beneficiaries of God's mercy in Scripture. (For a more thorough treatment of the Hebrew and Greek words rendered "mercy" in English, see chapter 2, the subheading entitled "God Is Compassionate.")

Wherever God and human misery intersect, God's mercy is present. As a consequence of the fall, Adam and Eve are shamefully aware of their sin and nakedness. God responds by providing them with clothes made from the skin of animals, presumably from the first sacrifice (Gen. 3:21). Cain murders. God marks him with mercy, so that no one in turn will kill him. Pharaoh decrees the slaughter of all Hebrew boys under the age of two. God saves Moses. The Israelites languish in slavery for four hundred years. God frees them. Jericho was in God's direct line of attack (Josh. 2:1–21). God preserves Rahab and her family (Josh. 6:22–25). Naomi loses her husband and sons. God gives her Ruth, who is better than many sons. David, inflamed by passion, commits adultery and kills a man. God forgives him and never removes him or Solomon, his son by Bathsheba, from the throne. Judah endures exile. God promises resettlement (Isa. 14:1). Although exiled Ephraim repeatedly rejects God and goes astray, God cannot forget this rebellious son (Jer. 31:20). In so many ways God is saying to a people who are not a people, "You are my people!" (Hos. 2:23).

In the New Testament, the stories are legion of Jesus extending mercy to the hungry (Mark 6:40–42), the thirsty (John 4:13–14), the barren (Luke 1:7, 57–58), the blind (Matt. 9:27), the paralyzed (Mark 2:3–5), the leper (Luke 17:12–13), the demon-possessed (Luke 11:14), and the bereaved (John 11:32–33, 43–44). Instead of leaving people on the sidelines and without hope, Jesus mercifully meets them at their point of need.

The common bond between recipients of mercy in both Testaments and in our society today is *our need*. No group can boast in the sight of God that they are self-sufficient. No one earns God's kindness or the right to be forgiven. For God says, "I will have mercy on whom I have mercy" (Rom. 9:15).

Jesus' story about the unforgiving servant (Matt. 18:23–35) explodes any presumption on our part of laying claim to God's largeness of heart. A certain king forgives his servant an astronomical debt. The same servant, then, refuses to cancel the relatively insignificant debt of another servant. Outraged, the king throws the merciless servant in jail. The parable pointedly shows that our response to other people's pleas for mercy reveals the depth to which we understand mercy. Only those who acknowledge their bankruptcy and ongoing debt to God can respond mercifully.

What the Pharisees as a group lacked was an awareness of their own need for God's mercy. To those who perceive themselves as well, Jesus responds that he has not come to heal *them* but the sick. Jesus challenges the Pharisees, who appeared pious and generous, "I desire mercy, not sacrifice" (Matt. 9:13). Jesus assures his hearers that no mint, dill, or cummin carried as sweet a fragrance as those who abide by God's judgment and mercy (Matt. 23:23). Jesus was not introducing a new concept to the Jews but restating the prophets, who called God's people "to act justly and to love mercy and to walk humbly with your God" (Micah 6:8 NIV).

In the sermon on the plain, Jesus instructs his audience "to be merciful, just as your Father is merciful" (Luke 6:36). The parable of Lazarus and the rich man makes the same point by illustrating the stark consequences of ignoring God's command. James states in slightly different language, but no less vividly, "Judgment will be without mercy to anyone who has shown no mercy" (James 2:13).

Why does God exhibit mercy to us? Paul elaborates in 2 Corinthians 1:3–4:

The Father of mercies and the God of all consolation . . . consoles us in all our affliction, so that we may be able to console those who are in any affliction with the consolation with which we ourselves are consoled by God.

God desires to transform those of us who acknowledge that we are recipients of God's mercy into conduits through which God's mercy can flow to others. The same progression of mercy occurs in the unfolding of the salvation drama. God's mercy first came to the Jews, and through the Jews to the Gentiles. Now having shown mercy to the Gentiles, God wants to show mercy to the Jews through the Gentiles (Rom. 11:30–31). The divine pattern repeats itself. God extends mercy to us in order for us to extend mercy to others.

Jesus Christ unveils God's greatest act of mercy. In the incarnation, crucifixion, and resurrection of Christ, we see the powerful marriage of God's holiness and mercy. Not sparing his own Son, God freely sacrificed him to save us from our sin. Every act of mercy on our part is based on this decisive and prior act of mercy on God's part: "God, who is rich in mercy, out of the great love with which he loved us even when we were dead through our trespasses, made us alive together with Christ" (Eph. 2:4–5). The marvelous part of the continuing story of redemption is God's insistence on using human vessels to convey a gift as precious as mercy.

Emphasizing Our Need of Mercy

We in the Chinese American church need to remind ourselves that our innate disobedience, not our ability to uphold the law, cries out for God's mercy.

In contrast to the Confucian educational system and social hierarchy, God introduces the church to the concept of mercy and radically alters the terms of acceptance in the community of faith. We belong, not because of what we have done, but because of what Christ has done for us. The church is constituted by those who have failed and received mercy. Recalling God's words to Israel, Peter proclaims, "Once you were not a people, but now you are God's people; once you had not received mercy, but now you have received mercy" (1 Peter 2:10). Peter was addressing Christians scattered throughout Asia Minor. Might a parallel be drawn between the exiles of the first century and the Chinese in diaspora today?

In search of an identity, Chinese Americans straddle two worlds: the one dominated by Confucian ethics, parental privilege, tradition, and reverence for the old, and the other dominated by American efficiency, independence, originality, and awe for the new. Both cultures stress the importance of self-reliance. The gospel challenges Chinese Americans to learn dependence on God and on others. We need to encourage one another to admit our needs, not only to family members, but to our brothers and sisters in Christ. To promote an atmosphere conducive to self-disclosure requires havens where trust and acceptance abound.

Recently I have been impressed by newsletters that I have received from Chinese American campus ministers. Their letters have revealed deeply personal chapters of their lives, including the forgiveness extended to a father and the words "I love you" spoken to a sick brother. While such disclosures may not be shocking to many readers, they are almost unheard of in traditional Chinese culture. A person would never share a lack in one's family with people outside of the family, and verbal affirmations of love are, on the whole, rare. Publicly expressing desire, need, failure, or affection is considered shameful.

Fearing loss of face makes an honest admission of need extraordinarily difficult, if not impossible. The alternative, much of the time, is to live a lie.

The concern with loss of face affects daily rituals, such as gift giving. Some of us Chinese Americans treat others generously, even beyond our means, in an effort to avoid embarrassment. Instead of seeing a gift as a free expression of another person's affection or appreciation, without any strings attached, we often construe a gift as something that must be reciprocated. To appear at a person's house empty-handed would be rude; to receive handouts from the government, unthinkable. Many Chinese Americans still feel that accepting anything unearned is to concede defeat. We could not make it on our own, so someone else had to help us.

In such a milieu, is it any wonder that Chinese Americans have difficulty understanding God's mercy and unconditional love? The precondition for obtaining mercy is admitting one's need, but in a Confucian-based culture, the public admission of need is taboo. The question is: When some of us finally muster enough courage to admit our need, what will the response of the Chinese American church be? For some of us the admission will not be nearly as dramatic as the profligate son's. For others it will be even more scandalous, because so much more was expected of us. But in either case, will our brothers and sisters rejoice over our repentance or will they shun us as a shame to the family?

Mercy as a Corrective to Our Lack of Joy

The beauty of mercy lies in its liberating power. A personal encounter with God's mercy can unleash our gratitude and release us from shame. No longer shackled by the opinions of others, we are free to share our experiences of God's mercy and to rejoice.

Irene Eng, a campus minister, recounted how God's mercy touched her anew while studying the story of the prodigal son:

> What I've come to realize is that the party our Father throws for us is so outrageously extravagant, lavish and rich, that there is no limit to the generosity he wants to show us. The celebration is so undeserved that it is ludicrous for us to think that we have earned it, or have done something to merit it, or can pay him back for his gifts. The party is a picture of our Father's mercy on us who have run away from home.

The choice, as she puts it, is:

> to continue in my works-oriented relationship with the Father, insisting that I've been the dutiful son and deserve better. . . . Or . . . realize that I don't really know the wild generosity and love of the Father and begin to enter into his joy.[33]

I am convinced that the same choice confronts all of us Chinese American Christians.

Perhaps, for Chinese Americans the place in which one can most freely experience God's mercy is outside the confines of the church building or the formal area designated for worship. We may feel freer to be ourselves in cars, restaurants, and our own living rooms. Personally, I have enjoyed fellowshipping with friends over food and praying with people on the telephone. By enlarging our sense of where we can do "business" with God, we expand the parameters of our experience of divine mercy and omnipresence.

Wherever the place, we have the responsibility of creating a safe place where people feel free to express their need for God and their joy over the ways God fills their need.

As church leaders, we need to model vulnerability by sharing our defeats as well as our victories. Recently, I have witnessed mercy entering the Chinese American pulpit more. I have watched ministers become agents of mercy to their congregations as they have shared intimate scenes from their personal lives. I recall vividly one Sunday when a guest speaker dynamically deconstructed the superman image most of us carry around about what a good Christian should be. He candidly confessed to the congregation instances of his own competitiveness, workaholism, and insecurity. These personal vignettes not only spoke powerfully to those of us who were listening, but made it far easier to believe in God's mercy, for we know that the preacher had already received the mercy he was describing.

A team approach to ministry can also heighten our awareness of God's mercy. A commitment to mutual accountability in the form of discipleship and partnership in prayer can promote the sense of trust needed for deep sharing. In addition, those of us who are called to be teachers and preachers need to encourage our people to seek Christian counseling and work at removing the traditional stigma associated with receiving such professional help. With all the academic and social pressures that our youth are facing, we need to assist our youth in finding constructive ways to deal with identity issues and other concerns.[34]

Most Chinese American churches provide opportunities outside the weekly worship service to share face to face. Once again, location can play a role in setting the tone. When fellowships meet at a member's home, where people can dress as they please and are free to linger, people feel freer to say how they are *really* doing.

A more relaxed atmosphere encourages people to share needs and to receive and to extend mercy. Laughter, smiles, tears, and applause also arise more spontaneously, contributing to honest and joyful sharing. Even when gatherings occur in a church building, there are ways to make the setting more conducive to genuine sharing. Icebreakers, small groups, and food, for example, can help people to bond.

A small group can be an ideal setting for cultivating deep and meaningful relationships. Discussions, activities, prayer, and Bible study can happen at a more intimate level. Individual personalities, backgrounds, and preferences can also be more easily accommodated. As nurture, care, and accountability arise, trust builds. And where the level of trust is high, mercy flourishes. Friends, after all, are far more willing to give and take than are mere acquaintances.

Mercy as a Corrective to Self-Righteousness and Social Apathy

Jesus provided mercy as an antidote to the self-righteousness of the religious leaders of his day. Similarly, we as Chinese American Christians can benefit by learning how to grow in mercy. Like the church James was addressing, we need to beware of showing favoritism to the "rich" (James 2:1–7). When considering leaders in the church, our roster of names should not consist exclusively of doctors and wealthy entrepreneurs. In fact, mercy will prod us to consider those who love God and others, but whose names society consistently overlooks.

Often immigrant families have worked incredibly hard to leave behind their past with its misery and hardships. The move to the suburbs marked their break with poverty and feeling like second-class citizens. As an increasing number of Chinese American churches have emerged in the suburbs, we must ask how we can show mercy to our neighbors, who may or may not be Chinese. Involvement in the local school system, volunteering at the library, working against drugs and violence, and participating in local politics are all ways in which Christians can demonstrate mercy and develop a deeper sense of belonging. For those churches situated in Chinatowns or predominantly Chinese neighborhoods, in addition to the above activities, Christians can serve as translators, English tutors, community organizers, and advocates to press for the needs of Chinese residents.

Fellowships can also prioritize acts of mercy by joining forces with various lobbying groups or serving at local soup kitchens, nursing homes, and prisons. Rubbing shoulders with others who acknowledge their need can remind us of our own need. By placing ourselves at the service of other people, we are asking for opportunities to be shown mercy and to show it, situations that lend themselves to true joy.

Furthermore, challenging the Chinese American church to exercise mercy could lead to a major readjustment of priorities. Instead of allowing a certain comfort level (such as having two cars and a home) to dictate our lifestyle, we may opt for a simpler life and use the money we save to invest in more worthy causes. Some Christians may actually decide to relocate to urban centers where there is a larger concentration of Chinese and other ethnic minorities. Others may seek employment that directly benefits the poor and the disenfranchised, such as teaching English as a second language, social work, immigration law, and politics. Demonstrating mercy in these concrete and tangible ways will point people to a God who genuinely cares for them in their particular situation. Keeping in touch with our Chinese American immigrant roots can also remind us of our humble beginnings and the tremendous mercies that God has poured out on us in the past and continues to lavish on us in the present.

Our Holy and Merciful God

Incredibly, the Bible presents a holy God who descends from heaven's lofty heights to cross the divide between the divine and the human. In the incarnation God becomes like us and lives among us (John 1:14). But God's intention does not stop there. God wants nothing less than for us to be like God. Although the idea of union with God may seem presumptuous, Christ prays that we may be one in God, God dwelling in us and we in God (John 17:20–23). To unite what was unholy with what is holy requires a divine sacrifice. Nothing short of God's mercy, extended to us on the cross, can reconcile us to God.

Similarly, under the former covenant God's condemnation of sin met God's desire for reconciliation in the Holy of Holies. Located between the cherubim and above the mercy seat (Exod. 25:20–22), God's presence filled the tabernacle, as God accepted the sweet-smelling sacrifices of a repentant people.

God's Spirit convicts us in order to restore us to intimacy with God and others, not to make us feel small or unloved. When we confront and confess our sinfulness, God does not berate us or shame us. God prepares a feast and rejoices over us. Reconciliation and union with our holy God are at the very heart of God's mercy.

On the final day, we will be free at last to sit down at the table and share in the divine banquet, not a symbolic meal with wine and bread, but a full ten-course banquet with as much food as we want and the company of the whole family. We will celebrate with the Lord and break out in *je nao*—with excitement, laughter, and loud voices characteristic of Chinese parties and family gatherings. We will also bow and worship God in silence and awe, kneeling as our ancestors who once prostrated themselves before family shrines. No longer caught between two worlds or cultures, we will finally be at home with our holy and merciful God.

As we have seen, the emphasis on holiness explored in this chapter comes from roots based both in the Bible, and as well in general revelation about God handed down in Chinese traditional religion. The next chapter explores these roots, particularly as exemplified in the descriptive names used for God in Chinese tradition.

Nine

Shang-di:
God from the Chinese Perspective

Tsu-Kung Chuang

Tsu-Kung Chuang, a Chinese born in Taiwan, is the Senior Pastor of Chinese Bible Church of Greater Boston in Lexington, Massachusetts. For the past several years, he is a popular evangelistic speaker among Chinese intellectuals. Before his call to full-time pastoral ministry in 1990, he already served fifteen years in chemical industry and a national research institute in Taiwan. He is a graduate of Northwestern University (Ph.D. in Chemical Engineering, 1983) and Trinity Evangelical Divinity School (Ph.D. in Intercultural Studies, 1995). Other than numerous articles, Chuang has written several books: *Ripening Harvest: Mission Strategy for Mainland Chinese Intellectuals in North America* (AFC, 1995) and *Interaction and Transformation: Christianity and The Way of Renewal of Chinese Culture* (in Chinese, CCI, 1997).

Chinese religion is unique. This is partly due to the fact that alone among the great religions of humanity, Chinese religion first developed in isolation, without the influence of the other great world religions. Confucianism and Taoism, two of the three faiths of China, developed their distinctive forms before there was any significant contact with the rest of the world.

An inquiry into the nature of religion in the Chinese context quickly reveals a fundamental working premise, namely, the belief that a continuity exists between the supernatural and the natural. The Chinese do not posit a radical distinction between the secular and the sacred nor do the Chinese seek to unfold the nature of Ultimate Reality by which all things exist. Rather, the Chinese view the world and the existence of all things after the "paradigm of life"—life which produces all things, permeates all things, and upholds all things.

The Swiss theologian Hans Küng describes the Chinese religions, which arose especially in the Yellow River basin, as a "river system" which set great value on a wisdom tradition.[1] However, Julia Ching prefers to call them "religions of harmony" because of the known Chinese effort in directing attention to harmony between the human and the cosmic, as well as harmony within society and within the self.[2] But the mention of the word "harmony" brings to mind certain arguments regarding whether Chinese civilization ever possessed a dimension of transcendence.

Frequently, the term "transcendence" is applied to Western religions like Christianity because of the centrality of the belief in God as the Other, and the clearness of a separation between this life and this world and the life beyond. In contrast, the Chinese tradition with its humanism appears to offer a clear alternative of immanence or of harmonizing oneself with nature or with others rather than worshiping the divine or wrestling with the question of the divine. But is this allegation accurate? Is the reality that simple?

First, we need to know that mainstream Chinese humanism has a certain openness to the transcendent, even if humanists themselves might be theists or atheists or agnostics.[3] Second, the idea of God, however different that is from the Christian Creator, was present from the very beginning of Chinese civilization until our own times, even if this idea has undergone evolution and transformation.

Therefore, in this chapter I am going to review the concept of God in ancient China, in the Confucian worldview, and in contemporary Chinese folk religion. I shall demonstrate that even as this has moved intellectually from a more personal understanding to a more transpersonal one, a practical and devotional theism has persisted in popular religious consciousness. Through some contemporary illustrations, I will demonstrate what is missing in understanding God (God as creator and God as transcendent) in the Chinese culture. Finally, I will conclude by reflecting on the missiological implications for the Chinese context of these ideas.

The Concept of God in Ancient China

The universe of the ancient Chinese was naturalistic, in the sense that it was characterized by the regularity which Western philosophy has called "law"—but it lacked the Western assumption of an outside "lawgiver."[4] Nevertheless, although the universe thus functions through the workings of "law without a lawgiver," the thinking of the ancient Chinese includes at the same time a personalized power of conspicuous importance.

Names of the Supreme God: Shang-di *and* Tian

At the dawn of Chinese history, two names of the most supreme deity, *Shang-di* and *Tian*, vied for prominence in China. The first, *Shang-di* (translated as "Lord-on-High"), was the supreme deity of the Shang dynasty (1766–ca. 1123 B.C.). *Shang-di* was a personal deity, associated with the ancestral cult, and in all probability represented the supreme ancestor of the royal family, capable of giving and protecting life and venerated above all deities.

However, *Shang-di* seems far from being the Almighty God of Western religions, for he had no clearly defined character and sent down no messages preserved in scriptures.[5] Rather, divination was necessary in order to know what he wanted or would tolerate. We still have the records of these divinations, the famous "oracle bones." The diviner, at the request of the king, would scrape thin some spot on a tortoise shell or piece of bone, position it above a flame, and read the cracks that appeared.

In the Chou dynasty (1122–256 B.C.), another name appeared and alternated with *Shang-di.* It was the word *Tian* (translated as "Heaven"). The conquest of Shang by Chou might lead to the subsequent usage of both *Shang-di* and *Tian* to designate the Supreme Deity, regarded as a personal God.[6] While the word *Tian* may refer to (1) the physical sky, or (2) the natural rhythmic movement of nature, or (3) *Tian's* ruling and presiding over all cosmic movement, and hence (4) to the fatalistic *Tian*—Heaven's unchangeable Ways (will), *Tian's* dominant use in Chinese religious literature was as (5) an ethical model of goodness.

Therefore, even though all the above meanings contributed to the conception of *Tian* as a supreme deity, *Tian* ultimately became a symbol for the universal, and inherently good, principle of creativity constantly functioning in the background as the source and origin of all things, permeating all things and unifying all things into a harmonious whole.

The Chou and subsequent emperors, because of their reputed close relation to Heaven, bore the title "*Tian Zi*" or "Heaven's Son." They worshiped *Tian* in the people's behalf at regular annual ceremonies. Every year at the time of the spring equinox (late January or early February in China), the emperor stood in the presence of *Tian* to report what had happened in his realm the previous year. As he presented his sacrificial offerings of grain or a bullock, he petitioned Heaven to continue good weather and crops and the well-being of his people. If things had been going badly, the emperor went before *Tian* with great anxiety because bad crops, famine, defeat in battle, or a plague meant that something was wrong and the emperor himself was responsible. He would then implore *Tian* to end such bad times and continue him and his dynasty in power.

Without this ceremony and its attendant appeals to the imperial ancestors, the people felt that the harmony between Earth and Heaven would be disrupted. *Tian*, as the regnant power among the supernatural forces of the world, and as the ultimate determiner of human affairs, dominated the entire course of Chinese religion down to the twentieth century, and the head of government (in classical times the emperor) has had a central role, especially ritually, in maintaining favorable relations between Heaven and Earth.

Reflection on the Duality of Names of the Supreme Deity

Julia Ching notes[7] that the presence of these two names for the Chinese supreme god (*Shang-di* and *Tian*) reminds us of the Old Testament, where there were also two different names for God. The first was *Yahweh,* which was explained to Moses in the burning bush as "I am who I am" or "I shall be what I shall be" according to more literal exegetes (Exod. 3:14). The other name was *Elohim,* a plural but used with the singular verb, meaning "God" or "Godhead" (Gen. 1:26).

The late Umberto Cassuto suggests that since in Genesis 1 the emphasis is on creation via the majestic God who speaks and it is done, thus the more generic name for God, *Elohim,* fits this emphasis admirably.[8] By contrast, the emphasis in Genesis 2:4–25 is more personal. The context here is not a universe but a garden. Also, the picture of man here is not of one with authority but of one under authority, a vassal in a covenant relationship. Therefore, *Yahweh* would be the proper designation for the deity at this point.

The emphasis of these two names of God (*Elohim* and *Yahweh*) in the Old Testament is parallel respectively to the two names of God (*Tian* and *Shang-di*) in China. However, in Judeo-Christianity, both terms had personal connotations, whereas, in the Chinese case, the term *Tian* would later take on pantheistic tones.[9]

Moreover, *Shang-di* or *Tian* is pictured in the ancient texts as being concerned with the actions of human beings, and as the source of the "mandate" from which the ruling dynasty received its legitimacy. But the ancient texts gave no hint that either was the creator of the universe or the cause of its functioning. It is only later, when the depersonalized *Tian* becomes the highest in a trinity of Heaven, Earth, and Human, that we might ascribe a God-like power to the Supreme Ruler. And yet even this Heaven of later times is not the Ultimate or the Absolute.

The Concept of God in Confucianism

The Latinized name, "Confucianism," is a Western invention which has come down from the seventeenth-century Jesuit missionaries. Confucianism is best known for its moral philosophy, propounded by Confucius (551–479 B.C.), Mencius (371–289 B.C.), and Hsun-tzu (298–238 B.C.). It is clearly grounded in the inherited religion of the *Tian*.

But for several hundred years after the master's death, no Confucian anywhere came to power long enough to make permanent changes in the official outlook on problems of government. However, the Emperor Wu Di of the Han Dynasty (who reigned 141 87 B.C.) put Confucians in charge of a government-sponsored system of education designed to train officials. Thereupon Confucianism became the dominant worldview among the intellectuals. Here we are using the term "Confucianism" broadly to include not merely the master's original teachings, but also those teachings of later disciples that became integrated into the school of Confucius or the doctrinal and ritual system called Confucianism.

The Teachings of Three Founding Fathers of Confucianism

Confucius stands as a prophet, giving an ethical teaching grounded in religious consciousness.[10] The basis of his teaching was the concept of humanity *(jen)*. But whereas most of Confucius's teachings stress the ethical dimension of humanity, he made it clear that it was *Tian* itself which protected him and gave him his message.

However, his attitude in religion was critical and discriminating, even marked by an evident restraint, for he was rationalistic and decidedly humanistic in his outlook. In his teaching he avoided discussing such subjects as prodigies, feats of strength, crime, and the supernatural, apparently because he did not wish to spend time discussing perturbing exceptions to human and natural law. He suggested to his disciples that "to devote oneself earnestly to one's duty to humanity, and, while respecting the spirits, to keep aloof from them, may be called wisdom" *(Analects of Confucius, VI.20)*.

Mencius projected the image of a teacher of mysticism.[11] He proclaimed an inner doctrine, alluding to the presence within the heart of something greater than itself. He attempted to show how the very essence of the Way of Heaven, the divine power of the cosmos, became human nature. He felt that if this human nature could be correctly cultivated and nurtured, even the common person could become a sage.

Mencius believed, like Confucius, in a guiding will or appointment of *Tian*. *Tian* sees and hears, and has an appointment for everything. *Tian* is that which creates the inner disposition. Mencius said:

> What belongs by his nature to the superior man cannot be increased by the largeness of his sphere of action, nor diminished by his dwelling in poverty and retirement;—for this reason, that it is determinately apportioned to him by *Tian*.[12]

Those who exercise their minds to the utmost and study their own natures know Heaven and Heaven's will. To look with sincerity into this inner disposition is to know *Tian* through it. For Mencius, it is thus that we may fulfill our destiny as *Tian* prepares it for us.

The third of the founding fathers of Confucianism, Hsun-tzu, is best remembered for his doctrine of ritual action *(li)*. He provides the practical side of Confucian religion. His genius was to demonstrate the power of correct ritual action needed to transform the normal mind, which is prone to err, into the mind of a sage.

However, his attitude toward *Tian* leaned far over in the direction of the Taoists' impersonal, naturalistic Way *(Tao)*. *Tian* is not to be anthropomorphically viewed, for it is just our name for the law of compensation operating within cosmic events, and one cannot ever expect it to respond to prayer.[13] All natural events, then, come to pass according to natural law. There are no supernatural agencies anywhere. So sure was Hsun-tzu of this that he took the radical step of denying the existence of spirits and deities.

Therefore, in the course of time, the meaning of the word *Tian* became ambiguous, shifting from the early reference to a supreme deity (Confucius), to a vacillation between that and moral force (Mencius), to the universe itself (Hsun-tzu).[14]

Tian in Neo-Confucianism

Confucian mysticism, especially in its second great phase, neo-Confucianism, leans more and more in the direction of pantheism. This is borne out by the later philosophers, Chang Tsai (1020–77), Chu Hsi (1130–1200) and Wang Yang-ming (1472–1529). In them Confucian religion and mysticism show the imprint of Taoist and Buddhist influences.

Those neo-Confucians started from a desire to reform the Confucianism of their day, and then sought to give practical guidance for the perfection of the mind. In actual fact, they all were primarily concerned with the task of achieving sagehood. Chu Hsi believed we must go through a long and arduous process of self-cultivation and ethical activity in order to reach sage.[15] Wang Yang-ming, on the other hand, agreed on the goal of sagehood, but rejected Chu Hsi's gradualist method. For Wang, only the "enlightenment experience" of the absolute unity of our minds with the mind of the Way would suffice to achieve sagehood.

Moreover, though Chu Hsi had gone pretty far toward rendering the older terminology no longer usable, he tried to make some concessions to the ancient conception of *Tian*. He refused to be anthropomorphic and, indeed, spoke of *Tian* in such abstract language that he encouraged the agnostic tendency in Confucianism.[16] But because his Great Ultimate is a rational principle, he sensed behind the cosmos something like an ordering will. In other respects he gave religion in its traditional forms little place. He denied that the souls of ancestors exist. Ancestor worship has the appropriateness and value that are derived from gratitude to forebears, piously felt and expressed.

In his personal practice, Chu Hsi found his spiritual and moral development best served by devoting a certain portion of each day to solitary meditation, which resembled the Buddhist *dhyana* or meditation.

But for Chu Hsi, the meditation had more a moral than a metaphysical or mystical bearing. Feeling that centrality is the order of the universe and harmony is its unalterable law, he wished "to get himself into the equable state that enabled him to apprehend this order and harmony and to feel at one with reason in it."[17] He has been called the Thomas Aquinas of Confucianism.

Therefore, after the Chou dynasty, the religious aspect was gradually taken out of the concept of *Tian*. This has become the "Major Tradition" among the Confucian intellectuals. The religious aspect of the spiritual world, however, through the influences of Taoism and Buddhism, was preserved among the common people and became the "Minor Tradition" in Chinese folk religions.

The Concept of God in Chinese Folk Religion

Folk religion refers to that body of beliefs and practices held by the common Chinese person in distinction from the educated and noble classes. Underlying this body of religious practices is a predominantly animistic perception of the world. By animism in the Chinese context is meant the belief that gods and spirits are capable of exerting good or evil influence on present situations and natural phenomena. While early animistic practices included the worship of sacred trees, mountains, and places, modern practice centers primarily on the relationship of living persons and the spirit world.

In general, the characteristic of Chinese folk religions is the mixture of Buddhism and "religious Taoism" that both began in the latter half of the Han dynasty (about A.D. 200).[18] Philosophical Taoism is reputed to have been founded by Lao-tzu and Chuang-tzu. Little is known about their lives, if indeed they ever existed. Adherents accepted the alternations of *yin* and *yang*, life and death, being and nonbeing, thus attaining present harmony with the underlying Way-of-Things. Religious Taoists, on the other hand, sought, in addition to health and long life, personal and individual immortality.[19] They revived belief in personal deities, practicing a ritual of prayer and appeasement.

Deification of Humans in Folk Religion

Regardless of the origin or significance of the deities in the Chinese folk religion, they are nearly all humanized. One reason for the numerical abundance of these deities stems from the belief that any person who exhibits the power of *ling* (meaning "spirit" or "spiritual power") may bcome deified. Therefore, these numerous deities are in most cases nothing more than deified humans whose prominence lies in their ability to act on behalf of living persons.

Some of the complexity and scope of folk religion can be seen in a survey which C.K. Yang made of temples in five provinces in different parts of China about 1949.[20] Only in two communities did he find a sizable number of Buddhist and Taoist temples. In six other communities he found Buddhist and Taoist temples greatly outnumbered by temples to other gods. And there were at least 298 gods, or 26.2 percent, with a historical background among a total of 1,138 gods.

However, not all deities were historical persons. Many were originally merely personifications of natural phenomena such as wind, rain, rivers, mountains, and stars, while many were legendary figures. Still others have been fabricated out of whole cloth and may be called fictitious, such as certain characters in a novel of the Ming dynasty (A.D. 1368–1644), called *The Canonization of the Gods.* Some are survivals of ancient nature worship, some are Taoist masters who attained immortality and the ability to work magic, some are Indian Buddhist importations or Chinese Buddhist creations, and some are famous statesmen or generals or just and merciful magistrates, some are men or women of the people who manifested strange, miraculous powers.

Once an individual achieves the status of a deity, a shrine is normally built so that prayers may be offered to the spirit of this person. Rumors might have spread and credibility might have been established through confirmation that the spirit responds to prayers. From then on the growth or decline of the cult results from the god's efficacy. This means that the death of the gods is also commonplace. When public confidence in the power of a deity has waned, he or she will be neglected and eventually forgotten.

As this discussion of deities indicates, the Chinese people express continuing devotion to Taoist deities as well as to various other gods and immortals. For most people, Buddhas and Bodhisattvas[21] function as deities, so they may be added to the pantheon of possibilities. Their specialization in power, rather than origins or titles, sets the deities off as individuals. They are not personifications of abstract virtues or passions or activities like Greek gods, but rather more like human officials who have the power to grant or withhold favors within the limits of their own jurisdiction.

Therefore, these gods of the Chinese folk religion are hardly more than human beings deified, possessed of mysterious and supernatural powers, of course, and yet far closer to humans than to God. Western Christians may beseech God to grant personal favors, and yet they like to think that they approach God fundamentally in a spirit of pure, disinterested worship, while the Chinese attitude before their deities seems in contrast so selfish, so devoid of the rapture of adoration. One is tempted to put it into an aphorism: Western Christians worship God as almighty because God made human beings; the Chinese demand service from their gods because human beings made the gods.[22]

Bureaucratic Heavenly Structure in Chinese Folk Religion

Nevertheless, the most striking characteristic of Chinese folk religion is that the divine world is but a recreation of the earthly bureaucracy on a heavenly scale. Chinese folk religion involves a number of gods, spirits, and heavenly beings, with a supreme God (*Yu-Huang-Da-Di*, or "Jade Emperor") standing above this spiritual host. Each god (e.g., City God) has his or her own domain of ruling which depends upon his or her ranking in heaven. The spirits (good or evil, *shen* or *gui* respectively) are lower than gods.

In the past two thousand years, the Chinese emperor had the power to appoint great historical personalities as folk gods. Thus gods of a historical nature played an intermediate role in the process of interactive integration between religion and politics in traditional Chinese society.

Therefore, from the sociological perspective, the Chinese concept of "social mobility" involves the following three interrelated status changes: (1) mobility within the human society, (2) mobility in the supernatural world, and (3) intermobility between human society and the supernatural world.[23] Mobility within human society gives people hope for life improvement. Mobility between human society and the supernatural world provides a great incentive for a long-term earthly achievement, which does not end with the death of the person.

Tian-shang Sheng-mu: Folk Religion in Taiwan

To illustrate some of the generalities expressed thus far we shall describe one of the major deities of the folk religion in present-day

Taiwan. *Tian-shang Sheng-mu,* Holy Mother in Heaven, is the most popular deity in Taiwan. She provides a classic example of the process by which "people become gods every day in China." The beginnings of the cult are obscure, but the generally accepted story is that she was born in the year the Sung dynasty was founded (A.D. 960) on the island of Meichou just off the coast of the Fukien province. Her birth was attended by auspicious portents. She was an exceptionally pious girl, and at the age of thirteen she met a Taoist master who presented her with certain charms and other secret lore. When she was sixteen she manifested her magical power by saving the lives of her father and elder brother, whose boat had capsized. Other tales of her supernatural intervention were told by grateful recipients of her mercies. When she died, still a young girl, a temple was erected in her community, seeking to attract her continuing favors.

As decades and then centuries passed, stories of miracles wrought by the goddess accumulated up and down the southeastern seaboard, and she became a familiar guardian spirit, particularly among seafarers. By mid-twelfth century the Imperial Court itself had learned of her reputation for spiritual power, and gave her official recognition as a deity of national importance. This meant that the state incorporated her worship in the schedule of sacrifices to be performed by the bureaucracy throughout the land.

The cult continued to grow until the goddess became one of the major deities of southeastern China and the most important deity of sailors, fishermen, and all who must hazard their lives upon the waters. She received high titles by imperial decree. For example, in 1409 she was called "Imperial Concubine of Heaven" who protects the country and shelters the people, looks after those who call on her with mysterious spirit, and saves universally by her great kindness. This imposing title was elevated by the K'ang Hsi Emperor in 1683 to "Consort of Heaven." To the people, however, she is more familiarly known as *Matsu,* a Taiwanese word for "grandma."

Chinese religion, at its best, highlights God's wisdom and holiness. As Christians we are reminded that the God in whom we believe is allwise and wants beliefs reflected in our way of life, ethics, morality, and wisdom. Humans need to be in harmony with God's will and with other people. However, the Chinese zeal for wisdom can be accentuated even further if God is also seen as a Creator who is transcendent.

The Creator God: The Missing Aspect of God in the Chinese Context

A distinct feature of Chinese cosmology is the absence of a well-accepted creation myth. Most of the educated Chinese simply regard the world as constituting a spontaneous, self-generating cosmos, having neither Creator nor Ultimate Cause external to itself. Some scholars, however, have argued that the *Pan-gu* legend is a distinct Chinese creation myth. According to this myth, a cosmic man, called *Pan-gu,* who grew ten feet a day, appeared when the world was still in chaos. During a period of eighteen thousand years, when the *Yang* or lighter elements of the chaos separated themselves and rose above the *Yin* or heavier elements, *Pan-gu* hewed out places in the heavens for the sun, moon, and stars, dug out the valleys on the surface of the earth, piled high the mountains, and finally enriched the scene of his labors by his own self-distribution.[24]

While the *Pan-gu* myth has been popular among the common people, Chinese intellectuals generally have ignored the myth as folklore, contending that the myth originally was an obscure tale in early China (perhaps owing something to an Indian source) and inadequate for undergirding a metaphysical theory.

Contemporary Chinese Attitudes toward God

Since Chinese people lack an accepted doctrine of creation, they postulated other origins for the universe. Atheism, pantheism, and agnosticism are the most popular alternatives among the contemporary Chinese people.

Atheism, which denies the existence of God, must either make matter eternal or find some other natural cause. It argues that every occurrence in the universe is due to the operation of the laws of nature. Humans' happiness and chances of success are thus dependent upon human knowledge of and cooperation with these laws. While the Scriptures recognize the existence of the laws of nature, they do not teach that they operate completely independently. They represent nature as neither self-directing nor self-sustaining. God concurs in all the operations of these laws, both of matter and of mind, and sometimes acts entirely independent of them. In this way the miracles of the incarnation and resurrection of Christ can be explained.

Pantheism, which posits that all reality is in essence divine, makes creation a part of God and has no real doctrine of providence. Since pantheists are obliged to make the governing cause also the author of sin, they destroy all possibility of true morality. Humans, being a part of this pantheistic god, cannot help sinning. Also, pantheists deny human freedom. Being part of this world system, human beings, too, act from necessity. From the Chinese perspective, even the deities can be bribed to do good for human beings. Therefore, the rise of folk religions in contemporary Taiwanese society has caused moral bankruptcy.

Finally, agnosticism says no one can know about God or his creation. This view may lead to fatalism, especially through the influence of Buddhism in China. Fatalism is to be distinguished from determinism. The former holds that all events are determined by fate or deeds in the pre-life of reincarnation, instead of by natural causes, and that nothing a person can will or do affects the course of events. Determinism, on the other hand, holds that events take place of necessity, but that they are made necessary by events immediately preceding, to which they stand in a relation of cause and effect. The fatalist may speak of the decreeing power as God, but it is certainly not the God of the Bible. The chief objection to fatalism is that it makes the originating cause arbitrary and nonmoral, and usually impersonal.[25]

The Significance of God as the Creator

The Christian view, however, affirms that God has not merely created the universe, together with all its properties and powers, and that he is preserving all that he has created, but that as a holy, benevolent, wise, and omnipotent Being, he also exercises sovereign control over it. Thus, Christianity affirms that creation came through the sovereign will and working of an infinite God, who, though immanent in his creation, also transcends his creation.

The Bible teaches more than the mere fact that God created the universe out of nothing (Gen.1:1–2). It also teaches that God created human beings in a special, personal way (Gen.1:26–27; 2:7, 21–22). The positive side of the fact that God created the universe and human beings is that this indicates that the universe and human beings have meaning and a purpose, namely, to bring glory to God. For example, Scripture represents humans' original condition by the phrase, "in the *image* and *likeness* of God" (Gen.1:26–27; 5:1; 9:6; 1 Cor. 11:7; James

3:9). But of what did that image and likeness consist? It was not a physical likeness; rather, it was a mental, moral, and social likeness.[26]

In making humans after his own image, God endowed them with those attributes (e.g., reason, conscience, and will) that belong to his own nature as a spirit. Humans are thereby distinguished from all other inhabitants of this world, and raised immeasurably above them. Therefore, Charles Hodge says:

> He (i.e., human being) belongs to the same order of being as God Himself, and is therefore capable of communion with his Maker. This conformity of nature between man and God . . . is also the necessary condition of our religious nature. If we were not like God, we could not know Him. We should be as the beasts which perish.[27]

Therefore, in sanctification a person is "being renewed in knowledge in the image of its Creator" (Col. 3:10 NIV). This likeness to God is inalienable, and since it constitutes human capacity for redemption, it gives value to the life even of the unregenerated (Gen. 9:6; 1 Cor. 11:7; James 3:9).

The image of God is clearly expressed not only in human rational nature, but also in moral conformity. If in regeneration the new person is "created to be like God in true righteousness and holiness" (Eph. 4:24 NIV), we can correctly infer that originally humans had both righteousness and holiness. This original holiness may be defined as "a tendency of man's affection and will, though accompanied by the power of evil choice, in the direction of the spiritual knowledge of God and of divine things generally."[28] It is distinguished from the sanctified holiness of the saints, as instinctive affections and childlike innocence differ from the holiness which has developed and been confirmed by temptation.

Finally, as God has a social nature, so he has endowed humans with a social nature. Consequently, humans seek companionship. In the first place, humans found this fellowship with God. God had made humans for himself, and humans found supreme satisfaction in communion with their Lord. But God also provided human fellowship. He created woman, for he said, "It is not good for the man to be alone. I will make a helper suitable for him" (Gen. 2:18 NIV). To make this a very intimate fellowship, he made the woman out of a bone taken from the man. And because of this intimate relation between the two, "a man will leave his father and mother and be united to his wife, and they will become one flesh" (Gen. 2:24 NIV). Thus, it is evident that humans were made with a social nature, even as God has a social nature. Human love and social interests spring directly from this element in human nature.

Therefore, the conception of the creation and the origin of humans taken literally from Scripture gives humans a dignity of being and a position of responsibility that no other theory (e.g., evolution) does, and lays the foundations for a sane system of ethics and redemption.[29]

The Immanence of God: From the Chinese Perspective

The term often used by Christians to speak of the fact that God is greater than creation and far above it is the word "transcendent." Metaphorically, this means that God is "above" the creation. On the other hand, the term used to speak of God's involvement in creation is the word "immanent," meaning "remaining in" creation.

The religious-philosophical notion behind the Chinese concept of a supreme deity, however, is noticeably different from that of the Christian notion of God. While certain similarities may be drawn, as Julia Ching notes,[30] the Chinese notion of God is that of an "immanent-transcendence" as distinct from the Western notion of "transcendent-transcendence" which emerges as a "being-in-himself," existing outside of time and controlling nature and history from that independent position.

While most Christian theologians might not agree with Julia Ching's allegation that Christians see God as "transcendent-transcendence," the debate is not so much in fundamental disagreement about Chinese religions as it is about the definitions of such terms as immanence and transcendence.[31]

The Characteristics of Chinese Cosmology

Not possessing a well-accepted creation myth, however, should not be taken to indicate that the Chinese lacked a specific and unique cosmology. The Chinese, in fact, possessed a distinct cosmology which conceived of the whole world with its inner structures and all processes of change after the paradigm of life.

The Chinese developed a notion of God within the context of an "immanent-transcendence" which conveys a "mystery of existence" not only in the structure of the universe, but also manifest in all living things.[32] The deity of Heaven, *Tian,* prompted in the heart of the Chinese person, more than any other natural symbol, a sense of awe and wonder toward this "mystery of existence" manifest in all things.

Cheng Chung-ying[33] calls this Chinese paradigm "life-ontology." This "life-ontology" approach enables the Chinese to grasp that "mystery" of existence permeating and sustaining all things. This paradigm, functioning more as an underlying theme rather than a descriptive expression, conveys a vision of existence—a vision of the ceaseless, creative, and transforming principle of internal life-movement. And since reality is more often "experienced" than "described" in Chinese thought, life merely expresses that general metaphysical entity by which all things come to be and are sustained in their being.

Because the Chinese believe that a continuity exists between Ultimate Reality and the human person, religion was perceived in the context of a "Way" *(Tao)* harmonizing these two dimensions and leading to an ideal moral state of existence.[34] Hence, the "Way" is not separated from the "human way." In fact, the human person stands at the center of Chinese thought, possessing the capacity to read the *Tao* and to bring the *Tao* to completion through the development of the moral core within human nature. And the person who actualizes this moral core is called a *ren-ren,* "a person of humanity."

The Chinese assert that humans should look deep within human nature and cultivate these innate moral tendencies. By developing these moral tendencies, humans can bring harmony both to self and to the world. To know and experience Ultimate Reality *(Tian)* merely requires a person to penetrate deeply into his or her own being. This maxim was to become better known in the later traditions, such as in Confucian and Taoist philosophers, to represent less a union between the divine and the human, and more a continuum or a communication between the two orders, moving more and more away from the originally anthropomorphic, to an increasingly pantheistic sense.[35]

Christian Perspective on the Immanence of God

In Christian thought, on the one hand, God is conceived as an absolute transcendent Being, the one and only Creator and Sustainer of all life, living in eternity and ruling the course of history from the beyond. While God is the Source of all things, God remains distinctly separate from all creation. This dichotomy naturally creates a separation between the human person and God.

But, on the other hand, God is also very involved in the creation, and the creation is continually dependent on God for its existence and its functioning. The God of the Bible is no abstract deity removed from his creation and uninterested in it. Rather, the whole history of the Bible is the story of God's involvement with his creation, and particularly the people in it (Acts 17:25, 28).

Thus the teachings of Scripture about the relationship between God and creation are unique compared to the religions of the Chinese. The Bible teaches that God is distinct from his creation. He is not part of it, for he has made it and rules over it. But God is both immanent and transcendent, and he is everywhere present in essence as well as in knowledge and power.[36] God's transcendence and immanence are both affirmed in a single verse when Paul speaks of "one God and Father of all, who is above all and through all and in all" (Eph. 4:6).

Missiological Implications in the Chinese Context

From a missiological perspective, there are several implications for the Chinese context. First of all, in ancient China the supreme God (*Shang-di* or *Tian*) was identified as a personal God. Although this concept of a personal God was gradually replaced by an impersonal *Tian* through the influence of Confucianism, the name of God is still an important issue in communicating the gospel to the Chinese people.

So far the question as to the correct connotation of these Chinese terms for God (*Shang-di* and *Tian*) remains open despite several centuries of discussions and investigations by Western scholars. Neither of the terms seemed a natural or logical choice as an appropriate translation for the "God" of the Bible because *Tian* was too impersonal to most Chinese people and *Shang-di* has been used by Taoists. A so-called term controversy erupted in Roman Catholic circles in the eighteenth century, which eventually concluded with the coinage of the term *Tian Zhu*, "Lord in Heaven." For a time, even this could not satisfy the more fundamentalist-minded, who preferred *Deusu* (Latin, *Deus*), as God was called in Japan.

Protestant translators of the Bible, on the other hand, also struggled between the two terms, with *Shang-di* being used predominantly in early (late nineteenth century) translations. Later Protestant translations, however, employed a new term, *Shen*. *Shen* in Chinese ancient pictography means the heavenly being who is the source and origin of all things. But in later Chinese literature *Shen* might also represent the good heavenly spirit.

Because *Shen* is a generic term for "heavenly being" without any religious connotation of Buddhism or Taoism, *Shen* was adopted by Protestant churches in China. However, depending upon the Chinese translation used, both terms (*Shen* and *Shang-di*) still occur, though the term *Shen* seems to have gained prominence in contemporary Protestant Christian worship.

Second, since God in the Chinese context was never seen as a Creator, this aspect of God should be stressed. The majority of Chinese people tend to be either pantheist or atheist in their worldview. Therefore, the "transcendence" of God has more or less been ignored or deemphasized in Chinese religions. This is one point that Chinese Christians could not ignore in their presentation of the faith.

Finally, the immanence of the divine nature was greatly emphasized in Chinese religions and philosophies. Indeed, this is the common ground of the Chinese religions. Thus after the Ming dynasty (1369–1644), many great religious thinkers sought to effect a harmonization of these three Chinese religions (Taoism, Buddhism, and Confucianism). This kind of syncretistic religious life is still very popular among Chinese people in Taiwan, Hong Kong, Southeast Asia, and China. But we need to emphasize that God is both immanent and transcendent. Although God created us in his image, he transcends his creation, including us.

Chinese cultural traditions provide us some insights as well as some misconceptions about God. For example, the Chinese, like the biblical believer, seek to be righteous and seek a way to an ideal moral state to experience mature wisdom and awe of this world. However, "being like God" must be balanced by "not being God." God is not limited by creation, as we are, but is outside of it. God is the transcendent unique Creator with whom humans can have personal fellowship. Only through this right perspective on God's attributes and essence can we know him and approach him correctly.

Like Chinese Christians, Korean Christians must also weigh the options carefully when seeking to appropriate from traditional usage the most accurate term for reflecting the biblical revelation of God's nature, as the next chapter reveals.

Communicating the Biblical Concept of God to Koreans

Bong Rin Ro

Bong Rin Ro, a Korean born and reared in Korea, received his Th.D. and S.T.M. in Concordia Lutheran Seminary, B.D. in Covenant Theological Seminary, and B.A. in history from Wheaton College, and B.A. in Bib. Ed. from Columbia Bible College. He has been an OMF missionary in Singapore, Taiwan, and Korea. He is also Professor of Church History and Missions at Torch Trinity Graduate School of Theology in Seoul, Korea, and Overseas Ministry Director of Korean Center for World Missions in Seoul. He has written many articles, essays, and books, including 1995 *World Directory of Theological Institutions, Korean Church Growth Explosion* (in its second edition), *God in Asian Contexts*, and *The Bible and Theology in Asian Contexts*.

How can one communicate the God of the Bible to Koreans with totally different concepts of God due to their traditional cultures and religions? How does a Christian interpret the religious experience of prayerful contemplation of a Buddhist in comparison with his own prayer to God? In Korea, Buddhist monks or devotees commonly pray or go through deep spiritual meditation in the temple. In the rural communities, many farmers believe in shamanism and the power of spirits that control their lives. Does some common ground exist between Christians and non-Christians to make possible religious dialogue?

These are some of the crucial questions that the Christians not only in Korea, but also in other countries are asking today. We are living in the age of religious pluralism and are very much influenced by the modern theological concept of contextualization. There have been numerous theological consultations on contextual issues in Korea, Asia, and the world. The Asia Theological Association held a theological consultation in Manila, Philippines, January 21–26, 1985, on the theme, "God the Creator and Redeemer," and published *God in Asian Contexts: Communicating the God of the Bible in Asia.*[1] Different Asian evangelical theologians compared the God of the Bible with the god(s) of their major religions of Asia, such as Hinduism, Buddhism, Chinese religion, Islam, tribal animism, and presented the best ways to communicate the gospel to the peoples in the non-Christian world.

The basic objective of this chapter is to gain a theological understanding of the Korean concept of God and how effectively to communicate the gospel to Asians, especially Koreans. In order to achieve this objective, I deal with three principal areas: How did the apostle Paul present the God of the Bible to the heathen in his missionary journeys in the first century? How do we analyze the complex Korean concepts of the deity? How do we apply scriptural principles for the purpose of communicating the God of the Bible to Koreans in the context of the twenty-first century?

Briefly, we will learn how some devout Koreans believe God can help one transcend the world. The Koreans have both a history of belief in one God and in many gods. What non-Christian Koreans do not have is an understanding of the personal, supreme God called "I will be," the God who brings meaning and purpose to the world and to one's life.

My hermeneutical approach is "from text to context," in other words, first to have the proper understanding of biblical texts on the God of the Bible and of how the people of God in the Bible have tried to communicate God to their people, and then to apply these texts to the Korean context. A common hermeneutical mistake among contextual theologians today has been to start their theology with context, and then try to apply different texts to prove their contextual theology. In other words, they put context at the foundation of their theology and use Bible passages as proof texts; consequently, they often misinterpret the scriptural texts in trying to prove their theology. In fact, many of the Asian contextual theologians today have utilized wrong hermeneutical methodology and produced Asian theologies that are not faithful to biblical teaching. The International Council of Accrediting Agencies, which is now called the International Council of Evangelical Theological Education, held a theological consultation on this very issue with the theme, "From Text to Context in Evangelical Theological Education," at London Bible College, London, England, July 9–13, 1991.[2]

Paul's Approach to the Gentiles in the First Century

Amazing similarities can be drawn between Ephesus of the first century and Asian cities today, including Korean cities, especially in three main areas. First, the crowded population of Ephesus then and that of Korea now is very similar. Ephesus, which was the capital city of the Asian province of the Roman Empire, had a population of about 300,000 people, representing the largest city in Asia Minor. It was also a very important seaport with much international trade and commerce and also boasted of a great amphitheater with 25,000 seats, a number of gymnasiums, baths, and many impressive public buildings. The big cities of Korea are similar. Seoul, with a population of 11 million people, is one of the most congested places in the world. Many other major cities, like Pusan, Inchon, Kwangjoo, and Taejon, are heavily populated with traffic jams and air pollution.

Second, Ephesus was a very religious city with its great temple of Artemis (or Diana, her Roman name), rated as one of the seven wonders of the ancient world. The temple of Artemis was situated just outside the city wall, and thousands of the Ephesians worshiped the goddess Artemis, known as the moon goddess, the goddess of hunting, and the patroness of young girls. Likewise, the Koreans were traditionally strong Buddhists, Confucianists, and shamanists until the Christian gospel was introduced to Korea in 1884. Today, South Korea has 12 million Protestant believers with 38,000 churches among its total population of 45 million. Nevertheless, the religious influences of Buddhism and shamanism are still very strong, controlling the spiritual minds of the people.

Third, Ephesus was a sinful city, as Paul described the moral condition of the Ephesians: "They have lost all sensitivity and have abandoned themselves to licentiousness, greedy to practice every kind of impurity" (Eph. 4:19). Today, we are facing a critical moral degeneration in Korea with crime, promiscuous sex, bribery, drugs, and so on.

Paul was preaching the life-changing message of the gospel of Jesus Christ in Ephesus; consequently, a small church was established with the membership consisting of Jewish and Gentile believers. This Ephesian church was facing an internal division between the "circumcised" and the "uncircumcised" Christians (Eph. 2:11–22), just as today's Korean Christians are deeply divided by many schismatic separations.

Therefore, how Paul interpreted the pagan religious conditions of the Ephesians and those of other cities he visited in his missionary journeys, and how he presented the gospel to these heathen in the first century teach us some important spiritual principles and methods of evangelism for the present generation. There are three passages from the writings of Paul that are extremely important to us today in the Korean context: Romans 1–2; 1 Corinthians 1–2; and Romans 7–8.

Humanity's Limited Religious Experience under Natural Revelation (Romans 1–2)

Paul discussed the natural person's ability to understand God and his attributes and to obey his commandments. How much did the Romans in the first century actually understand about the concept of the true and living God of the Bible and obey his statutes before the gospel entered into Rome? Likewise, how much did the Koreans truly understand God through their natural revelation prior to the coming of Western missionaries into Korea in 1884? Paul had a very interesting analysis of the spiritual condition of the Gentiles in the first century.

Paul emphasized that God has revealed himself to humans through natural revelation, which is manifested through the beauty of God's creation and human conscience. First, God clearly manifests himself through nature in Romans 1:19–21:

> For what can be known about God is plain to them, because God has shown it to them. Ever since the creation of the world his eternal power and divine nature, invisible though they are, have been understood and seen through the things he has made. So they are without excuse; for though they knew God, they did not honor him as God or give thanks to him, but they became futile in their thinking, and their senseless minds were darkened.

Second, God manifests himself in human conscience; the law of God is written in people's hearts as Paul described in Romans 2:14–15:

> When Gentiles, who do not possess the law, do instinctively what the law requires, these, though not having the law, are a law to themselves. They show that what the law requires is written on their hearts, to which their own conscience also bears witness; and their conflicting thoughts will accuse or perhaps excuse them.

Paul makes it very clear that humans who are made in the image of God are able to know God through natural revelation by observing his creation and by their conscience. Nevertheless, Paul also emphasizes that humans have lost that ability to know God, because their sins have entered into their lives and marred their spiritual sensitivity. Paul lists at least twenty-five different sins in Romans 1:24–31:

> Therefore God gave them up in the lusts of their hearts to impurity, to the degrading of their bodies among themselves, because they exchanged the truth about God for a lie and worshiped and served the creature rather than the Creator, who is blessed forever! Amen. For this reason God gave them up to degrading passions, (homosexuality mentioned). . . . wickedness, evil, covetousness, malice. Full of envy, murder, strife, deceit, craftiness, they are gossips, slanderers, God-haters, insolent, haughty, boastful, inventors of evil, rebellious toward parents, foolish, faithless, heartless, ruthless.

In other words, humans lost their spiritual eyesight to know God. Paul says in 2 Corinthians 4:4, 6:

> The god of this world has blinded the minds of the unbelievers, to keep them from seeing the light of the gospel of the glory of Christ, who is the image of God. . . . For it is the God who said, "Let light shine out of darkness," who has shone in our hearts to give the light of the knowledge of the glory of God in the face of Jesus Christ.

Koreans cannot know the true God of the Bible through their natural revelation because their minds have become distorted by human sin and idolatry. Consequently, their attempts to understand God through the superstitious practices and meditations of the traditional religions of Buddhism, Confucianism, Taoism, and shamanism have produced false concepts of God; therefore, they fall under God's judgment (Rom. 1:20; 2:1).

True Understanding of God through God's Special Revelation (1 Corinthians 1–2)

Since the natural person through natural revelation cannot fully comprehend the mystery of God, Paul mentions that the only way to know God fully is through supernatural, special revelation. In the city of Corinth, where the Greek philosophy of Plato and Aristotle was so prevalent and people tried to untie the mystery of the universe and explore the mystery religions of many gods (1 Cor. 8:5), Paul compares the epistemological differences between a Christian and a non-Christian. There are distinctive differences in the understanding of God between a believer in Christ and a heathen as mentioned in 1 Corinthians 1 and 2. The following chart shows Paul's explanation of the epistemological differences between these two kinds of people in Corinth in the first century.

Comparison of Epistemology between a Christian and a Non-Christian (1 Cor. 1–2)

Christian Faith

2:2 Paul desired only to know Christ.
2:4 Paul did not use words but a demonstration of the Spirit and power.
2:5 Faith rests on God's power

Non-Christian Doubt

1:21 The world through its wisdom did not know God.
2:1 Paul did not use superiority of speech or wisdom.
2:4 Paul did not use persuasive words of wisdom.
2:5 Faith rests on human wisdom.

God's Wisdom

2:7–9 God's secret wisdom is hidden; no eye has seen, no ear has heard, no mind has conceived what God has prepared for those who love him.
1:25 The foolishness of God (the cross) is wiser than human wisdom.
1:27 God chose the foolish and weak things of the world to shame the wise.
1:30 Christ has become God's wisdom.
1:24 Christ is God's power and God's wisdom.

Human Wisdom

2:6 Paul does not speak of the wisdom of this age or of the rulers of this age.
1:21 The world through its wisdom did not know God.
2 Cor. 4:4 The god of this age has blinded the minds of unbelievers.
2:13 Paul speaks in words not taught by human wisdom.

God's Revelation

2:10 God has revealed it to Christians by the Spirit. The Spirit searches all

Human Contemplation

2:11 A human knows his thoughts by his spirit.

things, even the deep things of God.
2:11 No one knows the thoughts of God except the Spirit of God.
2:12 Christians have received the Spirit from God.
2:13 The Spirit teaches spiritual truths in spiritual words.

2:12 Non-Christians have received the spirit of the world.

Spiritual Human
2:15–16 The spiritual person knows the mind of Christ.

Natural Human
2:14 A natural person does not accept the things from the Spirit of God.

Christians have both general and special revelation and know God by faith, which is based on the historical events of the cross and the resurrection (Luke 1:2–3). A person of worldly wisdom, even with a Ph.D., cannot understand God, Christ, and the spiritual realm of truth.

God's special revelation to us is essential in order to comprehend what God wants to accomplish for humanity in this world. God communicated his message to humans through his special revelation. This special revelation is found both in the Old and New Testaments. For example, in the Old Testament, God spoke directly to Abraham (Gen. 12:1), Moses (Exod. 3:4; 4:4, 19), and the prophets, and appeared to humans through angels (Gen. 16:7–13; 18:1–5; 19:1–5). The writings of the prophets commonly read, "Thus saith the LORD," to communicate God's messages to the people of Israel (Jer. 6:16; Amos 1:6).

God's full special revelation also came through Jesus Christ, who was with the Father before his incarnation and who knows the Father. Jesus said, "No one knows the Father except the Son" (Matt. 11:27). Jesus was sent to the world by his Father in order to accomplish the work of salvation for humanity (Matt. 1:21; John 3:16; 1 John 5:20).

God's special revelation also was given in the inspiration of the Bible. Paul says, "All Scripture is God-breathed and is useful for teaching, rebuking, correcting and training in righteousness" (2 Tim. 3:16 NIV; cf. 2 Peter 1:20–21). Therefore, if a person wants to know who God is, what God wants, and how he can go back to the Father, he can get all the information through Jesus Christ and the Scripture.

Spirit-Filled Life vs. I-Centered Life (Rom. 7–8)

Paul also compares the Spirit-filled Christian experience of God with the flesh-filled experience of the carnal Christian in Romans 7 and 8. The Christian life should be a Holy Spirit-filled life (Rom. 8:1–30), not the naturally oriented human life centered around himself (Rom. 7:7–25). The former life produces joy and victory and the latter life is one of failure and despair.

Spirit-Filled Life	I-Centered Life
(Rom. 8:1–30)	(Rom. 7:7–25; 8:5–9)
(The "Spirit" is mentioned 18 times.)	"I," "my," "me" are mentioned fifty times (NIV).
8:5 Their minds are set on what the Spirit desires.	8:5 Those who live by their sinful nature have their minds set on what that nature desires.
8:9 They are controlled by the Spirit, if the Spirit of God lives in them.	7:15 "I do not understand my own actions. For I do not what I want, but I do the very thing I hate."
8:14 Those "who are led by the Spirit of God are children of God."	7:20 "It is no longer I that do it, but sin that dwells within me."
8:23 Christians have "the firstfruits of the Spirit."	8:9 They are controlled by their sinful nature.
8:26 The Spirit intercedes for believers	7:24 "Wretched man that I am! Who will rescue me from this body of death?"
	8:7–8 The sinful mind is hostile to God, does not submit to God's law, and cannot please God.

Paul teaches, therefore, that the Holy Spirit is necessary to comprehend the true and the living God through God-given general and special revelation (1 Cor. 1–2), a knowledge unattainable by fallen human wisdom. Likewise, the Holy Spirit is necessary for a person to experience God in daily life. An "I-centered" sinful life cannot have this experience of God.

Korean Traditional Concepts of God

One of the important tasks of missionaries in their initial stage of work is to translate the Bible into vernacular languages, and one of the most important words in any translation is the word *God.* Mateo Ricci, Jesuit missionary to China (1581–1610), used *T'ien Chu* ("Heavenly Lord") to describe the God of the Bible, and later the Protestant missionaries used *Shang Ti* or *Shen* for God. All three words for God came from the Chinese traditional words to describe the Chinese concept of God. The Japanese *Kami* and the Indonesian *Allah* for God in their respective Bibles also came from the common usage of these peoples to describe their traditional gods.

However, the Korean Christians call God *Hananim* ("One Lord"), which is very close to the traditional name of God, *Hanoonim* ("Heavenly Lord"), but is not the same word. The Korean national anthem uses the word, *Hanoonim* ("who protects the country"). Since there are at least thirteen different terms used to refer to god or gods in Korea, it is quite necessary to look into the historical background of the religious life of the Korean people.

Religious Life of the Korean People

Traditionally, the Koreans have been associated with three main religions: Buddhism, Confucianism, and shamanism (old animism or nature-worship).[3] An American educator, Homer B. Hulbert, who came to Korea along with two other educators in September 1886 at the request of King Kojong, observed the religious life of the Koreans:

> As a general thing we may say that the all round Korean is a Confucianist when in society, a Buddhist when he philosophizes, and a spirit-worshipper when in trouble. Now if you want to know what a man's religion is, watch him when he is in trouble. Then his genuine religion will come out, if he has any. It is for this reason that I conclude that the underlying religion of the Korean, the foundation upon which all else is mere superstructure, is his original spirit-worship. In this term are included animism, shamanism, fetishism and nature-worship generally.[4]

Confucianism, which originated in China, came to Korea before the Koryo dynasty (935–1392). Chi-Won Choi, the great Confucian scholar known as the father of Korean literature, returned to Korea from China in 885 and introduced the study of Confucian classics. Confucianism, which teaches moral and ethical conduct with the doctrine of the Five Human Relationships and *Jen* ("love"), introduced ancestor worship to the Koreans. Confucianism in Korea was not significant in its influence upon the people during the Koryo dynasty but became very influential from the Yi dynasty (1392–1910). Since Confucianism still emphasizes ethical philosophy more than religious beliefs, it has remained among the small minority intellectual class in society.

Buddhism, on the other hand, as a religion has made very significant influences in the country not only in the religious realm of life, but also in all spheres of life, including art, music, education, ethics, and so on. Buddhism was first introduced to Korea from China in 372 and reached its Golden Age during the Koryo dynasty. Buddhist politicians controlled the government against the Confucian politicians during the Koryo dynasty, but during the Yi dynasty the Confucian politicians were in control of the government and expelled the Buddhist influences from the cities by not allowing Buddhists to build their temples in the cities. This is why we find only a small number of Buddhist temples in cities like Seoul; most temples are found in the mountains.[5] This situation is very different from that of Taiwan where Buddhist temples are built in the midst of people in the cities.

During the Yi dynasty, Confucianism, which was prevalent among the elite, educated people, did not touch the spiritual life of the vast majority of illiterate people. Buddhism, on the other hand, also lost its control in the nation by the expulsion of Buddhist politicians from the government by the Confucian politicians and also by the ban of Buddhist temples in cities. This is why Korea has not seen much spiritual influence of traditional religions among the people for many years, until the mid-1980s. I wrote about this spiritual vacuum of the Korean people in the *Korean Church Growth Explosion:*

> The majority of the people do not practice Buddhism and Confucianism in the form of cultic exercises. Many experience a spiritual vacuum, and for a significant number, Christianity has filled the void. . . . This is explicitly expressed in the survey statistics which show that the majority of people do not practice any religion at all. When the former President Chung-Hee Park of South Korea was asked whether he was a Christian, his reply reflected a typical feeling, "My father and mother were Buddhists, but I am nothing."[6]

Today, however, Korea has had a reform movement within Buddhism since the mid-1980s, making its impact upon the nation spiritually and politically.

Shamanism, however, is still popular among the people, especially in rural areas. In practice, it is basically animistic and superstitious, in close conjunction with ancestor worship. The people are afraid of spirits, especially evil spirits. Koreans traditionally believed that a human has three souls. One goes to hades upon death or wanders around the earth; another goes to the grave; and the last one goes to the ancestral tablet in the house.[7] With the government policy of reviving traditional culture and religions, shamanism, in particular, has been revived with many superstitious practices to appease ancestral spirits and other good and bad spirits.

In Korean shamanism, both the *mudang* and *pansu* play very important roles. The *mudang*, or woman sorceress, is invited to a home to hunt the spirits. She dances around in the house with the gong and drum and shakes an oak rod in her hand to point to the spirits in order to appease those that cause sickness and misfortune in the family. People believe that she has the power to expel evil spirits and demons, *kwesin*, from the house. The *pansu*, a blind man exorcist, deals directly with evil spirits and drives them away by repeating exorcisms from a book handed down from the earliest ages.[8]

Nature worship in shamanism was very popular in olden days, even in cities. The pantheistic concept of god was prevalent among rural people, because they believed that many objects possess their deities, as James S. Gale describes:

> Every hill, every path, every mountain, every stream and every house site, house, kitchen and almost every room has its deity or demon; and surrounded by this host of enemies, it is to be wondered at that the Korean has as good a time as he has.[9]

Spirit-trees are commonly seen on the roadside, especially gnarled pine trees, beautifully decorated with different colors of pieces of cloth for veneration. The people rub their hands in prayer in front of the trees for divine blessing and healing. Others worship before the rocks, and the passersby put small stones one on top of another, piling up the stones and offering prayer for divine blessing. Another common sight is the "Guardians of the Roads," which are two wooden statues standing with male and female heads with the Chinese characters written vertically, stating that they are the guardian generals to protect men and women on the roads. The worship of the spirits is the basis for Korean shamanism, because these spirits must be appeased in order to bring happiness and fortune.[10]

Chinese Influences on the Korean Concept of God

Korea has been called "a sandwich nation," because it is squeezed between the three giant nations of China, Russia, and Japan. Many wars and battles in the past have occurred among these nations in order to control this small nation of Korea. Historically, for centuries Korea has been more closely linked with China than with Japan and Russia. Korea has a history of an extensive exchange of trade, culture, religion, and education with China, because the Korean peninsula is geographically connected with Manchuria and China. Since sea navigation was not well developed until the nineteenth century, communication between Korea and the island nation of Japan was very difficult. Therefore, Korea had often depended upon China politically for protection from foreign invasions, especially from the Japanese, and from the internal conflicts and wars among the Korean kingdoms. During the expansion of the Mongolian empire in the thirteenth century, the Mongols invaded the capital city of the Korean dynasty (935–1392) in 1231, but could not destroy it. However, the Koryo dynasty had to surrender to the Mongols in 1259. Therefore, Korea received religious and cultural influences from both China and Mongolia.

When Buddhism came to Korea from China in 372 during the Kokuryo dynasty (33–668), Koreans transmitted it to Japan in 552 during the Paikche Dynasty (18 B.C.–A.D. 935). Many Buddhist monks, especially during the Koryo dynasty, had gone to China to learn Chinese Mahayana Buddhism and imported many Buddhist scriptures to Korea and spread Buddhism among the Koreans. The Buddhist monks carved the most famous "80,000 wooden block Buddhist scriptures" in 1237, which were used to print thousands of Buddhist scriptures for wider distribution. The famous original copies are still kept at the Haein Temple, located in the southeast part of Korea. Even though Buddhism experienced a setback during the Yi dynasty, it is still the strongest religion in Korea. According to the Ministry of Information statistics in 1990, the largest religious population in South Korea is in Buddhism, representing 25 percent of the total population, while Christianity, Roman Catholicism, and Confucianism represented 23 percent, 5 percent, and 19.7 percent respectively.[11] Some of the Korean concepts of God are definitely related to Chinese Buddhism.

The impact of Chinese Confucianism on the Koreans is very crucial in the formation of Korean concepts of God. Chi-Won Choi went to China to study Confucianism and returned to Korea in 885 and became a strong promoter of Confucian education. Yool-Kok Lee (1535–86) was the best known neo-Confucian scholar and strongly supported ancestor worship. Confucianism reached its highest scholarship during the sixteenth century. The Confucian concept of God known as *T'ien* ("Heaven") was adopted by Korean scholars, and several Korean concepts of God today are related to Confucianism.

Although the Korean alphabetical language was invented by King Sejong in 1446, the elite minority Confucian scholars had ignored the use of the Korean alphabet for over 450 years until Western missionaries came to Korea in 1884. The twenty-four letters in the Korean alphabet are simple to learn in comparison with the thousands of Chinese characters. The Confucian scholars wanted to maintain their elite educational privileges. Consequently, the vast majority of people were illiterate and readily accepted shamanistic concepts of God for themselves. However, even Korean shamanism and the Korean mythological story of the beginning of the Korean race are also influenced by Chinese religions.

Korean Concepts of God

Yong-Bok Rha, in his Th.D. thesis at Boston University in 1977, "An Analysis of the Terms Used for God in Korea in the Context of Indigenization," provides useful information on the concepts of God in Korea and lists thirteen different terms for God in Korea, which I will divide into three categories. The first category of gods is definitely influenced by Chinese concepts of gods. The second category of gods is related to Korean indigenous shamanism, and the third category has to do with the mythological story of the foremost ancestor of the Korean race, *Tangoon.*

Names of God Related to the Chinese Concept of Heavenly Rulers

Chun *("Heaven"),* Sang Che *("Heavenly Ruler"),* and Shen *("God")*

A number of names of God in Korea are related to the ruler(s) of the heavens, because the Koreans believed in the heavenly rulers just as the Chinese did. The Chinese used three terms for their God: *Shang Ti* ("Heavenly Ruler," called *Sang Che* in Korean), *T'ien* ("Heaven," *Chun* in Korean), and *Shen* ("God," *Shin* in Korean). During the Golden Age of China in the twenty-third century B.C., according to the Book of History, Emperor Shun offered sacrifice to *Shang Ti* to celebrate his accession to the throne, and offered at Tai Shan other sacrifices to the hills and streams, and a burnt offering to *T'ien*. *Shang Ti* is a personal God, the supreme ruler of all the rulers of the earth, while *T'ien* represents an impersonal heaven or providence. *Shen* is used as a technical term for god, often conveying the meaning of spirits or good spirits in contrast to evil spirits called *Kwei*.[12]

Koreans still use the words, *Chun (T'ien), Sang Che (Shang Ti),* and *Shin (Shun),* which came from the Chinese characters, when they refer to God. *Chun* was mainly used by Korean Confucianists, while *Sang Che* was used by the first Protestant missionaries in their Bible translation until the Korean Christians and the first missionaries decided to drop it and used rather the Korean colloquial language for God. We have to understand that many Korean words derived from Chinese characters, but most of the other vocabulary came directly from the Korean language without any connection with the Chinese language. Therefore, Koreans commonly used the words *Ha Nul Nim,* or *Han Ool Nim,* or *Ha Nu Nim* for God. *Chun Do Kyo* ("Heavenly Way Religion"), which is an indigenous religion founded by Soo-Woo Choe in 1860, who tried to combine Western Christianity with Eastern Learning, used *Sang Che* for a time but his followers do not use it any longer.[13]

Chun Chu *("Lord of Heaven"),* Chun Shin *("Gods of heaven"), and* Ok Hwang Che *("The Supreme Emperor" or "the King of Kings")*

When Mateo Ricci began to work on the book, *T'ien-Hsueh-Shih-I* ("The True Doctrine of T'ien's Teachings"), in 1591, he chose *T'ien Chu (Chun Chu)* for "God." Since then, the Roman Catholic Church, both in China and Korea, used this word until 1971 when the Korean Bible Society decided to produce a joint New Testament translation for Roman Catholics and Protestants using *Ha Nu Nim* for "God" instead.[14]

Chun Shin means "gods in heaven," signifying personified heaven and representing some nature gods as well as spirits in shamanism in Korea. Since the Confucianists believe in heavenly powers, *Chun Shin* represents natural powers that control wind, rain, storms, mountains, rivers, and the like. For shamanists, *Chun Shin* refers to gods or spirits that control all aspects of human life and particularly relate to rural and agricultural settings.

Ok Hwang Che, which means "the Supreme Emperor among the rulers," is the name of the deity for the Taoists in Korea. There is a hierarchical structure among the heavenly celestial beings, and this concept of gods conveys a thought of the Supreme One among many powerful rulers of the universe. Since Taoism deals with harmony with nature, it has many superstitious practices to communicate with gods and spirits in this world.[15]

Bu Chu Nim *(Buddha) in Buddhism*

When Gautama (ca. 560–480 B.C.) lived in northeast India, his main concern was human suffering *(dukha)* and how to extinguish suffering to the status of nirvana rather than whether the existence of god(s) is significant or not; therefore, some Buddhist scholars consider Buddhism as atheistic or agnostic. The Theraveda Buddhism does not consider Gautama Buddha as deity, but in Mahayana Buddhism, which is prevalent in China, Korea, Japan, and Vietnam, Gautama has been deified as the Absolute and the eternal Buddha essence.

Koreans worship Buddha as deity and revere Bodhisattvas (whose statues stand in the temples). These Bodhisattvas supposedly could reach the status of nirvana but abdicated the privilege in order to help others. There are hundreds of Buddha and Bodhisattva statues in Buddhist temples to which the Buddhists pay their tributes. Korean Buddhists are very polytheistic as are other Mahayana Buddhists in Asia.

Ha Nul Nim, Han Ool Nim, *and* Ha Nu Nim *(words associated with "Heavenly Lord")*

The most common words used to describe deity in Korea were associated with the Heavenly Lord or "the One who rules heavens" (*Ha Nul* in Korean). *Ha Nul Nim* means "Heavenly Lord." *Ha Nul* is the Korean translation of the Chinese character *Chun,* which means "Heaven," and *Nim,* which means "Lord." Therefore, the Korean concept of God has been very closely associated with the one who rules heaven. Confucianists and shamanists have used this phrase for "God."

Han Ool Nim is the term used for God by the *Chun Do Kyo* ("Heavenly Way Religion"). There is a difference of opinion among Korean scholars on the origin of the term *Han Ool Nim.* One view is that *Han* means "great" and *Ool* is an abbreviation of the word "Oori," meaning "great we"; therefore, *Han Ool Nim* means "Our Great God." Another view is that this term for God comes from *Ha Nul,* which means "Heaven"; therefore, *Han Ool Nim* has the same meaning of *Ha Nul*

Nim, "Heavenly Lord." *Ha Nu Nim* is the most commonly used traditional term for "God." The etymology of the word *Ha Nu* is the same as for *Ha Nul:* "Heavenly Lord." The Roman Catholic Church has adopted *Ha Nu Nim* for "God."[16]

The Names of God Related to Shamanism

The majority of Koreans before the coming of Western missionaries at the end of the nineteenth century had little education or were kept illiterate under the feudalistic society. The farmers and rural people were very much affected by shamanistic animism and worshiped many gods and spirits. Besides the *Chun Shin* ("Heavenly Spirits") mentioned above, which are associated with nature gods in shamanism and Confucianism, two other main terms are used for God by the rural people.

Shin Ryung *("Gods and Spirits")*

Korean shamanists believe in pantheism and polydemonism, in other words, that the spirits or gods are living in natural objects such as trees, rocks, hills, waters, houses, as well as in living and dead persons. The fear of evil spirits plays an important role in a person's life, so that he or she has to offer sacrifices to the spirits in order to appease them; otherwise, the power of the evil spirits will bring misfortune, sickness, and death to a family. Therefore, exorcists such as *mudangs* or *pansus* are brought into the family to appease the spirits. *Shin Ryung* is still popular among the people not only in rural areas, but also in cities.

Ha Na Nim *("One Great God")*

One very significant fact that we have to understand in Korean shamanism is the recognition of one Supreme God above other gods and spirits. Koreans used to utilize the word *Ha Na Nim,* in which *Ha Na* means "one" and *Nim* means "Lord" or "God." The hierarchical structure of gods and spirits in Korean shamanism has placed One Supreme God or Spirit as the head, which leads to the concept of monotheism. C. A. Clark, a renowned American missionary in Korea, states:

> Ha Na Nim is unique. There is scarcely a question that he goes far back into the dim ages of Korean history long before any of the foreign religions came

into the country. In the earliest history of Shamanism, we noted how Ye Kook people worshiped Ha Na Nim. It was Ha Na Nim whom Tangoon worshipped on his high altar on Kang Hwa.[17]

In contextualizing the biblical concept of the trinitarian God, Korean Protestant Christians adopted this term *Ha Na Nim* for God. This is quite different from the Chinese concepts of polytheism in Buddhism and of the impersonal Lord of Heaven, *T'ien,* of Confucianism. Furthermore, Koreans have one unified culture and language among 70 million people both in North and South Korea. This is one of the important reasons for Koreans' acceptance of the monotheistic God of the Bible; consequently, the churches have grown very rapidly among the Korean people.

Tangoon Mythological Concept of God ("Trinitarian God"): *Han Ul Nim* ("One Great Spirit") and *Sam Shin* ("Trinitarian God")

Each nation usually has its own mythological story of the beginning of its race. The Korean people also have their mythology, known as Tangoon Mythology. An indigenous religion, *Tangoon Kyo,* was established from this mythology, with its name changed to *Tai Chong Kyo* in October 1904 by Bong-I Paik, who claimed to receive special revelation at Mount Paiktoo. The *Tai Chong Kyo* has a membership of over a half million people.

According to the Tangoon mythological story, *Han Im* ("Father the Creator") lived with *Han Woong* ("Teacher, Leader") and *Han Kum* ("King, Governor") in heaven. *Han Woong* wanted to establish an earthly kingdom and received permission from his father *Han Im*. He descended upon Mount Tae Paik near Pyungyang with three thousand spirits and proclaimed himself as the "King of the Universe" under an ancient "Paktal" tree. He governed the universe through three vice-regents, the "Wind General," the "Rain Governor," and the "Cloud Teacher." Since he wanted to become a human being, he heard a dialogue between a tiger and a bear about becoming human beings. These two animals heard a voice coming out of the void saying that if each would eat twenty pieces of garlic and a piece of artemisia and retire in a cave for twenty-one days, they would become human. The active tiger could not remain in the cave for twenty-one days, but the patient bear stayed there for twenty-one days and became a woman whose first wish was to have a son. *Han Woong,* the Spirit King, saw her sitting beside the stream, circled around her, and breathed upon her. She finally conceived and bore a son whose name was *Tangoon* or *Han Kum,* the foremost ancestor of the Korean race in 2333 B.C.[18]

Rha points out three important points in *Tai Chong Kyo:*

1. It conveys the monotheistic concept in *Han Ul Nim* ("One Great Spirit"), and *Han Im, Han Woong,* and *Han Kum* are three functions of *Han Ul Nim.*
2. *Han Ul Nim* became incarnated into *Tangoon* or *Han Kum* and lived in this world (Korea) and ruled the people.
3. A trinitarian theology based on Tangoon Mythology was developed in Korea in 1963 by Sung-Bum Yun, professor of theology at the Korean Methodist Seminary in Seoul.[19]

In conclusion, Koreans, like many other Asians, have worshiped many gods and spirits. Nevertheless, the monotheistic concept of God can be discovered even in the traditional religions of Korea. The similarity of words such as *Ha Nu Nim* ("Heavenly Lord") and *Ha Na Nim* ("One Great Spirit") of shamanism, and the Christian usage of *Ha Na Nim* for the God of the Bible has certainly helped Korean Christians to witness to non-Christians about the gospel, opening their closed spiritual eyes.

How Can We Communicate the God of the Bible to Non-Christians?

Common Ground of Natural Revelation

If a Western missionary or a national Christian tries to communicate the gospel to non-Christians by condemning their idolatrous tradition and superstitious shamanistic practices, he may soon discover the strong defense mechanism built in their hearts against the gospel. Consequently, his communication with non-Christians is soon cut off, and his witness faces difficulty. Therefore, it is useful to start on the common ground between a Christian and a non-Christian after a personal relationship and confidence are first established between them. It is my experience that religious discussion often creates heated debate and even anger from non-Christian friends. I use three areas of common ground with an emphasis on God's natural revelation.

Humans are made in the image of God.

All human beings, regardless of whether they are Christians or non-Christians, are made in the image of God according to the Scripture:

> Then God said, "Let us make humankind in our image, according to our likeness; and let them have dominion over the fish of the sea." . . . So God created humankind in his image, in the image of God he created them; male and female he created them. (Gen. 1:26–27)

God's own response to his creation of humans on the sixth day is very interesting to notice: "God saw everything that he had made, and indeed, it was *very good*" (Gen. 1:31 italics mine). God's response to his creation of light, waters, sky, vegetation, fruit trees, lights, and living creatures during the previous five days of creation was just "good"; as the Scripture says, "God saw that the light was *good*" (Gen. 1:4; also, 1:10, 12, 18, 21).

I can make one appropriate illustration. I once took my family to a zoo in Taichung, Taiwan, and came to a big chimpanzee in a cage. We saw this huge animal in the iron bars looking straight at us. When the chimpanzee saw the Coca Cola I was drinking, he clapped his hands and put his hairy right hand through the iron bars asking for the drink, but I ignored him and finished it. When this animal knew that he was ignored, he went back to a corner and began beating his chest. When I saw this scene, I was really amazed to realize that this chimpanzee could think and act like a human. However, I was reminded of Genesis 1, that tells us humans alone are made in the image of God and that this chimpanzee, although it had desires, did not have the ability to understand God, because he was not made in the image of God.

Therefore, it is very important to emphasize that all humans are made in the image of God; consequently, all people have received natural revelation especially revealed in God's creation (Rom. 1:20–21) and in human conscience (Rom. 2:15). Humans have the ability to know God if they earnestly and honestly seek God. God's common grace has been extended to all, even to Buddhist monks and to superstitious shamanists, even though their knowledge of God became marred by their idolatry, superstitions, and sins.

Material things and sensual pleasures in this world cannot really satisfy people's longing hearts.

In the Korean consumer-oriented, capitalistic society of today where materialism, secularism, and hedonism are prevailing, Christians, Buddhists, and Confucianists all agree that humans do not acquire true happiness and peace as individuals and as a community from the things of this world. Inner peace must be found somewhere else. Paul's conclusion in Romans 7 is that an I-centered life is a life of failure. As he said, "Wretched man that I am! Who will rescue me from this body of death?" (v. 24).

Here is another good illustration on this subject. I had an automobile made by Daewoo Company when I was residing in Seoul. This car can use only unleaded gas. The "Unleaded Gas Only" sign is clearly marked on the fuel gauge indicator in front of the driver's seat. Nevertheless, if I keep putting in cheaper leaded gas instead of unleaded gas to save money, I will soon discover that the car does not run smoothly and has real problems. The car is not made to use leaded gas.

Likewise, since humans are made in the image of God, they are made to have relationships with their Creator; therefore, it is *normal* for humans to recognize God and to live according to God's statutes. Nevertheless, humans say they do not need God and do not want to live according to God's commandments, and instead they live just for themselves in sin. This kind of selfish life becomes *abnormal* in the sight of God. Without God, humans are incomplete; therefore, humans without God cannot find real happiness, even if they experience material prosperity and achieve the highest reputation.

Creating harmonious coexistence in the world is important.

One of the important Confucian tenets emphasizes harmonious human relationships. Confucius taught five basic human relationships: between king and subjects, husband and wife, parents and children, among children, and with people outside the family. Harmony and cooperation are the key words for the betterment of humanity and for the peace of society. Buddhism also teaches this harmonious and loving relationship among people. We find a similar emphasis in the teachings of both Jesus and Paul. Paul deals with the question of harmonious human relationships in Ephesians 5:18–6:9.

However, one important question which divides Christians from non-Christians is: "Can humans create harmonious coexistence in the world by themselves?" Confucius taught that man has the ability to create harmony and peace in the family, society, and nation, for he was a true humanist. However, the Bible teaches that God must be at the center of everything, even at the center of human activities. The following diagrams show the fundamental differences between Christians and non-Christians in their worldviews.

Distinctive Differences between Christians and Non-Christians

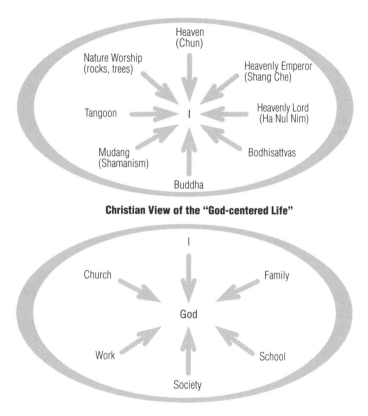

Christian View of the "God-centered Life"

Christians have both natural and special revelation.

One basic difference between Christians and non-Christians is that the former have both natural and special revelation. Paul makes it very clear in his teaching in 1 Corinthians 1 and 2 that humans are able to know God and God's will because God has revealed himself to humans through Jesus Christ, who is God's special revelation. I have already discussed this matter in the second section. Our sin-blinded minds cannot understand God and what he thinks unless he reveals those truths to us. That is what God did for us through Jesus Christ and through the Bible.

God has revealed his truth to us through Jesus Christ.

Jesus Christ was with God the Father from the beginning. God himself became human in Jesus Christ (John 1:1–14). Since Jesus came from the Father, he could tell us who God is, what kind of life God wants us to live, and how we can go back to the Father. If we want to know God, we should ask Jesus Christ, who came from God the Father. Certainly, non-Christians do not understand the mystery of the gospel, for they do not believe in Christ.

The Christian shares the purpose and meaning of his life with non-Christians.

Generally, non-Christians do not have a real meaningful purpose for their lives. There is no dynamic spiritual force within a person's life that dominates his mind and behavior. This purpose brings to a Christian a tremendous desire to share a testimony as to what Jesus Christ means in a person's life, just as Paul testified to others in the first century: "For to me, to live is Christ and to die is gain" (Phil. 1:21 NIV); "I have been crucified with Christ and I no longer live, but Christ lives in me. The life I live in the body, I live by faith in the Son of God, who loved me and gave himself for me" (Gal. 2:20 NIV).

Let the Holy Spirit Work

In the final analysis of our Christian witness either in Korea or elsewhere, the Holy Spirit is the one who brings non-Christians to the saving knowledge of Jesus Christ. God uses Christian witness and testimony for his glory; therefore, the Christian responsibility is to share the gospel with others through discussion, debate, and many other ways, and then to pray that the Holy Spirit would work in their hearts.

Many Christians have no doubt found sharing the God of the Bible with non-Christians increasingly difficult in Korea and in other parts of Asia where there has been a resurgence of traditional cultures and religions promoted by the government and where the Christian population represents a small minority. Yet, the God of the Bible is still greater than any gods or spiritual powers in the world.

Conclusion

Korean concepts of God today are very similar to the concepts espoused by the Greco-Roman world during the time of Paul. Paul went to Athens during his second missionary journey and saw an altar with the inscription, "To An Unknown God." He told the Athenians on Mars' Hill that they were very religious, worshiping this unknown god in ignorance. He declared that the God who made the heavens and the earth does not dwell in temples made by human hands and that this God, the Creator, requires repentance from everyone. He preached Jesus' cross and resurrection for the forgiveness of sins (Acts 17:22–34).

Paul and Barnabas went to Lystra during Paul's second missionary journey, and Paul healed a crippled man unable to walk from his birth. When the people saw this miracle, they shouted in the Lycaonian language, "The gods have come down to us in human form!" They then hailed Barnabas and Paul as gods, Zeus and Hermes, who were the two most popular gods in the Roman world, and their priest wanted to make sacrifices of animals to Barnabas and Paul, but these apostles refused to accept their sacrifices (Acts 14:8–13). Therefore, the people in Athens and Lystra in the first century did not have a clear picture of who God was because sin hindered their understanding of God from natural revelation.

Likewise, all traditional Asian religions of Buddhism, Taoism, Confucianism, Shintoism, shamanism, and Hinduism, based on natural revelation, do not give a clear picture of God but rather paint a picture of "unknown gods." The Korean understanding of God, which also falls into the category of natural revelation, was very much influenced by the Chinese concept of heavenly rulers *(T'ien)* of Confucianism and the polytheism of Buddhism. Shamanism also played a very important role for rural people in developing their religious practices.

Koreans were as religious in their pagan practices as the Chinese before the coming of the Western missionaries at the end of the nineteenth century. The only difference was the historical factor. In China, Christianity was rejected by the Chinese gentry class in the nineteenth century due to the dominant Western colonialism in China. The Chinese believed that Christianity was a forerunner of Western imperialism. Consequently, the Christian population in China had never exceeded over one percent of the total population.

However, the political situation in Korea was just the opposite from that of China. The colonial power in Korea was not Westerners but the Japanese who colonized Korea for thirty-six years (1910–1945). The only way to expel the Japanese from Korea was to invite Western powers; therefore, the Koreans opened their arms to Western intervention, including Christianity. In addition to this colonial situation, Buddhism, which reached its golden years during the Koryo dynasty (935–1392) in Korea, lost its influence for over five hundred years during the Yi dynasty (1392–1920). As a result, there was a spiritual vacuum among the people. Christianity took this opportunity to fill the spiritual gap.

The Korean term for "God" in shamanism, *Ha Nu Nim*, which means "One Great Lord" among the heavenly rulers, certainly acknowledged the Supreme One in the pantheon of gods, and helped Christianity to utilize the concept with the term *Ha Na Nim*, "the Only Great God." The special providence of God has been upon the Korean people in political, religious, and linguistic situations and has helped the church to grow faster than in any other nation in Asia.

The Korean church still has the challenge of reaching the remaining 75 percent non-Christian population among 45 million people in South Korea, plus 25.5 million in the North. God has selected the Korean people as one of the chosen peoples for today in order to proclaim his message of salvation around the world. As the apostle Peter says, "You are a chosen people, a royal priesthood, a holy nation, a people belonging to God, that you may declare the praises of him who called you out of darkness into his wonderful light. Once you were not a people, but now you are the people of God; once you had not received mercy, but now you have received mercy" (1 Peter 2:9–10 NIV).

Using the test case of Koreans coming to North America, the next chapter considers how Koreans in other lands find themselves struggling to hold on to their Christian understanding of God and not regress to reducing God to the utilitarian demands of atavistic shamanism.

The Korean American Dream
and the Blessings of *Hananim* (God)

Tae-Ju Moon

Tae-Ju Moon (B.A. from International Bible Institute in England, B.Th. from Chongshin College in Korea, M.Div. from Mapdong Presbyterian Theological Seminary, Th.M. from Ontario Theological Seminary, and D.Min. from Gordon-Conwell Theological Seminary) is senior minister of Ottawa Korean Community Church, Ottawa, Canada. Born and reared in Korea, he is a former general secretary of the Korean Youth-Workers Mission, Seoul, South Korea. He was visiting scholar at Regent College, Canada, in 1995, and is the author of *What Happiness Is, Who Has It, and Why* (Seoul: Agape, 1995), *Love: The Greatest Gift in the World* (Seoul: Agape, 1996), and *God of Love and Human Sufferings.*

The reception of Protestant Christianity in Korea in the 1880s was determined partly by Korean history and affected by Korea's isolation from the rest of the world. Early Western writers referred to Korea, the last nation on earth to forbid European travel and settlement, as "the Hermit Kingdom" and as "the last outstanding and irreconcilable scoffer among the nations."[1]

Though the Korean Protestant Church is slightly over 110 years old,[2] the growth of the Korean church is generally recognized as the most remarkable in the world in the twentieth century. The numerical growth of the Korean church is phenomenal by any estimation. There are over 12 million Christians and 37,000 churches in Korea today.[3] Korean immigrant churches have also become a noteworthy factor in North America. Their number has grown at an unprecedented rate; from about 75 churches in 1970 to about 2,000 in 1988,[4] and to approximately 3,500 in 1996 (or one church per about 350 Koreans). This is an increase of forty times in less than three decades. A popular saying among Korean North Americans seems to contain a kernel of truth: "When two Japanese meet, they set up a business firm; when two Chinese meet, they open a Chinese restaurant; and when two Koreans meet, they establish a church."

In comparison with their counterparts in their homeland, Korean churches in North America appear to be influenced by cultural differences in every aspect. Most Korean immigrants undergo cultural adjustment problems. The problems may vary depending on individual characteristics and backgrounds, but the new external pressures imposed on them present serious difficulties in adjusting to their new life. The problem definitely affects Christians, often causing serious drawbacks to their spiritual lives.

This chapter focuses on the ways in which Korean immigrants are dealing with the new reality they encounter in North American society in general, and particularly in their experience of the Korean church and their perceptions of the blessings of *Hananim*. I will use data from sociological census studies and about Korean religious institutions to understand the Korean immigrant in North America. Then I will show how the shamanistic heritage helps Koreans understand the power of God, the Blessing Healer (as in Exod. 15:26), but it hinders Koreans from understanding that God also is a holy, giving, kingdom-making God.

The Sociocultural Marginality of Korean Immigrants

The earliest Korean immigrants to North America were more than seven thousand, predominantly male, laborers who came to work on sugar plantations in Hawaii between 1903 and 1905. After Korea's tragic annexation to Japan in 1910, about nine hundred intellectuals and students, as well as approximately one thousand so-called picture-brides, came to America. The end of the Japanese occupation in 1945 brought about a slightly larger number of immigrants. Approximately ten thousand students, war brides, war orphans, and others came between 1951 and 1964.[5] The quota system under the new Immigration Act of 1965 brought about a dramatic increase of Korean immigrants to the United States. About 90 percent of Koreans residing in the United States today are the new immigrants who came after 1965 and their descendants.

The 1970 census reported about 70,000 Koreans in the United States and about 5,000 Koreans in Canada. From then on, approximately 30,000 Koreans have been admitted annually to the United States. In the decade of 1970, 244,732 Korean immigrants arrived in the United States. That number increased to 333,765 in the 1980s. The estimate of the number of Koreans in 1996 ranges anywhere between one million to 1.2 million in North America (about 70,000 of those are residing in Canada). The Population Reference Bureau's projections indicate that the size of the Korean population in the United States will reach 1,320,759 in the year 2000.[6]

The Korean immigrants' predicament in North America, in one word, is "marginality." Marginality means that Korean immigrants experience a social and cultural displacement or uprootedness. They are no longer in their home country, nor are they really part of a newly adopted country. They are in a totally new third culture, living in between these two cultures.

This sociocultural marginality, or the imposed limitation in the assimilation of Korean immigrants, has resulted in so-called adhesive or additive assimilation, and strong and apparently permanent ethnic attachment. Unlike some other immigrant people, the Koreans' acculturation or length of stay in North America does not weaken their attachment to the Korean cultural ethos and the Korean ethnic community.[7] One of the prominent factors that has led Korean immigrants to a strong ethnic attachment is the Caucasian dominant group's maintenance of a social distance from them. Hurh and Kim write:

> The immigrants' perception of such structural limitations and definition of their own limited adaptive capacities and resources would invoke in the immigrants a defense—their desire to maintain and even enhance their ethnic attachment and identity.[8]

The second-generation Korean North Americans (native-born children), by virtue of their particular situation, face a more difficult predicament than do their elders. They are more deeply involved in the white North American world than the first generation is. They are self-consciously aware, much more acutely than their parents are, of their marginalization. Contrary to the first-generation Koreans who have their ethnic culture and community to turn to, those of the second generation cannot find a shelter in their ethnic community because their ethnic attachment is not strong enough. They have never belonged deeply to the Korean culture or social world and, therefore, cannot return to it. They are truly in a wilderness, in the world of in-betweenness and homelessness.

Korean Immigrants' Church Participation

For Korean immigrants, church participation is so extensive that it occupies a significant portion of their lives in North America. Church has functioned as the central social institution for the Korean community and as a bridge to American or Canadian culture. Church life is a sociocultural resource that is readily available to many Korean immigrants in their struggle to satisfy the basic needs of immigrant life, such as a sense of belonging in a new place and personal support or comfort in their difficulty to secure a settlement. For most Koreans, churches are still the only organizations in North America available to satisfy both primary and secondary relational needs.

According to a Chicago survey, about 52 percent of Korean immigrants were already affiliated with Christian churches in Korea. Most of these preimmigration church affiliates currently attend churches. Additionally, many of the respondents who did not go to church in Korea are also currently affiliated with churches. About 77 percent of the respondents are affiliated with churches. The majority of the church affiliates (83.5 percent in the Los Angeles sample and 78.3 percent in the Chicago sample) attend church at least once a week.[9] This implies that about half of the non-Christian Korean immigrants join churches after their arrival in North America. The rate of church affiliation for Koreans in North America is very high, especially compared with that in Korea (about 25 percent).

In the Chicago sample, almost half of the preimmigration Christians were members of Presbyterian churches in Korea, 14 percent were Methodists, and the remaining one-fifth were Catholics. The denominational distribution of the current church affiliates in the Chicago sample is similar. About 40 percent of the current Christians belong to Presbyterian churches, 14 percent are affiliated with Methodist churches, and 13.6 percent are Catholics.[10]

Reasons for Korean Immigrants' Heavy Church Affiliation

Why is there such an unusually high degree of church participation among Korean immigrants? What kind of factors have led to an unusually heavy church affiliation of Korean immigrants? How is this extensive church involvement to be explained? From a social-scientific point of view, several factors have been proposed: (a) the high degree of preimmigration church affiliation; (b) the legacy of the church's heavy sociocultural role as the community center since the days of the earliest Korean immigrants; (c) the inclusive character of Korean churches in terms of the variety of people who are accepted into these churches and the regularity and frequency of church gatherings; and (d) the religious pluralism inherent in North American society, and the public acceptability of minority ethnic associations under a religious (especially Protestant) pretext.[11]

More important than any of the above reasons, however, most Korean immigrants attend Korean immigrant churches primarily to meet religious needs ("to worship God," "for strengthening faith," "for eternal life and salvation," and "to encourage their children's religious faith"). Secondarily, they go to find psychological comfort and to meet social needs ("to see friends and meet with other Koreans"). The vast majority of respondents (86 percent) gave a religious reason as their primary motivation for church affiliation. Of equal significance, 96 percent identified their communal need as their secondary reason for church attendance.[12]

The Korean Immigrant Church and Daybreak Prayer

The Korean church in Korea is often regarded as a praying church. Prayer is, indeed, one of the distinguishing characteristics of the Korean church. Historically, prayer has been emphasized and has enabled the Korean church to grow qualitatively and quantitatively. The Korean church has developed a tradition of revivals and strong prayer habits. The practices of daybreak prayer, all-night prayer, and fasting and praying at prayer mountain houses are common. Almost all churches open from 4:00 to 5:00 A.M. for early morning prayer services. Though not all Korean Christians participate daily in these meetings, daybreak prayer is the main source of vitality in the Korean church.

The situation in North America is, however, very different from the experience of Korean immigrant Christians in Korea. According to a recent survey dealing with the prayer lives of Korean immigrant Christians in Canada, many indications show that they cannot follow the same prayer habits in North America as are followed in Korea. Such habits include the daybreak prayer service, prayer at prayer mountain houses, and all-night prayer meetings.[13]

Two main reasons explain why Korean immigrant churches are having difficulty in maintaining the daybreak prayer service. First, most Korean immigrant churches in North America do not possess their own facilities. They meet in the buildings of preexisting American or Canadian congregations. Consequently, they usually have a service in the afternoon on the Lord's Day unless the church building is large enough to permit dual services in the morning. Only about 20 percent of Korean immigrant churches in Canada and about 30 percent of those in the United States own their own buildings.[14] Thus, most Korean Christians do not have ease of access to church buildings.

Second, most Korean immigrants are engaged in small individual enterprises such as variety shops, convenience stores, laundries, and the like. Several factors seem to relate to the tendency of Korean immigrants to concentrate in small businesses. One is the language barrier. Deficiency in the English language results in labor-intensive occupations in North America. They prefer small businesses that do not require fluency in English. Another factor involved is the nature of small business itself. Running such a business guarantees work opportunity for every able member of the family. The capital and labor resources can be utilized at maximum capacity. They also provide the psychological satisfaction of holding ownership.

Since the majority of Korean immigrants are disadvantaged in the segmented labor market (with low skills, long hours of work, unfavorable work conditions, and low earnings), most of their spouses are mobilized into the labor force to supplement the family income. Therefore, attending such a prayer meeting early every morning is almost impossible for most Korean immigrant Christians.

Schism of Korean Immigrant Churches

The Korean church has a strong congregational nature. Although Presbyterian or Methodist in polity, denominational reins are very loose, and for a denomination to discipline a local congregation or to prevent its changing allegiance, such as their going independent or joining another denomination, is virtually impossible. This congregational nature of the Korean churches, combined with the Korean sense of personal loyalty to individuals at the expense of institutions and principles, has contributed to the many splits and divisions in the denominations. When a dynamic church leader disagrees on matters of doctrine, polity, or even church position, personal followers tend to join in with that leader in dissociating themselves and forming a new church or a denomination.

The frequent breaking up of Korean churches has become a serious problem in Korean society. Many non-Christian Koreans indicate that one of the most negative problems of the Korean church in Korea is the frequent splitting and dividing of congregations and denominations.

In North America, the schismatic situation of Korean immigrant churches is worse than in the homeland churches. Conflicts are magnified by the fact that church members are highly diversified in their social backgrounds, current occupations and interests, and personal beliefs or orientations. For most Korean immigrant Christians, the church is one of the few places available to provide focal points of social belonging. The Korean immigrants' deprivation of the fulfillment of their social roles in the larger North American society is precisely what makes the holding of church offices, such as elder or deacon, so important. This same factor is behind so much of the intrachurch conflict that arises regarding the election of officers. Also, many ordained immigrant ministers have few alternative clerical work opportunities. As a result, Korean immigrant churches are often plagued with internal church politics, serious schisms, faction fighting, and empire building. Often, Korean immigrant churches proliferate by church schisms and internal fighting, with the result being the split of one church into two or three churches.

The American Dream and Shamanistic Blessings

Korean immigrants came to North America for their own personal and very human reasons: for financial well-being, for a better education, for political or religious freedom, for greater career opportunities, and the like. They came to this new land in search of a better country, chasing after the American dream. The cornerstone of the American dream has always been financial freedom: having enough money to attain personal fulfillment.

For many people in the world, religion becomes a means for finding a "good or better life." Of course, what counts as "good or better" is dependent on the values of a particular culture. For most Koreans, a good life implies material prosperity, physical health, and long life. Korean Christians want a faith that works toward a good life. The danger is that God and faith can become merely instrumental to human purposes, rather than humans having their lives subordinated to the purposes of God.

This desire to see faith made real is manifest in the desire for what is called "victorious Christianity," the roots of which find their origin in the Keswick Bible Conference movement of the end of the last century.[15] A similar emphasis is found in the so-called wealth and health gospel: "Serve God and get rich and be healthy," although it actually has very little of the character of Christ's gospel in it. In some forms of California Christianity, this "gospel" features an emphasis on positive thinking and a focus on self-esteem. For Korean Christians, however, their pursuit of earthly blessings is rooted in a shamanistic cultural background.

Shamanism has exercised a profound influence on the development of Korean attitudes and practices. Because shamanism is the oldest religion in Korea, brought to the peninsula by the first settlers, its influence pervades many aspects of Korean life and the major world religions that were imported at a later date. Prior to the introduction of the Christian gospel, three major religions—Confucianism, Buddhism, and Taoism—existed in a state of harmony for several centuries in Korea. These three major religions also came to Korea from other countries and took root in a shamanistic religious environment. Buddhism and Confucianism have been shamanized to a certain degree and Christianity has also been influenced.

Korean shamanism has undergone prolonged and intensive interaction with the four religions. It has always been an undercurrent of Korean culture, shaped by a long history of oppression and foreign domination. The end result is a general impression of the long-ingrained habit of religious syncretism. Therefore, in Korea, there is

Buddhist shamanism, Taoist and Confucianist shamanism, and, undoubtedly, Christian shamanism. Based on twenty years' experience of pastoral ministry in the Korean church (ten years in Seoul, Korea, and twelve years in London, England, and Ottawa, Canada), without any hesitation, I can say that one of the most destructive problems among Korean Christians is the shamanistic belief of earthly blessings.

According to a survey conducted by a Korean Protestant church's monthly magazine, *Pastoral Ministry and Theology* (June 1992), of 1,500 non-Christian university students about 20 percent (the largest number group among opinions) have also indicated that the most negative problem of the Korean church is a wish for blessings in this life *(kibok-sasang)*. The shamanistic earthly blessings offer a human-centered, rather than a God-centered Christianity.

Shamanism in Korea

As one of the most primitive natural religions of the world, shamanism is classified by anthropologists as an archaic magico-religious phenomenon in which the shaman is the great master of ecstasy. Shamanism itself was defined by the late Mircea Eliade as a technique of ecstasy.[16] A shaman may exhibit a particular magical specialty (such as control over fire, wind, or magical flight). The most common magical specialty is a power of healing. The distinguishing characteristic of shamanism is its focus on an ecstatic trance state in which the soul of the shaman is believed to leave the body and ascend to the sky (heavens) or descend into the earth (underworld). The shaman makes use of spirit helpers, with whom he or she communicates, all the while retaining control over his or her own consciousness.

Shamanism in Korea is a pragmatic belief system, primarily concerned with the seeking of fortune and the avoidance of misfortune with the aid of the power of a superhuman or shaman *(mudang)*. It has been customary among some ethnologists to relate the ideas of fortune and misfortune to the distinction between gods and spirits: benevolent gods bring fortune while malevolent spirits cause misfortune. In times of sickness, ill-fortune, or death, the shaman is usually present. Although not recognized officially as a religion, shamanism remains the most prevalent form of religiosity in Korea.

Korea was kept basically agricultural before and during the Japanese occupation and did not have much knowledge of the Industrial Revolution until World War II and the Korean War. Thus, shamanism, not surprisingly, has persisted, being that it accommodates itself to an agrarian society. What is amazing is that it has not disappeared since the industrial spurt of the last three decades, which has placed South Korea eleventh in the world in terms of gross national product.

In modern Korea, numerous challenges toward shamanism have all become serious threats to its continued existence. Internationalization, globalization, urbanization, industrialization, the rapid development of computer science and communications technology, and the vigorous propagation of Christianity have all exacted a heavy toll. To those who would drag Korea into Western modernization at any cost, shamanism is a disgrace which is better forgotten. Most educated Koreans are embarrassed if shamanism becomes a topic of conversation. They are quick to deny that shamanism has had anything to do with decent folk, and even quicker to terminate the discussion by proclaiming that it is no longer a part of Korean life.

Shamanistic beliefs and the accompanying worldview may have weakened and even disappeared in many ways. However, after so many centuries of indoctrination in these tenets, Koreans could hardly be said to have discarded the customs, habits, and thought patterns derived from that system. The shamanistic understanding of blessings (wealth, health, power, honor, and so on) and curses (disease, poverty, failure in business, and the like) captures as many Koreans as ever.

For example, shamanistic geomancy is a popular method of divination for locating favorable sites for cities, residences, and burial grounds in Korea. This belief holds that happiness and prosperity will prevail over a house built on an ideal site *(myongdang)*. The site of the ancestral grave must be ideal as well, as the location is believed to exert a lasting and decisive influence over the destinies of descendants. Without exception, powerful families concentrate their attention on securing such places for residences and burial grounds.

Shamanism and Korean Christianity

Because the culture and tradition of shamanism are so strong in Korea, Korean Christianity has adopted many of its characteristics. All of the Protestant churches have adopted a critical attitude toward shamanism, but most of them are influenced by it to a greater or lesser degree. Korean traditional shamanism seems to have carried over into Korean Christianity in many ways. It would be surprising if such socially significant and individually meaningful approaches to life as those in the indigenous religion did not carry over into a new religion when first adopted.

The spiritual world of Korean shamanism may be divided into six classes: the Supreme Being, the gods of the air, the gods of the land, the gods of the water, nameless lesser spirits, and the ancestral spirits.[17] The head of the Korean's shamanistic pantheon is *Hananim*. The name has been variously translated. *Hanal* is the ordinary word for the sky and *Nim* is honorific, so that the ordinary idea has been that the name meant "Honourable Heavens," or "Sky Master." James Gale, taking a suggestion made several hundred years ago by one of the ancient poets, says that the word comes not from *Hanal* ("Heaven"), but from *Hana* ("One") so that it would mean "the Only Great One."[18]

In Korean shamanism, *Hananim* is unique and a supreme god above all gods or spirits. People believe that he sends the harvest and the rain, that by his grace we live and breathe. It was *Hananim* whom Tan-gun (the mystic founder of the country, half divine and half human) worshiped on his high altar on Kanghwado (an island in midwest Korea). The Rain Bringing Ceremonies *(Kiwooje)* are addressed to *Hananim*. Charles A. Clark, one of the early missionaries to Korea, described *Hananim* of shamanism as follows:

> In times of mortal danger, almost the first cry of the Korean is to *Hananim*. He seems to dominate their lives, since his name is continually on their lips, but curious to note, they seem never to really worship him, unless we except the Rain Ceremonies. They say that he sends the harvest, yet in the Fall they offer their sacrifices not to him, but to the gods of the hills, or to the house gods, or to the ancestral tablets. He seems to be everything to them, and then again he seems to be nothing, judging from the way in which they disregard him when all goes well.[19]

The Korean Protestant Church has seized upon this word *Hananim* and has defined it until, for Christians, it holds all of the content in the English word for "God." The Korean Roman Catholic Church uses the Chinese word *Chonjunim* ("The Honourable Lord of Heaven").

Some of the influences of shamanism in Korean Christianity are: (1) a concern with power, and the attraction of a God who can dominate other spirits and protect human proteges; (2) the belief in ubiquitous and potentially dangerous spirits; and (3) the hope of tangible results from faith in Christianity, just as shamanism was often a religious means to specific familial, medical, or financial objectives.[20] These elements are still manifested among Korean churches both in Korea and North America, mostly without their origin being fully recognized. These elements continue to exist, though, in order to attract more people.

The Blessings of *Hananim* between Shamanism and Christianity

In Korean churches, what becomes very apparent is the excessive emphasis in sermons on the believers' earthly blessings. Bong-Ho Son wrote:

> The majority of Korean churches, mostly Presbyterian, Methodist, and Korean Evangelical, remain rather sound, but very few remain totally unaffected by this shamanistic mysticism. The main temptation is to emphasize the promise of earthly blessings in order to attract the shamanistically attuned Korean populace.[21]

In Korea, shamans serve four functions: (1) They act as priests, mediating between human beings and gods and spirits; (2) they offer healing and exorcism, expelling bad spirits to bring relief from physical and mental pain, grief, and distress; (3) they explain abnormal phenomena and predict both bad and good fortune; and (4) they arrange for recreation, providing communal good times of singing, dancing, eating, and drinking, as persons participate together in festive occasions.[22] Korean pastors, both in Korea and in North America, are looked upon and treated almost as shamans by many new believers rather than as spiritual leaders who teach them the Word of God.

After comparing the role of a shaman *(mudang)* and Yong-Gi Cho, the pastor of the Full Gospel Central Church in Seoul (the biggest and perhaps richest church in the world), Boo-Woong Yoo concluded:

> His role in Sunday morning worship looks exactly like that of a shaman or *mudang*. The only difference is that a shaman performs his wonders in the

name of the spirits, while the Rev. Yong-Gi Cho exorcises evil spirits and heals the sick in the name of Jesus.[23]

The visible example of Cho's success has made an enormous impact upon all Korean churches in the world. Numerous pastors attempt to imitate Pastor Cho's "threefold blessings of God," which is based on 3 John 2: "Beloved, I pray that all may go well with you and that you may be in health; I know that it is well with your soul" (RSV). This verse is the basic Scripture text of the so-called gospel of prosperity. Cho interpreted this verse as follows:

1. "all may go well with you" means business or material prosperity;
2. "you may be in health" means good health and longevity;
3. "it is well with your soul" means protection from evil spirits.[24]

Cho and his friends' interpretation of this verse is totally subjective and arbitrary. The Greek word translated "well" *(euodoomai)* means "to go well with someone." This combination of wishing that "all may go well" and for the recipient's "good health" *(hugiainō)* was the standard form of greeting in a personal letter in antiquity. To extend John's wish for Gaius (the recipient of 3 John) to refer to financial and material prosperity for all Christians of all times is totally foreign to the text. John neither intended that, nor could Gaius have so understood it.[25] Thus, Cho's interpretation cannot be the plain meaning of the text.

Koreans have a flair for decorating things with Chinese ideographs, the most common being *su*, meaning long life, and *pok*, bliss. The marks of these two Chinese characters decorate so many everyday articles, such as spoons and pillowcases. Of these two characters, preference is for the former. First is long life, and then well-being. Wealth, a good career, and health are considered factors of bliss. Rev. Cho's threefold blessings certainly connect with the shamanistic belief of *su-pok*, and this kind of preaching satisfies the needs of the majority of the Korean people, both in Korea and North America.

The Christian Bible certainly teaches that Christ's followers may expect earthly as well as spiritual blessings from God. Our God is a God of all the blessings in heaven and earth. When God created Adam and Eve, his first action was to bless them (Gen. 1:28). "I will bless you," said God to Abraham, "I will make your name great, and you will be a blessing" (Gen. 12:2 NIV). God promised to his servant Moses: "In every place where I cause my name to be remembered I will come to you and bless you" (Exod. 20:24). Paul says, "Blessed be the God and Father of our Lord Jesus Christ, who has blessed us in Christ with every spiritual blessing in the heavenly places" (Eph. 1:3). God the Father is the source or origin of every blessing we enjoy.

The biblical *Hananim*'s blessings, since they are that of an omniscient, omnipotent, omnipresent God, are always fully effective, both in supplying human needs in this life and eternal life in the world to come. Therefore, children of God can pray for wealth, health, and longevity on the earth. In order to attract the attention of the shamanistically oriented Koreans, we can legitimately tell them that God is the source or origin of every conceivable blessing. Our presentation of God's blessings, however, has to be pertinent, and done with care. With this matter, at least two things should be deliberated.

The Carefree Attitude toward Earthly Blessings

Earthly blessings of wealth and health, though not excluded, are not the only blessings promised to Christians, nor are they the most important ones. Actually, the carefree attitude toward wealth and possessions, for which neither prosperity nor poverty is a value, is thoroughgoing in the New Testament. "In the full biblical view," says Gordon Fee, "wealth and possessions are a zero value for the people of God. Granted that often in the Old Testament—but never in the New—possessions are frequently related to a life of obedience."[26]

"For the love of money is a root of all kinds of evil," warns Paul to us, "for which some have strayed from the faith in their greediness, and pierced themselves through with many sorrows" (1 Tim. 6:10 NKJV). Then he remembers those who happen to be rich. They are to treat their wealth in this present world with indifference; they must not put their hope in wealth. Rather, they are to be generous and willing to share, for this is true wealth (1 Tim. 6:17–19). The point is, in the kingdom of God, wealth and possessions are simply of zero value for all God's children.

In North America, Korean Christians should practice Jesus' instruction that "it is more blessed to give than to receive" (Acts 20:35). Blessing in giving and sharing is something which is entirely unknown in shamanism and is increasingly being neglected by many Korean Christians. Their scramble for a foothold in North America sometimes brings them into conflict with other ethnic groups, particularly the African American community. In the early 1990s, in New York, Los Angeles, and other cities, publicity and boycotts escalated cases of personal disputes between Korean shopkeepers and African American customers into ethnic confrontations.

So when the April 29, 1992 acquittal of the police officers who beat Rodney King stirred outrage among Los Angeles African Americans, Korean immigrants found themselves among the objects of attack. Of some fifty deaths, only one was Korean American, but it shook the community deeply. Koreans suffered perhaps half of the almost one billion dollars of property damage. Hundreds of businesses, representing years of hard labor by entire families, were looted, burned, or totally destroyed overnight. Their American dream became an American nightmare.

African Americans sometimes accuse Koreans of disrespect toward African American customers and of not putting resources back into the poor neighborhoods from which they draw their income. Korean immigrant Christians should play a significant role in resolving black–Korean tensions. They should learn to give more than just wanting to receive.

Holiness of God

Unlike Christianity, shamanism has almost no ethical teachings. As for ideas of sin and questions of ethical behavior, shamanism does not seem to have exercised much influence. It is not that shamans have taught evil to others. Outside of their example in cultivating the intimate friendship of the evil spirits and the rumored suggestions as to their own private lives, shamans had no message or interest in the matter. They had no doctrine of a judgment day or anything resembling it. It was outside their line of vision.[27] Innumerable spirits are believed to bless and curse human beings according to the spirit's whims. Neither blessings nor curses are morally deserved. We can hardly expect from shamanism such ethical or moral values as justice, righteousness, love, responsibility, and forgiveness.

The Bible calls *Hananim* "holy" (Lev. 11:44–45; Isa. 5:16; 6:3; 41:14; Amos 4:2; John 17:11; Rev. 15:4). The word "holy" signifies everything about God that sets him apart from us and makes him an object of awe, adoration, and dread. God's holiness is entire freedom from moral evil, on the one hand, and absolute moral perfection on the other.

Justice, which means doing right in all circumstances, is an attribute of God which manifests his holiness. God displays his justice as legislator and judge, and also as promise-keeper and pardoner of sin. His moral law, requiring behavior that matches his own, is "holy and just and good" (Rom. 7:12). Since God is infinitely perfect, he must be impartial in his judgments and always treat his creatures with equity. "Far be it from you to do such a thing," said Abraham to the Lord, "to kill the righteous with the wicked, treating the righteous and the wicked alike. Far be it from you! Will not the Judge of all the earth do right?" (Gen. 18:25 NIV).

When God justifies the ungodly through faith in Christ, he does so on the basis of justice done; that is, the punishment of our sins in the person of Christ our substitute. Thus, the form taken by his justifying mercy shows him to be utterly and totally just (Rom. 3:25–26), and our justification itself is shown to be judicially justified.

Holiness is the characteristic mark of a believer in both the Old and the New Testament (Deut. 30:1–10; Eph. 4:17–5:14; 1 Peter 1:13–22). He that would stand in the holy place to worship God must have clean hands and a pure heart and not have sworn to a lie (Ps. 24:3–4). Because God is holy, we must be holy too. In this sense, the biblical *Hananim* differs totally from the shamanistic *Hananim*. Korean churches should emphasize God's holiness before earthly blessings.

Conclusion

Both Canada and the United States are immigrant countries. Without exception, all North Americans are either immigrants themselves or the descendants of immigrants. Most anthropologists believe that the first Native Americans also migrated from Asia in the Old Stone Age. Thus, the population of North America today consists entirely of immigrants or the children of the immigrants. North America is the product of immigration. Its history and society have been woven from successive waves of immigrants.

My family lives in the western suburbs of Ottawa, Canada. In the house next to us lives a single mother with two small children, all of whom are Italian posterity. Next to them is a young couple of French and Polish descent. Across the street is a Jewish family. Next to them is a middle-aged widow of Greek heritage. And on our other side is a retired couple who are Irish immigrants. Next to them is a Brazilian immigrant family. Their next door neighbors are of Chinese descent. Each family in this miniature sample of our North American society maintains its ethnicity, yet we all cooperate together in community events, respect each other's ethnic identity, and we care for each other. Who is the owner of the land of North America? The whole universe belongs to God, the Creator, *Hananim*. The world is God's farmland and a gift to human beings. The land and its fruits are to be shared. The land of North America belongs not only to the people who came early, but to all its residents. The age of the melting pot is gone. Ours is now the age of the salad bowl or buffet where our distinctive and unique identity should give its own distinctive color and unique flavor, thus making the meal more pleasant and abundant.

However, no matter where we live, and what color and flavor we have, <u>human beings are only aliens and strangers on earth</u>. In God's appointed time, every person must go into the shadowland, leaving behind all earthly riches. The mirth of the world endures but a while, and six feet of earth makes all people equal. Korean immigrant Christians, therefore, should know that neither ethnic particularity nor participation, nor health, wealth, and longevity in the North American world are an end in themselves, or the ultimate goal. These are rather the means toward a greater goal—the task of participating in God's own work of establishing his reign in the world. Our dream should be changed from the American dream to the dream of *Hananim-Nara* ("the kingdom of God"). The land of North America has become a mission field. So many people, including the Korean second generation in this land, need the saving power of the Lord Jesus Christ. The following expression clearly states the problem of Korean immigrant churches: When Korean children graduate from high school, they also want to graduate from Korean immigrant churches. The future prospect of Korean immigrant churches depends on the evangelization of the second generation. We are here as messengers of the Lord Jesus Christ, bridge builders between two worlds—God's kingdom and the pagan world. Let the dream of *Hananim-Nara* be our priority.

Conclusion

Throughout the years, from ancient times to these contemporary times, a newsworthy person comes to the attention of people from many cultures. When someone moves into prominence, in a flash, a score of microphones are thrust in his or her face and dozens of newspeople take photographs. Later, when we see these photographs in print, we see the subject, still recognizable, but from varied stances. Or, if the newsperson has a movie camera, we, the audience, see various action shots—walking, standing, climbing. However, in all these perspectives, clearly the same person is perceived but from different aspects. The goal of this book is to capture different perspectives (because of the different cultural stances) of the one God.

Through these subtleties of perception, a united image of the paradoxical attributes of God, operant in various cultures that comprise today's world, emerges: loving power (chapter 2), righteous love (chapter 3), holy strangeness (chapter 4), transcendent immanence (chapter 5), unique creating (chapter 6), traditional uniqueness (chapter 7), merciful holiness (chapter 8), transcendent presence (chapter 9), purposeful holiness (chapter 10), and kingdom-making healing (chapter 11).

Some shot their pictures with a wide-angle lens, depicting God in contrast to the paganism left behind. Others used an eight-millimeter, reacting to the setting of the Christian community and picking God out of its foibles. What we need to remember is that the crowd of photographers is a fluid group of people. Even though one ethnic or gender group, for example, might tend to stay far away while another might tend to run up close, these tendencies are not limited to culture or sex. A cultural group known for its demure, reticent photographers might also have its pushy photographers, or a group known for its assumption that closeness is part of life may have its more reticent members. We have learned that not only is God "one," but also humanity is "one."

Even though perspectives in a culture tend to be similar at points, within each culture are people who exemplify every perspective of every culture here described. Not only is God "global," but humanity is "global" too. By understanding reactions to larger cultural traditions, we can better understand that individuals in our culture may be the way they are because they may have reacted to influences in their own lives, influences similar to entire cultures. In other words, possibly in every microcosm we find other microcosms.

In each culture we find people who have a tendency to want to advance their own power. They need to learn that the God of power is also a God of love (chapter 2). Other people do understand that God is love, but they misunderstand the nature of love. God's love is insepa-rable from both individual and corporate righteousness (chapter 3). This righteousness extends even to strangers, demanding justice for them and of them wherever they may wander (chapter 4). Some people understand that God is transcendent (holy and unknowable), but they need to discover that God is also immanent (one who reveals truths about the divine self, choosing to be known, and drawing people to approach and worship) (chapter 5). Many have perceived God through the general revelation of God's handiwork as the Creator of the world, but they need to learn also that God enters specific relationships with humanity and is a unique and jealous God (chapter 6). Many will look as well for knowledge of God in their traditions. They also need to know that God is above all traditions and has created God's own one in Christ (chapter 7). When some people's emphasis on holiness has made them legalistic, they need to learn to emphasize as well God's mercy (chap-ter 8). Some need to rediscover God at work in history, having stressed God's otherness from creation, and avoid making belief in God merely a stage of spirituality (chapter 9). Others who do not understand the "I Will Be" who works in history are confused about whether God is one or many and stress a holiness unfocused on the purpose and mean-ing of life (chapter 10). Others know too well the power of God to heal and provide good things, neglecting to consider God's primary and ultimate design to be a holy, giving, kingdom-making Ruler (chapter 11). Each of these snapshots enlarges our composite picture of the one great God, viewed from differing perspectives.

Notes

Chapter 1: The God of the Bible

1. Col. 1:15; 1 Tim. 1:17; Heb. 1:3; 11:27. See also Murray J. Harris, *Jesus as God: The New Testament Use of* Theos *in Reference to Jesus* (Grand Rapids: Baker, 1992).

2. For further reading, see Aída Besançon Spencer, *Beyond the Curse: Women Called to Ministry* (Peabody: Hendrickson, 1985), ch. 5; *The Goddess Revival* (Grand Rapids: Baker, 1995), chs. 6–7.

3. Francis Brown, S. R. Driver, and Charles A. Briggs, *A Hebrew and English Lexicon of the Old Testament*, trans. Edward Robinson (Oxford: Clarendon, 1907), 994–95; Phyllis Trible, *God and the Rhetoric of Sexuality*, Overtures to Biblical Theology (Philadelphia: Fortress, 1978), 33, 45, 61.

4. In contrast, Naomi feels deceived by God "Almighty" when she loses her two sons (Ruth 1:5, 20). "Almighty" seems to be related to "breast in Gen. 49:25. Blessings of the "Almighty" are synonymous to "blessings of the breasts and of the womb." The plural for "womb" is compassion. Trible, *Rhetoric*, 62–63.

5. John 6:35, 51; 8:12; 9:5; 10:7, 9, 11; 11:25; 14:6; 15:1.

6. Exod. 3:18; Josh. 24:2; Judg. 4:6; 6:8; 1 Sam. 2:30. In 2 Kings 20:5 and Isa. 38:5, Hezekiah is reminded of "the Lord, the God of your ancestor David."

7. Lev. 19:36; 25:37–38, 47–55.

8. Lev. 26:3–13; Num. 15:37–41; Deut. 11:1–12; 2 Chron. 7:22; Neh. 9:9–17; Jer. 32:20–24.

9. Num. 1:3–4, 26; 31:5, 32, 48, 53; 32:27; Deut. 20:9; Josh. 4:13.

10. Brown, Driver, Briggs, *Lexicon*, 838.

11. 1 Sam. 1:2, 11; 2:4–5.

12. Jer. 33:2–5. Paul also highlights God's role in creation when communicating to Gentiles (Acts 14:15; 17:24). See also John 1:3–9.

13. The early Christians also refer to this title as a reminder to God of God's power over the Gentiles (Acts 4:24–30) and even over Israel (Rom. 11:25–36).

14. Exod. 20:4–5; Deut. 4:23–24; 5:9; 6:14–15.

15. Brown, Driver, Briggs, *Lexicon*, 933.

16. Henry George Liddell and Robert Scott, *A Greek-English Lexicon*, eds. Henry Stuart Jones and Roderick McKenzie, 9th ed. (Oxford: Clarendon, 1940), 1628.

17. Luke 7:13; Matt. 9:36; 20:34.

18. In the parables this deeply felt compassion also always results in action. The father, upon seeing the repentant son from a far distance, runs to him, hugs and kisses him, and celebrates his return (Luke 15:20–22). The Samaritan goes to the robbed man, stripped of clothes, beaten, and alone, gives him first aid, takes him to a hotel, and pays his expenses (Luke 10:33–35). The king releases from bondage and forgives the debt of the slave (Matt. 18:25–27).

19. Nah. 1:2–3; Jer. 9:24–25. See also Aída Besançon Spencer and William David Spencer, *Joy through the Night: Biblical Resources for Suffering People* (Downers Grove: InterVarsity, 1994), ch. 3.

20. Brown, Driver, Briggs, *Lexicon*, 338–39; Karl Feyerabend, *Langenscheidt Pocket Hebrew Dictionary to the Old Testament* (New York: McGraw-Hill, 1969), 104.

21. Gen. 19:19; 39:21; Ruth 2:20; Ezra 7:28; 9:9; Neh. 1:5–6.

22. Num. 14:19; Pss. 25:7; 51:1.

23. Pss. 21:7 [8]; 32:10; 36:7 [8]; Gen. 24:12; 32:10 [11]; Ps. 31:16 [17].

24. 1 Chron. 16:41; 2 Chron. 5:13; Pss. 103:17; 136:1; Lam. 3:22.

25. Brown, Driver, Briggs, *Lexicon*, 52, 54.

26. Josh. 2:12; Deut. 7:9; Prov. 11:19 [18]; Isa. 61:8.

27. See also 1 Cor. 1:9; 10:13.

28. Neh. 9:19–31; Pss. 51:1–2; 86:15–16; 103:8; 145:8–9; Isa. 43:25; Dan. 9:4–5; Eph. 2:4–6; 1 Tim. 1:15.

29. Pss. 71:21; 86:17; 119:82; Isa. 51:3; 52:9.

30. Isa. 12:1; 40:1–2; 49:13.

31. Ps. 23:4; Isa. 51:12 [13]; Zech. 10:2 [1].

32. Gen. 37:35; 50:21; Ruth 2:13; 2 Sam. 10:2; 12:24; 1 Chron. 7:22; Job 2:11; Isa. 22:4; 61:2; 66:12–13; 2 Cor. 1:3–4; 7:6.

33. 2 Kings 14:5–6; 2 Chron. 25:4; Jer. 31:30; Ezek. 18:4, 20.

34. Luke 24:26–27; 1 Cor. 2:2; 2 Cor. 5:21; Heb. 9:11–14; 1 Peter 3:18; 1 John 4:9–10.

35. Lev. 20:26; Isa. 6:3; 1 Cor. 3:17; 2 Cor. 7:1; 1 Tim. 6:15–16; 1 Pet. 1:15–17; Rev. 4:8.

36. Lev. 19; 21:8.

37. Luke 6:2–5; Acts 10:11–15; Heb. 10:14; Gal. 4:10–11; 1 Tim. 4:4.

38. John 17:11, 16; Acts 3:14; 7:52.

39. Lev. 19:18; Matt. 22:36–40.

40. The two earliest Greek uncial manuscripts, Sinaiticus and Vaticanus, support "movement of turning shadow."

41. For further explanation, see Spencer, *Goddess Revival*, ch. 5.

42. See also Matt. 6:24; 19:5–6; 25:40; 28:1; Luke 10:42; 15:7; John 17:11, 21–23; Acts 4:32; Rom. 3:30; 5:15–19; 12:4–5; 15:5–6; 1 Cor. 6:16; 10:17; 12:4–20; Gal. 3:28; Eph. 4:4–6; Col. 3:15; 1 Tim. 3:2; 5:9; Titus 1:6.

43. On the significance of widows in the Bible, see William David Spencer and Aída Besançon Spencer, *The Prayer Life of Jesus: Shout of Agony, Revelation of Love. A Commentary* (Lanham: University Press of America, 1990), 48–50.

Chapter 2: God of Power versus God of Love: The United States of America

1. Bartolomé de las Casas, *History of the Indies*, I, trans. and ed. Andrée Collard (New York: Harper, 1971), 112.

2. Present attempts to explain the existence of evil by limiting the capability of God, as well intentioned as these may be, are simply not the scriptural view. The biblical writings are overwhelming in their revelation of an omnipotent, good God who permits human evil out of tolerant love not out of weakness or the presence of evil in the divine character. Those who would like our further views on this distinction may consult our practical theodicy: Aída Besançon Spencer and William David Spencer, *Joy through the Night: Biblical Resources for Suffering People* (Downers Grove: InterVarsity Press, 1994).

3. All translations are from the New Revised Standard Version of the Bible or by the author.

4. Meanings are gleaned from Francis Brown, et. al., eds., *A Hebrew and English Lexicon of the Old Testament* (Oxford: Oxford University, 1968) and Karl Feyerabend, *Langenscheidt Pocket Hebrew Dictionary to the Old Testament* (New York: McGraw-Hill, 1969).

5. King Ferdinand and Queen Isabella, "Privileges and Prerogatives Granted to Columbus, April 30, 1492," *Documents of American History*, ed. Henry Steele Commager (7th ed.; New York, Appleton-Century-Crofts, 1963), 1.

6. Christopher Columbus, "Discovery of the New World: March 14, 1493," *The Annals of America*, ed. Mortimer Adler (Chicago: Encyclopedia Britannica, 1968), 1, 1. In his journal Columbus recorded many scenes as this one: "Many came and many women, each with something, giving thanks to God, throwing themselves on the ground and raising their hands to the sky, and then shouting to us that we should land" (October 13). Christopher Columbus, *The Journal of Christopher Columbus*, trans. Cecil Jane (London: Anthony Blond, 1968), 28.

7. Columbus, *Journal*, 3.

8. Bartolomé de las Casas, *History of the Indies*, III, 8. Father Casas' own plea that the newly discovered mainland be set aside as a place for missionaries with a ban on soldiers and adventurers following was refused, since "a territory occupied by priests would bring no income to the king" (*History*, III, 138).

9. Casas, II, 43.

10. Ibid., 11.

11. Ibid., 1.

12. Casas, *History*, III, 117.

13. Casas, *History*, I, 96.

14. Casas, III, 145.

15. Casas, II, 1.

16. Casas, I, 93.

17. Casas, II, 43.

18. Casas, III, 117.

19. Ibid. See Matthew 7:21–23, near the end of Jesus' Sermon on the Mount, where he warns, "Not everyone who says to me, 'Lord, Lord,' will enter the kingdom of heaven, but only the one who does the will of my Father in heaven. On that day many will say to me, 'Lord, Lord, did we not prophesy in your name, and cast out demons in your name, and do many deeds of power in your name?' Then I will declare to them, 'I never knew you; go away from me, you evildoers.'"

20. Ibid. Sadly, Casas himself seized on controlled African slavery as a desperate measure to save the Taino-Arawak. When it got out of control, he realized he had merely helped displace the evil and involve more innocent lives in misery and he berated himself bitterly as having been duped. "The clergyman," he writes of himself, "soon repented and judged himself guilty of ignorance. He came to realize black slavery was as unjust as Indian slavery and was no remedy at all, even though he had acted on good faith, and he was not sure that his ignorance and good faith would excuse him in the eyes of God." Rather than helping the Amerindians, he realized bitterly, "What Casas had achieved to help the Spaniards sustain themselves on the land while freeing Indians turned into a business proposition that was no small obstacle to the securing of Indian freedom" (Casas, *History*, III, 29).

The African slave trade that filled the Caribbean islands with slaves, of course, was a sophisticated business operation between African chiefs and European traders. Africa had had slavery centuries before the European slaving vessels ever lumbered down its shores. In 1324, 170 years before Columbus stumbled on the Americas, Emperor Marsa Musa of Mali on the upper Niger went on pilgrimage to Mecca with five hundred slaves. Chiefs regularly traded convicted criminals and prisoners of war. Secret societies, like the Poro Society, sold violators of its rules and split profits among members. The Asante were traders and when European demand for gold was augmented by a demand for wageless labor, they readily obliged. Religions not only sanctioned, but in some instances organized, the slave trade. Enslavement by both Islamic and indigenous slavers, having preceded the European market by centuries, was able to be diverted at once to fill the new need. On the upper Niger

River the slave trade was even controlled by an African traditional religion priestly society, or oracle. Islamic traders began expanding and taking over traditional routes in the 1100s, centuries before Europeans implemented slavery in the Americas. Even today religious fetish slavery of women is still practiced by traditional shrines in Ghana (see Walter Pinpong, "Ministry Breaks Slavery Bonds," *Christianity Today,* 16 Aug. 1993:54).

As the faithful priests in Columbus's time, missionaries and indigenous Christians have been the consistent opponents of Africa's slavery, for the Bible condemns slave traders (1 Tim. 1:10). While African traditional religion is a "power" religion and is commensurate with slavery, Christianity is not and should work steadily to eliminate this great evil.

21. On March 25, 1586, while Shakespeare was still getting ready to entertain the London of Elizabethan England, Sir Walter Raleigh was granted a charter to attempt to plant a colony where his half brother Sir Gilbert Humphrey had failed. The "Virgin Queen" Elizabeth graciously granted him "Virginia" with "free libertie and licence . . . to discover, search, finde out, and view such remote, heathen and barbarous lands, countries, and territories, not actually possessed of any Christian Prince, nor inhabited by Christian People . . . to have, holde occupie and enjoy to him . . . for ever, with all prerogatives" (Queen Elizabeth I, "Charter to Sir Walter Raleigh, March 25, 1584," Commager, *Documents,* 6). Without a thought for the prior claim of the Amerindians, but with deference to the claims of other "Christian" rulers, Roanoke Island was settled.

By April 10, 1606 when Elizabeth's successor King James was issuing the First Charter of Virginia, he had been conditioned to apportion out the rights to North America in a quite obviously highhanded manner. He granted his pioneers to "begin their said first Plantation and Habitation, at any Place upon the said Coast of *Virginia* or *America,* where they shall think fit and convenient." And, with a mere nod at not commandeering land "now actually possessed by any *Christian* Prince or People," he invested them with "Power and Authority to take and surprise by all Ways and Means whatsoever, all and every Person and Persons, with their ships, Vessels, Goods and other Furniture, which shall be found trafficking, into any Harbour or Harbours, Creek or Creeks, or Place, within the Limits or Precincts of the said several Colonies and Plantations . . . under our Obedience." Toward the Amerindians he excused this flagrant encroachment as "so noble a Work, which may, by the Providence of Almighty God, hereafter tend to the Glory of his Divine Majesty, in propagating of *Christian* Religion to such People, as yet live in Darkness and miserable Ignorance of the true Knowledge and Worship of God, and may in time bring the Infidels and Savages, living in those Parts, to human Civility, and to a settled and quiet Government" (King James, "First Charter of Virginia, April 10, 1606," *Documents,* 8–10).

22. These and other examples can be found in George Bullin's introduction to the 1887 edition of Harriet Beecher Stowe's *Uncle Tom's Cabin* (Boston: Houghton Mifflin, 1887), ix–x.

23. From a report of Jamaica's Committee of Assembly, January 28, 1832, quoted in Mavis Christine Campbell, *The Dynamics of Change in a Slave Society* (Madison, New Jersey: Fairleigh Dickinson University, 1976), 213.

24. John L. O'Sullivan, "Our Manifest Destiny," *Annals,* 289.

25. Ibid., 291–92.

26. Ibid., 289, 291.

27. From a letter from Theodore Roosevelt to Henry Cabot Lodge, cited in Charles A. Beard and Mary R. Beard, *The Beards' New Basic History of the United States* (Garden City: Doubleday, 1944), 320–21. Thomas Bailey captures the pugnacious spirit of Roosevelt's and Mahan's times when he observes, "A dangerous spirit of bellicosity was abroad in the United States by 1898. Our people craved new sensations, for many were bored with thread-bare issues like the tariff and free silver. America had not fought a rousing war for over thirty years. The restless younger generation was jealous of the Civil War veterans, with their idealized tales of 'tenting on the old camp ground.'" Small wonder that the Civil War photographic

chronicler Matthew Brady died in poverty in the alms ward of New York City's Presbyterian Hospital. His thousands of photographs were squirreled away in some government bin, having been bought for a pittance at public auction. His graphic record of the horror of the Civil War did not fit the national mood. Instead, as Bailey continues, "War scares with Germany, Italy, Chile, and Britain had whetted the national appetite, while leaving it frustrated. If we were going to show the world that we were 'some pumpkins,' we might have to fight somebody. If we were going to 'keep up with the Joneses,' we would have to acquire overseas real estate, as the other powers were doing." Thomas Bailey, *The American Pageant: A History of the Republic* (Boston: Heath, 1956), 612. This is the kind of lethally competitive attitude that escalates the arms race and precipitates pointless, devastating wars.

28. Alfred Thayer Mahan, "Sea Power and History," *Annals*, 11, 311.

29. Rena M. Atchison, "The Perils of Unrestricted Immigration," *Annals*, 11, 506.

30. Enrique's inspiring story can be found in Casas' *History of the Indies*, III, 125ff.

31. Betsey Stockton's and George Leile's exciting histories can be found respectively in Eileen F. Moffett, "Betsey Stockton: Pioneer American Missionary," *International Bulletin of Missionary Research* (April, 1995): 71–76, and Clement Gayle, *George Leile: Pioneer Missionary to Jamaica* (Kingston: Jamaica Baptist Union, 6 Hope Road, Kingston 10, Jamaica, 1982).

32. In addition to the books already identified, those who would like to read more about these positive contributions can find the records of Christian protest to the witch trial madness in Marion L. Starkey's excellent *The Devil in Massachusetts: A Modern Inquiry into the Salem Witch Trials* (New York: Dolphin, 1949). A corroborating resource is David Levin's *What Happened in Salem?* (New York: Harcourt, Brace & World, 1960). Frederick Douglass tells his account in his books: 1845's *Narrative of the Life of Frederick Douglass, An American Slave* (New York: Dolphin, 1963) and *Life and Times of Frederick Douglass* (New York: Collier, 1962). Harriet Beecher Stowe is the author of the epoch-changing novel *Uncle Tom's Cabin*. Abraham Lincoln's deep and abiding faith can be found in his diaries. After the battle of Gettysburg, he is reported to have made his confession to Christ, telling it to Dr. Gurley, the pastor of New York Avenue Presbyterian Church, where he attended. His attention had wandered during the play "Our American Cousin" and he was telling his wife of his plan to visit Israel and see Bethlehem and Jerusalem when he was shot at Ford's Theater (see syndicated columnist Mike McManus' "Lincoln's Faith Revealed in his Diaries" *New England Church Life*, Feb. 1990: 2). The exciting achievements of women in the church can be found in the outstanding chronicle by Ruth Tucker and Walter Liefeld, *Daughters of the Church: Women and Ministry from New Testament Times to the Present* (Grand Rapids: Zondervan, 1987) and the educational accomplishments of women are catalogued in Barbara Miller Solomon's *In the Company of Educated Women* (New Haven: Yale, 1985). For reference to the missionaries mentioned, see Sydney E. Ahlstrom, *A Religious History of the American People* (New Haven: Yale, 1972), 40, 52, 43–44, 61–62, 103 respectively. These resources give but the merest glimpse of the merciful acts God has done and is doing through those who worship the God of primary love in the United States of America.

33. Statistics are gathered from Otto Johnson, exec. ed., *Information Please, Almanac Atlas and Yearbook* (48th ed.; Boston: Houghton Mifflin, 1995), 824–40, 63, and Bureau of the Census, *Statistical Abstract of the United States: 1994* (114th ed.; Washington, D.C.: U.S. Department of Commerce, 1994), 1–26.

34. Quotations are from Martha L. Girard and Trudy H. Peterson, *The United States Government Manual 1994–95* (2d ed.; Lanham, Md: Office of Official Registrar, National Archives and Records Administration, 1994), 539, 627–28, 699, 749–50. See also J. Robert Dumochel, *Government Assistance Almanac* (Washington: Regnery Gateway, Inc. / Foggy Bottom Publishers, 1988).

35. Office of Research Services of the Presbyterian Church (U.S.A.), *Presbyterian Panel Summary (Listening to Presbyterians): Volunteerism and Other Issues, November 1994* (Louisville: Congregational Ministries Division, Presbyterian Church (U.S.A.), 1994), 1–4.

36. Hugh Davis Graham and Ted Robert Garr, *Violence in America: A Report to the National Commission on the Causes and Prevention of Violence, June, 1969* (New York: Signet, 1969), xv.

37. One caution: mine is not a romantic call for a unilateral disarmament, for, as the lesson of Hitler warned us in this past century, expansionist greed is not the exclusive dream of the Spanish conquistadores, the British empire, the United States, and so on. Just war is a sad but true reality of life in a fallen world. But, mutual, verifiable reduction of arms should be prioritized and encouraged for all nations by Christians of all nations working together globally (with the wisdom of serpents against being duped by partisan political opportunists and the gentleness of doves to ensure safety and just treatment for all).

Chapter 3: The Complementarity of God's Love and God's Righteousness: The United States of America

1. George Orwell, *Animal Farm* (New York: Penguin Books, 1951),114.

2. "The modern civil rights movement began with Rosa Parks' refusal to surrender her seat on a bus to a white man on December 1, 1955 in Montgomery, Alabama. Her arrest for violating the city's segregation laws was the catalyst for a mass boycott of the city's buses, whose ridership was 70 percent black.... The boycott continued until December 20, 1956, when a Supreme Court order declaring Montgomery's segregating seating laws unconstitutional was served on city officials. The next day blacks returned to the integrated buses, but not without violent incidents." *Current Biography Yearbook, 1989* (New York: H.W. Wilson, 1989),431.

3. For example, specifically church-related organizations include the Southern Christian Leadership Conference, Evangelicals for Social Action, The Christian Legal Society, Bread for the World, and Habitat for Humanity.

4. It should also be noted that respected religious pollster George Barna finds that "the percentage of religiously conservative Christians is declining nationwide." Reported in *The Christian Century*, 14 Dec 1994: 1185.

5. Commenting on the notion that the United States is losing its "cultural purity," John Wilson, managing editor of *Books & Culture*, observes: "The reality is much different. Culturally we are all mulattos," Nov./Dec. 1995: 4.

6. Reported in *The New York Times*, 14 March 1996: A16.

7. Thomas A. Harris, *I'm OK—You're OK: A Practical Guide to Transactional Analysis* (New York: Harper & Row, 1969).

8. James M. Wall, "God as a Hobby," *The Christian Century*, 6 Oct 1993: 923.

9. The First Amendment to the United States Constitution reads: "Congress shall make no law respecting an establishment of religion, or prohibiting the free exercise thereof; or abridging the freedom of speech, or of the press, or of the right of the people peaceably to assemble, and to petition the Government for a redress of grievances."

10. So Dietrich Bonhoeffer: "Man has learnt to deal with himself in all questions of importance without recourse to the 'working hypothesis' called 'God'.... [S]o in human affairs generally, 'God' is being pushed more and more out of life" (*Dietrich Bonhoeffer: Selected Writings* [London: HarperCollins, 1995], 157, 165).

11. So A.W. Tozer: "God, being infinite, must possess attributes about which we can know nothing" (*The Knowledge of the Holy* [San Francisco: Harper & Row, 1961], 13).

12. God's love is described as eternal lovingkindness in the Old Testament (Ps. 136; Isa. 63:7; Jer. 31:3) and as self-giving sacrifice in the New Testament (Mark 10:45; John 3:16). Love expresses itself in the wideness of God's mercy (Jonah 4:11) and in compassionate yearning for union with the loved ones (Luke 13:34). Love never seeks its own, and never fails the loved

one (1 Cor. 13). God's righteousness incorporates holiness, integrity, wholeness, justice (Pss. 9:8; 11:7; 37:28; 45:6–7; 82:3; Isa. 30:18). God is love (1 John 4:16); God is also our righteousness (Jer. 23:6; 33:16; 1 Cor. 1:30).

13. Oswald Chambers, *The Love of God* (Fort Washington, Pa.: Christian Literature Crusade, 1973), 22.

14. So world religion scholar Houston Smith, *Newsweek,* 1 April 1996: 68.

15. Unfortunately, in the rush to distance themselves from past acts of discrimination, many well-meaning Christians have concluded that it is inappropriate to share their faith. Increasing unwillingness to witness publicly will only undermine our First Amendment right to freedom of religion, and encourage that easy assumption that a firm believer is a bigot.

16. Erich W. Segal, *Love Story* (New York: Harper & Row, 1970), 91, 131.

17. So George F. Will, "Our Expanding Menu of Rights," *Newsweek,* 14 December 1992, 90.

18. "A World without *Roe,*" *The New Republic,* 20 Feb. 1989: 20. In addition, when reporting on civil rights legislation passed by the city of New York, one attorney declared: "This law is a moral statement as much as anything else, and that moral statement has completely transformed the feel of day-to-day life for gay people here. Civil rights acts reflect society and propel it forward" (*The New York Times,* 21 March 1996: B1).

19. Plenary Address, Christian Legal Society National Conference, Oct. 23, 1986.

20. *The New York Times,* 26 Nov. 1994: 23.

21. *The New York Times,* "News of the Week in Review," 3 Oct. 1993: 3.

22. Ibid.

23. So convicted rapist Mike Tyson: "I'm an ex-felon. . . . I've been in prison three and a half years. Treat me fairly" (*The New York Times,* 23 March 1996: 33). Tyson complained further: "No one gives me any justice" (*Newsday,* 23 March 1996: A41).

24. James Patterson and Peter Kim, *The Day America Told the Truth* (New York: Prentice-Hall, 1991), 27.

25. Alyce M. McKenzie, "'Different Strokes for Different Folks'—America's Quintessential Postmodern Proverb," *Theology Today,* July 1996, 211.

26. A. W. Tozer, *Knowledge,* 27.

27. See more comprehensive treatment of the biblical bases of human liberty and human rights in: Gretchen Gaebelein Hull, "Discrimination and Human Rights," *Applying the Scriptures,* ed. Kenneth G. Kantzer (Grand Rapids: Academie/Zondervan, 1987), 333–51.

28. United Nations, General Assembly, Dec. 10, 1948, *Universal Declaration of Human Rights* (DPI/15–14792), article 1: 3.

29. Hull, *Applying,* 343.

30. Quoted in *The Christian Century,* 22 Feb. 1995: 195.

31. Internal inconsistencies within each pole of the abortion debate only add to the difficulties. So Michael Gorman: "Some actively oppose abortion and call themselves 'pro-life.' But many of them also support a large military budget, further deployment of nuclear weapons, decreased aid to the poor and hungry, and other policies that are hardly pro-life. Their concern for the sanctity of life decreases rapidly after birth; they are more 'pro-birthers' than 'pro-lifers.' On the other hand, those who are working to reverse the arms race and to stop hunger are nearly always 'pro-choice.' Their concern for social justice does not include justice for the unborn. Neither group is able to see its own inconsistency, and each accuses the other of gross disrespect for life" ("Shalom and the Unborn," *Transformation,* January/March 1986: 26–27).

32. New York State Congressman Sherwood Boehlert has wryly observed: "Under the First Amendment, you cannot yell 'Fire!' in a crowded theater. I don't understand people who think the Second Amendment should enable you to fire into a crowded theater" (*The New York Times,* 29 March 1996: B1).

33. "Religious Freedom: Cornerstone of Human Rights," *Christian Legal Society Quarterly*, 3 May 1984: 7.

34. Possibly the most extreme example of a formal presentation of the ideology that "Love is all that matters" was the 1991 Majority Report of the General Assembly Committee on Human Sexuality (Presbyterian Church U.S.A.) in which the conclusion was essentially "almost anything that feels good is good." This report was rejected by a 94% majority of the Commissioners to General Assembly, which action reaffirmed the denomination's allegiance to the authority of Scripture rather than cultural authority.

35. So William Temple, who stated as far back as 1934 that "the atheist who is moved by love is moved by the spirit of God; an atheist who lives by love is saved by his faith in the God whose existence (under that name) he denies" (William Temple, *Nature, Man, and God* [New York: Macmillan, 1934], 405).

36. *The New York Times*, 21 March 1996: A12. Such thinking overlooks the fact that in God's eyes "all have sinned, and fall short of the glory of God" (Rom. 3:23). The wonder of God's love is that "while we still were sinners Christ died for us" (Rom. 5:8) and that all who believe in Christ become "new creations" (2 Cor. 5:17). It is in the light of this new creation that we strive to know and follow God's call to righteousness, which may be entirely counter to current human cultural notions of righteousness.

37. *The New York Times*, 16 March 1996: 27.

38. So one correspondent to the General Assembly Special Committee on Human Sexuality (PCUSA): "If we profess to believe in God's continuing revelation to us, perhaps we should consider that this includes a reevaluation of our definition of 'sin' in terms of the changing mores of our society" (Lines 772–74, "Keeping Body and Soul Together: Sexuality, Spirituality, and Social Justice" [Louisville, Ky., PCUSA Distribution Management Service, 1991]).

39. Question asked in Harper Torch video, "Maybe We're Talking about a Different God" (winter 1996 Catalog, 20).

40. One parishioner of an Episcopal church that is pastored by a practicing homosexual minister believes her children will benefit by seeing "that relationships filled with love are more important than relationships that follow a certain formula" (*The New York Times*, 16 March 1996: 27).

41. *The New York Times*, 18 March 1996: 1.

42. *The New York Times*, 23 March 1996: 9.

43. An important *caveat* is that Christians uphold God's wisdom in a winsome and not abrasive manner, and a manner that recognizes the civil rights of all persons and not only those persons with whom the Christians might agree. Case Hoogenborn gives this insight: "The evangelical community must fight to maintain the right to shape the moral character of its institutions and its members. It must never give up the power of social censure and ostracism even though the force of those powers has weakened considerably in recent years. Yet, as a reconciling force in a pluralistic society, it must lead the way in issuing a call for civil rights and justice for all people and groups regardless of race, religion, saintliness, or sexual preference. Only then will its actions support the witness of the Word it proclaims" ("Gay Rights and Wrongs," *Eternity*, June 1981: 19).

44. Bonhoeffer, *Writings*, 69, 150, 159.

45. Joseph Fletcher, *Situation Ethics: The New Morality* (Philadelphia: Westminster, 1966), 15.

46. Fletcher, *Situation*, 45. Fletcher emphasizes this unique "otherness" of love by stating categorically: "Everything else without exception, all laws and rules and principles and ideals and norms, are only *contingent*, only valid *if they happen* to serve love in any situation" (p. 30).

47. Ibid., 33.

48. In some ways, certain branches of the church have contributed to this slippage by suggesting that there is a sort of "two-phase" conversion experience, whereby one can accept God's free gift of salvation by believing in the work of Christ but then make a later (and perhaps optional) decision to commit to Christ as Lord. Such separation of Christ's saviorship from Christ's lordship (however well-meaning) can encourage persons to think that being a "carnal Christian" is regrettably possible, rather than a contradiction in terms. A return to the scriptural teaching of Romans 6:1–14 is a much needed corrective.

49. A. W. Tozer, *Knowledge*, 15. Tozer observes: "The doctrine of the divine unity means not only that there is but one God; it means also that God is simple, uncomplex, one with Himself. . . . Between his attributes no contradiction can exist. He need not suspend one to exercise another, for in Him all His attributes are one."

50. Ibid., 15.

51. So A. W. Tozer: "Holy is the way God is. To be holy He does not conform to a standard. He is that standard" (Ibid., 105).

52. Jesus by his own testimony did not come to overturn, annul, or erase the Hebrew Scriptures (which are embodied in the term "the law and the prophets"). Rather (Matt. 5:17–20), Jesus came not to abolish but to fulfill, with the word "fulfill" having the sense of what completely permeates and draws out the full depth of meaning. Referring to the Law and the Prophets, John Chrysostom commented that Christ's sayings "were no repeal of the former, but a drawing out and filling up of them" (*Homilies on the Gospel of St. Matthew*, I, trans. G. Prevost [Oxford, 1843], 229).

53. So Merill C. Tenney: "The command 'Stop sinning' presupposes the possibility that the man's affliction may have been caused by his own sin" (*The Expositor's Bible Commentary* 9 [Grand Rapids: Zondervan, 1981], 63). Significantly, John's Gospel teaches belief, not good works, as the entry point into new life in Christ (John 1:12; 3:16; see also Eph. 2:8–9). However, Jesus' interchange with the disabled man in John 5 contains no mention of belief in Christ as Savior, but rather focuses on the man's moral responsibility for specific actions. ("Do you want to be healed?" "Do not sin any more.") To consider any future moral lapse now to be cause for the man's eternal damnation (something "worse" happening) raises a severe problem. Such an interpretation would not only make the man's eternal security dependent on forever after living a sinless life, but would conflict with 1 John's teaching as to the impossibility of sinlessness in this life and therefore the need to deal with the on-going struggle against sin (1 John 1:9–2:2). See also G. Campbell Morgan, *The Gospel according to John* (Old Tappan, N.J.: Revell, n.d.), 89–90.

54. Although not canonical, John 7:53–8:11 is considered by many to be a true tradition and can be invoked in support of tolerating specific moral transgressions by highlighting only John 8:1–7 (so the 1991 PCUSA Majority Report on Human Sexuality, lines 2677–2682). However, the entire passage reveals Jesus inseparably linking loving forgiveness with the command to return to righteousness (v. 11).

55. The recognition of being God's covenant people seems largely lost to many Christians today. When that is the case, there can be a decreasing recognition that Christians are called to uphold God's name and reflect God's standards. In Asian cultures (including that of Asian Americans) where the concept of family honor is still strong, the concept of God's honor will also be strong among Christians influenced by that culture. But in the wider United States culture, with the breakdown of the traditional family and also with the greater mobility that has destroyed neighborhood ties, the concept of upholding family honor is practically nonexistent. Consequently there can be a corresponding lack of any imperative among those who claim to be children of God to uphold God's honor and righteousness. There is much appreciation of the freedom of the child of God as against the servant status (cf. Galatians), but all too often little thought is given to the responsibilities inherent in the privilege of being a family member.

56 Joseph Fletcher, *Situation*, 146. He writes: ". . . . there are no rules—none at all" 55.

57. James Patterson and Peter Kim, *The Day America Told the Truth* (New York: Prentice-Hall, 1991), 25.

58. Ibid., *Day*, 25–26.

59. Houston Smith, *Newsweek*, 1 April 1996: 68 (italics mine).

60. Deborah Tannen, "I'm Sorry, I Won't Apologize," *The New York Times Magazine*, 21 July 1996: 35.

61. Plenary address, Christian Legal Society National Conference, 23 Oct. 1986.

62. P. D. James, *Devices and Desires* (New York: Alfred A. Knopf, 1990), 328.

63. Walter Burghardt, "What Does the Lord Require of You? Do Justice," *Bread for the World Newsletter*, March 1996: 6.

64. For example, even in 1996, child hunger in the United States remains a significant problem. Compare Arthur Simon, *Bread for the World* (Grand Rapids: Eerdmans, 1975), 86, with David Beckman, "Reforming Welfare, Ending Hunger," *The Christian Century*, 31 July–7 August, 1996: 760. Internationally, the United Nations Organization, of which the United States was a founding member state, has not only failed to achieve its stated goal of eradicating war even among its members, but UN humanitarian aid to developing countries has sadly declined (so Secretary-General Boutros Boutros-Ghali, *Confronting New Challenges: Annual Report on the Work of the Organization* [New York: United Nations, 1995], 1).

65. Increasingly in mainline denominations the assurance of pardon is offered but any call to repentance is by-passed. Such an underemphasis on the need to repent is as unbalanced as a paralyzing overemphasis on guilt. True, "in Jesus Christ we are forgiven," but the entry point into that forgiveness is repentance and then belief in the saving work of Christ.

66. So Darrell Jadock: "The contemporary culture war is about the body, yes, but 'body' as a whole unit including mind, body, spirit, soul. We must continue to reflect on the role and importance of physicality, but also on the priority and shape of community—our life together. . . . [O]ne kind of body cannot be understood apart from the other and neither can be fully understood except as a gift from God" (*The Christian Century*, 1–8 February 1995: 107).

67. "Naked and Exposed," *Books & Culture*, March/April 1996: 28.

68. "Since God is perfectly personal and relational, and since we are created in the image of God, then we will be most like God when we live out our personhood in a manner that conforms to who God is" (Catherine Mowry LaCugna, "The Practical Trinity," *The Christian Century*. 15–22 July 1992: 682).

69. Richard J. Foster, *Freedom of Simplicity* (San Francisco: Harper, 1981), 36.

70. W. E. Sangster forcefully observes: "A Church boldly challenging this present social order, and giving visible evidence of our Lord's power to reshape it nearer to his own desire, would open to evangelism millions of people to whom the offer of changed feelings seems a well-intentioned but pitiful irrelevance" (Frank Cumbers, ed., *Daily Readings from W. E. Sangster* [London: Epworth, 1966], 271).

71. Darrell Jadock, "Confused about the Body," *The Christian Century*, 1–8 Feb. 1995: 107. Jadock continues: "Individualism has become so pervasive that we think of the body as a private possession. Not so: the body is the dimension of selfhood that permits communication with others. It is the public self and therefore to some degree a public as well as a private responsibility."

72. Tom Sine, *Cease Fire: Searching for Sanity in America's Culture Wars* (Grand Rapids: Eerdmans, 1995), 134–35.

73. So John Stott: "To proclaim the uniqueness of Jesus is one thing: to proclaim the superiority of Western civilization or ecclesiastical culture is something quite, quite different" (Leadership Luncheon, following the 1983 National Prayer Breakfast, Washington, D.C.).

74. So President George Bush, in addressing the American people when the Gulf War began on January 16, 1991, and similarly with Bush's proclamation regarding Feb. 3, 1991,

as National Day of Prayer, asking God to give America victory. William Willimon warns: "Such a prayer sounds Christian. But it is idolatrous and pagan, the same sort of prayer Caesar always prays to Mars before battle" (Stanley Hauerwas, *In Good Company: The Church as Polis* [Notre Dame: Univ. of Notre Dame Press, 1995], 55).

75. George MacDonald, *Creation in Christ* (Wheaton: Harold Shaw, 1976), 24.

76. In America's national euphoria over the quick conclusion of the Gulf War hostilities, few Americans analyzed the true cost of that war. Lyn Cryderman sadly observed: "Our carefully controlled media coverage lifts before us the remarkable number of only 69 Americans killed in action, and we are grateful that so few of our own lost their lives. But what about the estimates that more than 100,000 Iraqis were killed? What about the estimated 300,000 (including 15,000 civilians) who were injured? The Kuwaitis scorched homeland? What about Iraq's cratered cities? The thousands of humiliated 'enemy' soldiers returning to an uncertain fate? This war, in both human and economic terms, was not cheap. While there is reason to rejoice, the Christian heart must also grieve" (Lyn Cryderman, "Weeping over Baghdad," *Christianity Today*, 29 April 1991: 12).

77. *Carl Henry at His Best* (Portland: Multnomah, 1989), 183.

78. Sadly, current figures show that both as a nation and as evangelical Christians, Americans give only a fraction of their available income to needy peoples. So David Beckman: "The trend in cutting back on foreign aid is global. But the United States is a leader of the trend, which will mean increased hardship for hungry people in poor countries" (*Bread for the World Newsletter*, Aug/Sept 1996: 9). Ronald J. Sider cites recent studies revealing that both American evangelicals and Christians worldwide give only the most minimal amounts of their disposable income to missions and other humanitarian causes (Ronald J. Sider, *One-Sided Christianity: Uniting the Church to Heal a Lost and Broken World* [Grand Rapids: Zondervan, 1993], 191–92).

79. Ronald J. Sider, *Completely Pro-Life* (Downers Grove: InterVarsity, 1987), 29.

80. T. R. Roosevelt's words are quoted on his graveside plaque, Young's Memorial Cemetery, Oyster Bay, New York.

Chapter 4: God the Stranger: An Intercultural Hispanic American Perspective

1. George G. Goodwin, "Fox," *Collier's Encyclopedia*, 1987 ed.; Roy Pinney, *The Animals in the Bible* (New York: Chilton, 1964), 121. See also Ezekiel 13:4.

2. In the Bible, see Matt. 13:32; Deut. 22:6; Ps. 104:16–17; Isa. 31:5; Jer. 8:7. Azaria Alon, *The Natural History of the Land of the Bible* (New York: Paul Hamlyn, 1969), 213–18.

3. Henry George Liddell and Robert Scott define *skēnoō* as "pitch tents, encamp," "live or dwell in a tent." *Skēnoō* refers to a "tent, booth" or "hut" (*A Greek-English Lexicon*, eds. H. S. Jones and R. McKenzie [9th ed., Oxford: Clarendon, 1977], 1608). "Tentmakers" *(skēnopoios)* is used literally in Acts 18:3. *Skēnoō* is used literally in Gen. 13:12; Judg. 5:17, 8:11. *Kataskēnoō* is used literally for "pitch a tent" in Josh. 22:19 (tent of Lord) and Ezek. 25:4 or, more generally, for "dwell" (Deut. 33:12, 28).

4. Matt. 12:46; Mark 3:21, 31; Luke 8:19.

5. See also Prov. 3:24; Ezek. 34:25.

6. Psychologist James Loder's view presented at a Princeton Theological Seminary lecture on "Educational Psychology" in 1971. Erik Erikson mentions that "true 'engagement' with others is the result and the test of firm self-delineation." A clear sense of oneself is a psychological counterpart to a physical space for oneself. Frieda Fromm-Reichmann helps us understand the disciples' desire to return home. She concludes that: "The genesis of anxiety may also be understood as a result of unresolved early emotional tie-ups with significant persons of one's early environment" (eds. Maurice R. Stein, Arthur J. Vidich, and David Man-

ning White, *Identity and Anxiety: Survival of the Person in Mass Society* [Glencoe: Free Press, 1960], 56, 142).

7. Daniel R. Rodríquez-Díaz, "Hidden Stories," *Hidden Stories: Unveiling the History of the Latino Church*, eds. Daniel R. Rodríquez-Díaz and David Cortes-Fuentes (Decatur: A.E.T.H., 1994), 3. Fernando F. Segovia discusses the different possible terms (Latin American, Latinos/as, Hispanic American, etc.) and their accuracy. "Aliens in the Promised Land: The Manifest Destiny of U.S. Hispanic American Theology," *Hispanic/Latino Theology: Challenge and Promise*, eds. Ada María Isasi-Díaz and Fernando F. Segovia (Minneapolis: Fortress, 1996), 37–40.

8. Justo L. González, *The Theological Education of Hispanics* (New York: Fund for Theological Education, 1988), 33–34. See also *Mañana: Christian Theology from a Hispanic Perspective* (Nashville: Abingdon, 1990), 41–42.

The imagery of exile is a recurring theme in contemporary secondary Hispanic American Christian literature. For example, Ada María Isasi-Díaz writes: "I am caught between two worlds, neither of which is fully mine, both of which are partially mine. . . . As a foreigner in an alien land, I have not inherited a garden from my mother but rather a bunch of cuttings. Beautiful but rootless flowering plants—that is my inheritance" (Isasi-Díaz, "A Hispanic Garden in a Foreign Land," *Inheriting Our Mother's Gardens: Feminist Theology in Third World Perspective*, eds. Letty M. Russell, Kwok Pui- Lan, Ada María Isasi-Díaz, and Katie Geneva Cannon [Philadelphia: Westminster, 1988], 92).

Fernando F. Segovia writes "an experience of marginalization and oppression" is "the key to the liberating message of the Bible" ("Toward Intercultural Criticism: A Reading Strategy from the Diaspora," *Reading from this Place* 2, eds. Fernando F. Segovia and Mary Ann Tolbert [Minneapolis: Fortress, 1995], 308, 319). He uses the term "diaspora hermeneutics" (*Reading*, 322). Isasi-Díaz entitles the conclusion "Strangers No Longer" and describes the Latino/Hispanic communities as "marginalized and oppressed people in the United States" (*Hispanic/Latino Theology*, 367). Allan Figueroa Deck, too, describes Hispanics as "Strangers in Their Own Land and Church" (*We Are a People! Initiatives in Hispanic Theology*, ed. Roberto S. Goizueta [Minneapolis: Fortress, 1992], 3). Isasi-Díaz begins *En la Lucha/In the Struggle: A Hispanic Women's Liberation Theology* with a poem by New Yorker Lourdes Casal which explains she will always remain a marginalized stranger even when she returns to the city of her birth. The marginality is within (Minneapolis: Fortress, 1993), vii. "A pilgrim people" is another imagery used for Hispanics. (See Justo L. González, "Hispanic Worship: An Introduction," *¡Alabadle! Hispanic Christian Worship*, ed. Justo L. González (Nashville: Abingdon, 1996), 18; Orlando E. Costas, *Christ outside the Gate: A New Place of Salvation* (MaryKnoll: Orbis, 1982).

9. Rodríquez-Díaz, *Hidden Stories*, 3–4.

10. González, *¡Alabadle!*, 20–22.

11. Allan Figueroa Deck, "Hispanic Catholic Prayer and Worship," *¡Alabadle!*, 39.

12. *The Journal of Christopher Columbus*, trans. Cecil Jane (London: Anthony Blond, 1945), 23.

13. Ana Maria Pineda, "The Oral Tradition of a People: Forjadora de rostro y corazón," *Hispanic/Latino Theology*, 112–13, 115.

14. Gen. 17:8; 23:4; 28:4; 37:1; Exod. 6:4.

15. Gen. 15:13; Exod. 22:21; 23:9; Deut. 23:7; 1 Chron. 16:19–20; Ps. 105:12–13.

16. Acts 10:34; Rom. 2:11; James 2:1, 9; Eph. 6:9; Gal. 2:6; Matt. 22:16. See Aída Besançon Spencer, and others, *The Goddess Revival* (Grand Rapids: Baker, 1995), 191–92.

17. Lev. 19:9–10; 23:22; 25:6; Deut. 16:9–12; 24:19–22; 26:11.

18. Jer. 7:5–7; 22:3–5; Ezek. 22:7; Zech. 7:10.

19. Deut. 29:10–12; 31:12; Josh. 8:33–35; 2 Chron. 30:23–25.

20. Lev. 22:17–19; Num. 15:14–16. Philo *Embassy to Gaius* XL mentions that the Roman emperor Augustus "gave orders for a continuation of whole burnt offerings every day to the Most High God to be charged to his own purse."

21. Exod. 20:10; 23:12; Lev. 16:29–30; 25:6; Deut. 5:14.

22. Exod. 12:19, 48–49; Num. 9:14.

23. Exod. 12:49; Lev. 24:22; Num. 15:29. Foreigners could be enslaved (Lev. 25:45–47) and charged interest (Deut. 23:20). They could not serve as ruler (Deut. 17:15). They could not be forced to forgive debts every seventh year (Deut. 15:3).

24. Lev. 17:8–16; 18:26; 20:2; 24:16; Num. 15:27–30; 19:10; Ezek. 14:7.

25. For succinct but clear examples of oppression of Hispanic women in the United States, see Isasi-Díaz, *En la Lucha*, 188–90.

26. For arguments that Zipporah was "black," see Charles B. Copher, "The Black Presence in the Old Testament," *Stony the Road We Trod: African American Biblical Interpretation*, ed. Cain Hope Felder (Minneapolis: Fortress, 1991), 135, 152, 156.

Sensitized Hispanics are conscious of their interracial heritage, "a mestizo people." According to Ismael Garcia, "North American Hispanics embody all major racial groups— African, Asian, Caucasian, and Indian" ("A Theological-Ethical Analysis of Hispanic Struggles for Community Building in the United States," *Hispanic/Latino Theology*, 289, 354). Isasi-Díaz summarizes this view with a proverb: "Aquí todos somos café con leche; unas más café, otros más leche, here we all are coffee and milk; some more coffee, others more milk" (*En la Lucha*, 15). González points out that "the *mestizo's* very existence is a challenge to the neat divisions and classifications that are used to justify the existing status quo of exploitation and segregation" (*¡Alabadle!*, 15). Teresa Chávez Sauceda has a chapter on "Becoming a Mestizo Church" in *¡Alabadle!*

27. Emmett Velten and Carlene T. Simpson, *Rx for Learning Disability* (Chicago: Nelson-Hall, 1978), 18.

28. Spanish was the most frequent language other than English spoken in United States' homes in 1990. In 76% of Hispanic homes, Spanish is spoken in the home (Ronald H. Brown, and others, eds. *Statistical Abstract of the United States 1995* [115th ed.; Lanham: U.S. Bureau of the Census, 1995], 51, 53). See also González, *The Theological Education of Hispanics*, 11–12.

29. Exod. 32:1–8, 19. See also Num. 12:2.

30. "Anomie, anomy," *Webster's New Universal Unabridged Dictionary*, 2d ed.

31. Matt. 7:23; 2 Cor. 6:14; Heb. 1:9; 10:17.

32. Josh. 6:23–25; Heb. 11:31; James 2:25.

33. For a similar view, see Don C. Gibbons and Joseph F. Jones *The Study of Deviance: Perspectives and Problems* (Englewood Cliffs; Prentice-Hall, 1975), chap. 6.

Chapter 5: Transcendent but Not Remote: The Caribbean

1. Abbot Mulago as cited by Ngindu Mushete, "The History of Theology in Africa: From Polemics to Critical Irenics," *African Theology En Route*, eds. Kofi Appiah-Kubi and Sergio Torres (Maryknoll, N.Y.: Orbis, 1981), 28.

2. Jose B. Chipenda, "Theological Options in Africa Today," *African Theology*, 71.

3. Examples of the domestication of theology by culture would include the kind of apologetics mounted for the conquest of the Americas by the European powers, especially Spain, the theology of racial superiority, the theology of tribalism, and so on (see chapters by W. D. Spencer in this volume).

4. See the excellent article by Timothy Erdel on "Theological Education and Religious Pluralism," *BINAH* 1 (1996): 34–50.

5. For example, when the Ghanaian theologian Osofo Okomfo Kwabena Damuah set about formulating his theology of African identity he purposefully set aside Christian ideas,

relying solely on traditional African Religion. See Kwame Dediako, *Christianity in Africa: The Renewal of a Non-Western Religion* (Edinburgh: Edinburgh University, 1995), 17–38.

6. In this regard, Gabriel Setiloane boldly asserts: "African myths concerning the origins of human beings and things make much more sense than the creation myths of Genesis. . . . We Africans are bringing to Christianity a view of Divinity much higher, deeper, and more pervasive" (Gabriel Setiloane, "Where Are We in African Theology?" *African Theology*, 62–63).

7. Merci Amba Oduyoye, "The Value of African Religious Beliefs and Practices for Christian Theology," *African Theology*, 110, 115.

8. Bediako, *Christianity in Africa*, 85.

9. Ibid., 84–85, 102–106.

10. William Dyrness, *Learning about Theology from the Third World* (Grand Rapids: Zondervan, 1990), 32. Here Dyrness is citing Sunand Suminthra in Bong Rin Ro and Ruth Eschenauer, eds., *The Bible and Theology in Asia* (Seoul: Word of Life, 1984), 220.

11. *Bible and Theology*, 32.

12. Ibid., 20.

13. Dale Bisnauth, *History of Religions in the Caribbean* (Kingston: Kingston Publishers Limited, 1989), 82.

14. Ibid., 178.

15. Trinidadian Shango refers to the Yoruba deity Elephon as "Eternal Father" or the head of the divine pantheon. However, in Yoruba belief, the supreme God is Olurun, not Elephon. Because of this, some scholars believe that the title attributed to Elephon is nominal, not substantial (see Bisnauth, *History of Religions*, 172).

Does this mean that the concept of a supreme being as a high god is absent from Shango? If the contention that the ascription of the title "father" to Elephon is correct, the question must be answered in the positive. However, could we not argue that the ascription of the title to a lesser deity means that the *concept* of the high god did survive the Middle Passage? In this case it would be the *name* of the high god that did not make it across the Atlantic.

16. In Revivalism "trumping" is an intense and forceful dance performed by worshipers in a counter clockwise direction to induce possession by the spirits.

17. In Haitian Vaudou, for example, dead twins, called Marassa, are often divinised as *loas*. In Jamaican revival cults certain deceased leaders, referred to as shepherds/shepherdesses, have become trumping spirits. In Shango, "certain deities (powers) are former cult leaders who have come to be regarded as powers" (George Simpson, *Religious Cults of the Caribbean* [Rio Piedra, Puerto Rico: University of Puerto Rico, 1970], 23; Bisnauth, *History of Religions*, 169; and L. Hurbon, *Dieu dans le Vaudou Haitien* [Port-au-Prince: Henry Deschamps, 1987], 151).

18. Joseph Moore, *Religion of Jamaican Negroes: A Study of Afro-Jamaican Acculturation* (Ph.D. Diss., Northwestern University, Evanston, Ill., 1953), 79.

19. Moore, *Religion*, 79.

20. Simpson, *Religious Cults*, 94.

21. Bisnauth, *History of Religions*, 178; Moore, *Religion*, 79.

22. Bisnauth, *History of Religions*, 86–87; Hurbon, *Dieu*, 188.

23. Cornelius Olowola, *African Religion and Christian Faith* (African Christian Press, 1993), 14. Also Bisnauth, *History of Religions*, 11.

24. Francis Osborne, *History of the Catholic Church in Jamaica* (Chicago: Loyola University, 1988), 11.

25. Ivor Morrish, *Obeah, Christ and Rastaman: Jamaica and its Religion* (Cambridge: James Clarke, 1982), 19–20. Also Hurbon, *Dieu*, 124.

26. Hurbon, *Dieu*, 123.

27. Morrish, *Obeah, Christ*, 19; George Mulrain, *Theology in Folk Culture: The Theological Significance of Haitian Folk Religion* (Frankfurtam Main: Peter Lang, 1984), 103.

28. Mulrain, *Theology*, 103.

29. Morrish, *Obeah, Christ*, 19.

30. Mulrain, *Theology*, 102.

31. Edward Seaga, "Revival Cults in Jamaica," *Jamaica Journal* 3, no. 2 (June 1969), 3–13 especially, 10.

32. Hurbon, *Dieu*, 150, 168–69.

33. Ibid., 178.

34. Ibid., 179–80.

35. Ibid., 182.

36. Ibid., 182.

37. Ibid., 185.

38. Ibid., 180–82, 198.

39. Ibid., 187.

40. Simpson, *Religious Cults*, 103; Hurbon, *Dieu*, 198.

41. William Dyrness, *Themes in Old Testament Theology* (Downers Grove: InterVarsity, 1979), 65.

42. Ibid.

43. Hurbon, *Dieu*, 185.

44. Ibid., 124.

45. Bisnauth, *History of Religions*, 84.

46. John Gray, "The Book of Exodus," *The Interpreter's One Volume Commentary on the Bible* (Nashville: Abingdon, 1971), 30.

47. Donald Guthrie, J. A. Motyer, eds., *New Bible Commentary: Revised* (Downers Grove: InterVarsity, 1970), 117.

48. Ibid.

49. See Stanley Grenz and Roger Olson, *Theology in the Twentieth Century* (Downers Grove: InterVarsity, 1993).

Chapter 6: Unapproachable God: The High God of African Traditional Religion

1. Oyetunde (1979).

2. Bruce K. Waltke, *Creation and Chaos* (Portland: Western Conservative Baptist Seminary, 1974), 3.

3. Victor C. Uchendu, *The Igbo of Southeast Nigeria* (New York: Holt, Rinehart & Winston, 1965), 11.

4. Basil Davidson, *A History of West Africa to the Nineteenth Century* (New York: Doubleday, 1966), 39–81.

5. Samuel Johnson, *The History of the Yorubas from the Earliest Times to the Beginning of the British Protectorate*, ed. O. Johnson (Lagos: CMS Bookshop, 1921), 67–72.

6. Eugene Ruyle, "Slavery, Surplus, and Stratification on the Northwest Coast: The Ethnoenergetics of an Incipient Stratification System," *Current Anthropology* 14 (1973): 630–31.

7. John S. Mbiti, *African Religions and Philosophies* (New York: Doubleday, 1970), 20.

8. Max Assimeng, "Toward an Understanding of Traditional Religion in Ghana: A Preliminary Guide to Research" (unpublished paper, University of Ghana, 1975), 12–13.

9. Uchendu, *The Igbo*, 13.

10. Simon N. Patten, *The Social Basis of Religion* (New York: MacMillan, 1911), 13.

11. Edwin W. Smith, *The Religion of Lower Races* (New York: MacMillan, 1923, 7.

12. Such a misconception as this has been strongly condemned by modern researchers under the light of better scientific investigations. See, for instance, E. Bolaji Idowu, *Olodumare: God in Yoruba Belief* (London: Longmans, Green, 1962), 64–67.

13. Ibid., 65.

14. Ernest Harms, "Five Basic Types of the Theistic Worlds in the Religions of Man," *Numen* 12 (1966): 205–40.

15. Some of the African writers such as J. B. Danquah, *The Akan Doctrine of God* (London: Lutterworth, 1944), and Harry Sawyerr, *God, Ancestor or Creator? Aspects of Traditional Belief in Ghana, Nigeria and Sierra Leone* (London: Longman Group, 1970), have argued that God in African perception is the great grand Ancestor. Others, such as Mbiti and Idowu, have identified God as the Creator.

16. Assimeng, "Traditional Religion in Ghana," 32.

17. P. M. Williams, "Ogboni Cult," *Africa* 30 (1960): 364.

18. See A. L. Kroeber and E. W. Gifford, "World Renewal, a Cult System of Native Northwest Coast of California," *Anthropological Records* 13 (1949): 1–156.

19. Of two hundred questionnaires used in ten African countries across the Sudan, 99% answered the question of life after death in the affirmative.

20. J. Awolalu Omosade, "Sacrifice in the Religion of the Yoruba" (Ph.D. diss., University of Ibadan, 1970), 34.

21. Jomo Kenyatta, *Facing Mount Kenya: The Tribal Life of the Gikuyu* (London: Martin Secker & Warburg, 1953), 266–67 and Mbiti, *African Religions and Philosophies*, 116.

22. A lot of debate has been transpiring among African scholars as to whether the Africans worship or venerate their ancestors.

23. See "400 Divinities" in Modupe Oduyoye, *The Vocabulary of Yoruba Religious Discourse* (Ibadan: Daystar, 1971), 17–20.

24. J. Olumide Lucas devoted the introductory part of his book to this subject. *The Religion of the Yorubas* (Lagos: CMS Bookshop, 1948), 3–30. While his philological efforts are praiseworthy, the present writer rejects his etymology for the word *orisa*.

25. Oduyoye, *The Vocabulary*, 18.

26. N. A. Fadipe, *The Sociology of the Yoruba* (Ibadan: University, 1970), 262.

27. See Samuel Johnson, *The History of the Yorubas*, 43; Idowu, *Olodumare*, 90; Lucas, *The Religion of the Yorubas*, 104.

28. Geoffrey Parrinder, *West African Religion* (London: Epworth, 1961), 38.

29. James D. Pritchard, *The Ancient Near East: An Anthology of Texts and Pictures*, vol. 1 (Princeton: Princeton University, 1958), 36.

30. G. T. Basden, *Among the Ibos of Nigeria* (London: Seeley Service, 1921), 219.

31. Idowu, *Olodumare*, 57–106; Idowu, *African Traditional Religion: A Definition* (New York: Orbis, 1973), 165–73.

32. Kwesi A. Dickson and Paul Ellingworth, eds., *Biblical Revelation and African Beliefs* (London: Lutterworth, 1969), 42.

33. Ibid.

34. Lucas, *The Religion of the Yorubas*, 51–98; Idowu, *African Traditional Religion*, 172.

35. Assimeng, "Traditional Religion in Ghana," 30.

36. Cited by Carl F. H. Henry, *God, Revelation and Authority*, vol. 1: *God Who Speaks and Shows* (Waco, Tex.: Word, 1976), 76–77.

37. P. A. Sarpong, *Ghana in Retrospect: Some Aspects of Ghanaian Culture* (Tema: Ghana, 1974), 4.

38. In biblical theology it is the heart of humans that is deceitful above all things and desperately wicked (Jer. 17:9). Spiritual regeneration is an internal work of the Holy Spirit in each believing sinner, replacing the heart of stone with one of flesh and writing God's laws upon it (cf. Jer. 31:33–34; Heb. 8:10). On the contrary, the Yoruba figure *okan* ("heart") cannot be reached to be washed. Thus salvation or destiny consists of the external. The point should not be missed, however, that regardless of perversion they perceive supernatural contact and control.

39. Sawyerr, *God: Ancestor or Creator?* (London: Longman Group, 1970), xi; Sawyerr, "African Concepts of Life and Death," paper presented at the Seminar on Moral and Religious Issues in Population Dynamics and Development, University of Ghana, Legon, 1974, p.e.

40. John Calvin, *Institutes of the Christian Religion,* trans. Henry Beveridge, vol. 1 (Grand Rapids, Eerdmans, 1972), 44; also T. H. L. Parker, *Calvin's Doctrine of the Knowledge of God,* rev. ed. (Grand Rapids: Eerdmans, 1959), 8. Luther, like Calvin, allows that "even the heathen have this awareness (sensum) by a natural instinct, that there is some supreme deity (numen) ... for this knowledge is divinely implanted in the minds of all men, even if they afterwards err in this, who that God is and how He wills to be worshiped" (Quoted by P. S. Watson, *Let God Be God* [Philadelphia: Muhlenberg, 1949], 80).

41. Mircea Eliade, *The Sacred and the Profane* (London: Epworth, 1958; Harper, 1959), 137.

42. K. O. K. Onyoiha, "Was the Black Man Ever a Pagan? If No, What Was He?" paper presented at a colloquium during the Second World Black and African Festival of Arts and Cultures, Lagos, January 15 to February 12, 1977, pp. 1–2.

43. Mbiti, *African Religions and Philosophies,* 63.

44. Lewis Sperry Chafer, *Systematic Theology,* vol. 1 (1973): *Prolegomena—Bibliography—Theology Proper* (Dallas: Dallas Seminary, 1973), 49, 52.

45. Chafer, *Prolegomena,* 49.

46. George W. Peters, *A Biblical Theology of Missions* (Chicago: Moody, 1972), 84.

47. In *Enuma elis* ("When on high") we have the account of the creation drama beginning with the birth of the gods. And in the Epic of Gilgamesh the earthly things, as humans and nature, love and adventure, friendship and combat, all culminating in the deluge are recorded. See Pritchard, *The Ancient Near East,* vol. 1.

48. Cases of myths of creation and/or "paradise lost" spread all over Africa. H. Baumann, in *Schopfund und Urzeit des Menschen in Mythus, der A africanischen Volker* (Berlin: Reimer, 1964), has analyzed two thousand African myths. In all of them he came to the conclusion that God is the explanation of human origin and sustenance.

49. Interview with the Reverend John Mpaayei, a well-educated Masai man of Kenya, Nairobi, Kenya, July 24, 1977.

50. Erich Sauer, *The Dawn of World Redemption,* trans. G. H. Lang (Grand Rapids: Eerdmans, 1973), 82.

51. *Westminster Shorter Catechism,* with an analysis by R. Boyd (New York: M. W. Dowd, 1860), question 11.

52. Charles Hodge, *Systematic Theology,* vol. 1 (Grand Rapids: Eerdmans, 1975), 575 ff.

53. D. Campbell, *In the Heart of Bantuland* (London: Oxford University, 1922), 245.

54. John Mbiti, *The Prayers of African Religion* (New York: Orbis; London: SPCK, 1975), 57.

55. P. Schebesta, *Revisiting My Pygmy Hosts,* vol. 2 (London: E. T., 1936), 171.

56. R. A. Lystad, *The Ashanti* (New Brunswick: Gospel Publications, 1957), 163–64.

57. S. Abiodun Adewale, "The Interaction of Religions among the Egba" (Ph.D. diss., University of Ibadan, 1976), 9–10.

58. In traditional Yoruba society, *Ifa* is of paramount importance. Before any major undertaking such as betrothal, marriage, childbirth, building a house, or going on a trip, *Ifa* is always consulted. It is like "augury" and "auspices" in Roman society.

59. The Reverend H. Townsend, letter, August 27, 1850, in "Proceedings of Church Missionary Society," 1851, 100–101.

Chapter 7: The God above Tradition Who Speaks to All Traditions: An African (Ghanaian) Perspective

1. The material in this chapter was drawn from my thesis, "Pastoral Care and the Ghanaian Tradition: Guidelines for Ministry" (D.Min. diss., Gordon-Conwell Theological Seminary, 1993).

2. *Webster's New Twentieth Century Dictionary*, (2d ed., 1977), 1934.

3. *Vine's Expository Dictionary of Bible Words* (Nashville: Thomas Nelson, 1984), 639.

4. *Webster's*, 1527.

5. *Chambers English Dictionary* (Edinburgh: W & R Chambers, 1988), 1240.

6. James Strong, *Strong's Exhaustive Concordance of the Bible* (Nashville: Abingdon, 1986), 47. The Greek rendering is *threskeia*.

7. Kwabena Amponsah, *Topics on West African Traditional Religion*, vol. 1 (Accra: Adwinsa, 1977), 13.

8. Kofi Asare Opoku, *West African Traditional Religion* (Accra: FEP International Private, 1978), 8.

9. Byang H. Kato, *Theological Pitfalls in Africa* (Kisumu: Evangel, 1975), 18.

10. Opoku, *West African Traditional Religion*, 3.

11. Ibid., 3.

12. Kato, *Theological Pitfalls*, 20.

13. Ibid., 21.

14. Opoku, *West African Traditional Religion*, 4.

15. Ibid., 4.

16. Kato, *Theological Pitfalls*, 22.

17. Ibid., 20.

18. Opoku, *West African Traditional Religion*, 8

19. Kato, *Theological Pitfalls*, 24.

20. Opoku, *West African Traditional Religion*, 9–17. This is the set of beliefs of the African traditional systems which is not different from that of the Ghanaian traditional religious systems.

21. Opoku, *The Black Experience in Religion*, 293–94.

22. The data is taken from Peter Barker's *Peoples, Languages and Religion in Northern Ghana* (Accra: Ghana Evangelism Committee, 1986). This is a preliminary study gathered from prepared questionnaires and personal interviews. Barker's report contains up-to-date information on the Northern peoples of Ghana.

23. Baafuor Kese-Amankwaa, *Indigenous Religion and Culture*. (Legon: Baafuor Educational Enterprises, 1980), 59.

24. Paul Makhubu, *Who Are the Independent Churches?* (Johannesburg: Skotaville, 1988), 65.

25. Tokunboh Adeyemo, *Salvation in African Tradition* (Nairobi: Evangel, 1979), 93.

26. Kese-Amankwaa, *Indigenous Religion and Culture*, 58.

27. Victor Lamont, *Ed. Risk* 7 (No 3, 1991): 57.

28. Adeyemo, *Salvation in African Tradition*, 96.

Chapter 8: Viewing God through the Twin Lenses of Holiness and Mercy: A Chinese American Perspective

1. While the term "second generation" can refer either to the first-generation immigrant or the first generation born in America, I have used the term to describe those born in the States to immigrant parents.

2 . I have relied on the Wade-Giles Romanization system for the transliteration of Chinese words.

3. Stanford M. Lyman, *Chinese Americans, Ethnic Groups in Comparative Perspective*, ed. Peter I. Rose (New York: Random House, 1974), 11.

4. Translation by Wing-Tsit Chan, ed., *A Source Book in Chinese Philosophy* (Princeton: Princeton University, 1963), 23. Wing-Tsit Chan's text is considered a standard translation and primer on Chinese philosophy. I found his introductions to key figures in Chinese thought, including Confucius, especially helpful.

5. Wing-Tsit Chan, ed, *Chinese Philosophy,* 14–17. I normally would correct the use of noninclusive language, but in the case of Confucius, I have chosen not to, because, historically, he was addressing the male sex exclusively in his discourse on virtue.

6. For more details on the civil service examinations, see Conrad Schirokauer, *A Brief History of Chinese Civilization* (2d ed.; New York: Harcourt Brace & Co., 1991).

7. An excerpt from the *The Doctrine of the Mean,* chap. 31, as quoted in James Legge, trans., *The Chinese Classics,* I (Hong Kong: Hong Kong University, 1960), 428–29.

8. Kenneth Uyeda Fong, *Insights for Growing Asian-American Ministries* (2d ed.; Rosemead, California: EverGrowing Publications, 1990), 95.

9. Fong, *Insights,* 95.

10. Wilberta L. Chinn, *Singles Sorting It Out: Discussion Guide* (Whittier, California: Peacock Enterprises, 1991), 39.

11. For the entire story, read Amy Tan, "Rules of the Game," in *The Joy Luck Club* (New York: G.P. Putnam's Sons, 1989), 89–101.

12. Judson Cornwall, *Let Us Be Holy* (Plainfield, New Jersey: Logos International, 1978), 17.

13. All Scriptural quotations are from the New Revised Standard Version unless otherwise noted.

14. Neh. 11:1, 18; Isa. 48:2; 52:1.

15 . Pss. 5:7; 65:4; Jonah 2:4, 7; Micah 1:2; Hab. 2:20.

16. Isa. 11:9; 27:13; 56:7; 57:13; 65:11, 25; 66:20; Ezek. 20:40; 28:14; Zeph. 3:11.

17. Wing Ning Pang, "The Chinese Church in North America, 1980–1990," CCCOWE-NA, Research Committee, unpublished draft, 62.

18. E.g., Sabbath (Exod. 16:23; 20:8); Passover (Exod. 12:16).

19. Num. 4:15, 19–20; 2 Chron. 5:5, 7.

20. Exod. 40:10; 1 Kings 15:15; 1 Chron. 9:29; 1 Chron. 22:19.

21. Walter C. Kaiser, Jr., *Toward Old Testament Ethics* (Grand Rapids: Zondervan, 1993), 6.

22. The New Testament authors repeatedly refer to God's people as "saints." See Acts 9:13, 32, 41; 26:10; Rom. 1:7; 8:27; 12:13; 15:25–26, 31; 16:2, 15; 1 Cor. 1:2; 6:1–2; 14:33; 16:1, 15; 2 Cor. 1:1; 8:4; 9:12; Eph. 1:1, 15, 18; 2:19; 3:8, 18; 4:12; 5:3; 6:18; Phil. 1:1; 4:22; Col. 1:2, 4, 12, 26; 1 Thess. 3:13; 2 Thess. 1:10; 1 Tim. 5:10; Philem. 5, 7; Heb. 6:10; 13:24; Jude 3; Rev. 8:3–4; 14:12; 16:6; 17:6; 19:8; 20:9.

23. Fong, *Insights,* 42.

24. Ibid., 42.

25. Lisa Tsoi Hoshmand and David Y.F. Ho, "Moral Dimensions of Selfhood: Chinese Traditions and Cultural Change," *World Psychology,* 1, no. 3 (1995): 52.

26. Num. 14:18, Deut. 5:10, Ps. 106:7, Lam. 3:22.

27. Ps. 103:13, Isa. 9:17, Jer. 31:20, Hos. 2:23.

28. Gen. 33:5, Exod. 33:19, Num. 6:25, Isa. 33:2.

29. Matt. 15:22, Mark 10:47, Eph. 2:4.

30. 2 Cor. 1:3, Phil. 2:1.

31. Mark 6:34 Luke 7:13; 15:20.

32. "Mercy," *The New Bible Dictionary,* 2d ed. (1988).

33. Irene Eng, Brown University, Providence, R.I., Letter to InterVarsity Christian Fellowship supporters, November 1995.

34. Joan E. Rigdon, "Exploding Myth: Asian-American Youth Suffer a Rising Toll from Heavy Pressures," *The Wall Street Journal,* 10 July 1991: A1, 4.

Chapter 9: *Shang-di:* God from the Chinese Perspective

1. Hans Kung and Julia Ching, *Christianity and Chinese Religions* (New York: Doubleday, 1989).

2. Julia Ching, *Chinese Religions* (Maryknoll: Orbis, 1993), 4.

3. Ibid., 5.

4. Lawrence G. Thompson, *Chinese Religion: An Introduction* (Belmont: Dickenson, 1969), 3.

5. David S. Noss and John B. Noss, *A History of the World's Religions* (New York: MacMillan, 1990), 254.

6. Ching, *Chinese Religions*, 34.

7. Ibid., 34.

8. U. Cassuto, *A Commentary on the Book of Genesis*, vol. 1: trans. I. Abrahams (Jerusalem: Magnes, 1961–64), 86–87. See also Victor P. Hamilton, *The Book of Genesis: Chapters 1–17*, New International Commentary on the Old Testament (Grand Rapids: Eerdmans, 1990), 153.

9. Kung and Ching, *Christianity and Chinese Religions*, 100.

10. H.H. Rowley has described Confucius as both reformer and statesman, as were the great Hebrew prophets like Amos, Isaiah, Jeremiah, and so on (H.H. Rowley, *Prophecy and Religion in Ancient China and Israel* [London: Athlone, 1956]). But Rowley also acknowledges that Confucius does not have what most distinguishes the great prophets of Israel: a very personal vocation from God as his direct messenger. See also John Berthrong, *Eerdmans' Handbook to the World's Religions* (Grand Rapids: Eerdmans, 1982), 248.

11. Berthrong, *Eerdmans' Handbook*, 248–49.

12. The American reprint of *The Works of Mencius* in Robert O. Ballou, *The Bible of the World* (New York: Viking, 1939), 460.

13. Noss and Noss, *History*, 308.

14. Berthrong, *Eerdmans' Handbook*, 250.

15. Ibid., 250–51.

16. Noss and Noss, *History*, 314.

17. Ibid., 315.

18. Thompson, *Chinese Religion*, 54.

19. Noss and Noss, *History*, 273.

20. C. K. Yang, *Religion in Chinese Society* (Berkeley: University of California Press, 1961).

21. "Buddha" literally means "the enlightened one," which is the title of Gautama, the founder of Buddhism. Bodhisattva, on the other hand, in Mahayana Buddhism is a saint or semidivine being who has voluntarily renounced nirvana in order to help others to salvation. In popular devotion, bodhisattvas are worshiped as symbols of compassion.

22. Thompson, *Chinese Religion*, 55.

23. Wen-hui Tsai, "Historical Personalities in Chinese Folk Religion: A Functional Interpretation," *Legend, Lore, and Religion in China*, eds. S. Allan and A.P. Cohen (San Francisco: Chinese Materials Center, 1979), 30.

24. Noss and Noss, *History*, 250.

25. Henry C. Thiessen, *Lectures in Systematic Theology* (Grand Rapids: Eerdmans, 1979), 128.

26. Ibid., 154–57.

27. Charles Hodge, *Systematic Theology II* (Grand Rapids: Eerdmans, 1952), 96–97.

28. Thiessen, *Lectures in Systematic Theology*, 156.

29. Ibid., 153.

30. Julia Ching, *Confucianism and Christianity: A Comparative Study* (Tokyo/N.Y.: Kodansha International, 1977).

31. Ching, *Chinese Religions*, 6.

32. Donald L. Alexander, "Religion in Chinese Context," *Christianity and China: Issues in Missions and Church History* (Wheaton: Wheaton College, 1991), 4–5.

33. Chung-ying Cheng," A Model of Causality in Chinese Philosophy: A Comparative Study," *Philosophy East and West* 26 (1976): 8.

34. Alexander, *Christianity and China*, 2.

35. Ching, *Chinese Religions*, 5.

36. Thiessen, *Lectures in Systematic Theology*, 78.

Chapter 10: Communicating the Biblical Concept of God to Koreans

1. Bong Rin Ro and Mark C. Albrecht, eds., *God in Asian Contexts* (Taichung, Taiwan: Asia Theological Association, 1988), 274.

2. Roger Kemp, ed., *Text and Context in Theological Education* (Springwood, NSW, Australia: International Council of Accrediting Agencies, 1994).

3. Ellasue Wagner, *Korea: The Old and the New* (New York: Revell, 1931), 128.

4. Homer B. Hulbert, *The Passing of Korea* (New York: Doubleday Page, 1906), 403.

5. Allen D. Clark, *A History of the Church in Korea* (Seoul: Christian Literature Society of Korea, 1971), 42–47.

6. Bong Rin Ro, ed., *Korean Church Growth Explosion*, 2nd ed. (Seoul: Word of Life, 1995), 167.

7. Daniel L. Gifford, *Every-Day Life in Korea* (Chicago: Student Missionary Campaign Library, 1898), 90.

8. Ibid., 109–11.

9. Wagner, *Old*, 135.

10. Ibid., 136–37.

11. The Ministry of Information, "1990 Statistics of Korean Religions," *1993 Directory of Korean Religions* (Seoul: n.p., 1993), 208.

12. Bong Rin Ro, "Chinese Concept of God and the God of the Bible," *God in Asian Context*, 167–71. See also Bong Rin Ro, ed., *Christian Alternatives to Ancestor Practices* (Taiwan: Asia Theological Association, 1985), 95–97, 126–27.

13. Yong-Bok Rha, *An Analysis of the Terms Used for God in Korea in the Context of Indigenization* (Th.D. diss., Boston University School of Theology, 1977), 64–65, 69.

14. Ibid., 69–70.

15. Ibid., 65–68.

16. Ibid., 71–73.

17. Ibid., 74.

18. Ibid., 87–94.

19. Sung-Bum Yun, "Tangoon Mythology Is 'Vestigium Trinitatis,'" *Christian Thought*, October 1963. See also Rha, *Analysis*, 94–96.

Chapter 11: The Korean American Dream and the Blessings of *Hananim*

1. Horace N. Allen, *Things Korean* (New York: Revell Company, 1908), 50; Horace G. Underwood, *The Call of Korea* (New York: Young People's Missionary Movement, 1908), 103; Everett N. Hunt, *Protestant Pioneers in Korea* (New York: Orbis Books, 1980), 46.

2. The year 1784 is generally regarded as the first year of the Roman Catholic Church in Korea, and the year 1883 is generally recognized as the first year of the Protestant Church in Korea.

3. According to *The Korea Christianity Yearbook of 1992* (Seoul: Kidokgoumoonsa, 1993), there are 2,571,062 Christians (over 25 percent of the Korean population), 37,190 churches, and 67,398 pastors, priests, and evangelists in the Korean church.

4. Sang-Hyun Lee, "Korean American Presbyterians: A Need for Ethnic Particularity and the Challenge of Christian Pilgrimage," *The Diversity of Discipleship: Presbyterians and Twentieth-Century Christian Witness*, ed. Milton J. Coalter (Louisville: Westminster/John Knox, 1991), 312.

5. Bong-Young Choy, *Koreans in America* (Chicago: Nelson Hall, 1979), 253–60; see also Hyung-Chang Kim, ed., *The Korean Diaspora* (Santa Barbara, Calif.: ABC-Clio Press, 1977); Won-Moo Hurh and Kwang-Chung Kim, *Korean Immigrants in America: A Structural Analysis of Ethnic Confinement and Adhesive Adaptation* (Rutherford, N.J.: Fairleigh Dickinson Univ., 1984), 46–49.

6. Kwang-Chung Kim and Shin Kim, "Korean Immigrant Churches in the United States," *Yearbook of American and Canadian Churches in 1995* (Nashville: Abingdon, 1996), 6–9; see also Sang-Hyn Lee, *Diversity*, 313–14.

7. Hurh and Kim, *Korean Immigrants*, 73–86.

8. Ibid., 86.

9. Won-Moo Hurh and Kwang-Chung Kim, "Religious Participation of Korean Immigrants in the United States," *Journal for the Scientific Study of Religion* 29, no. 1 (1990): 19–20; see also Kwang-chung Kim and Shin Kim, *Yearbook*, 7.

10. Kim and Kim, *Yearbook*, 7.

11. Hurh and Kim, *Journal*, 29–32.

12. Hurh and Kim, *Korean Immigrants*, 131–32; see also Kim and Kim, *Yearbook*, 6–7.

13. For a more detailed description about the prayer life of Korean Christians both in Korea and in North America, see Tae-Ju Moon, *The Korean Church and Prayer: Prayer Emphasis in Korean Christians and an Evaluation of Their Prayer Life* (D.Min. diss., Gordon-Conwell Theological Seminary, 1994).

14. See Dan Moul, "For Koreans in America, Growth and Growing Pains," *Christianity Today*, March 1989, 57.

15. It began as an annual gathering in Keswick, England, in 1875 with the aim of "the promotion of Practical Holiness."

16. Mircea Eliade, *Shamanism: Archaic Techniques of Ecstasy* (London: Arkana, 1989).

17. James H. Grayson, *Korea: A Religious History* (Oxford: Clarendon, 1990), 260.

18. Charles A. Clark, *Religions of Old Korea* (New York: Garland, 1981),195.

19. Ibid., 196.

20. Griffin Dix, "Personal Faith or Social Propriety: An Interpretive History of Christianity in a Korean Village," in *Culture and Christianity: The Dialectics of Transformation*, ed. George Saunders (New York: Greenwood, 1988), 79–80.

21. Bong-Ho Son, "Some Dangers of Rapid Growth," in *Korean Church Growth Explosion*, eds. Bong-Rin Ro and Marlin L. Nelson (Seoul: Word of Life, 1983), 338–39.

22. Dix, "Personal Faith," 80.

23. Boo-Woong Yoo, "Pentecostalism in Korea," in *Pentecost, Mission, and Ecumenism*, ed. Jan A. Jongeneel (Frankfurt am Main: P. Lang, 1992), 174.

24. Yong-Gi-Cho, *Church Growth*, vol. 3 (Seoul: Youngsan, 1983), 33–34.

25. Gordon D. Fee, *The Disease of the Health and Wealth Gospels* (Costa Mesa, Calif.: The Word for Today, 1979), 4.

26. Ibid., 7.

27. Clark, *Religions*, 217.

Subject Index

Scripture Index

277